Practice *Planners*

W9-BYL-285

Arthur E. Jongsma, Jr., Series Editor

Helping therapists help their clients . . .

Practice *Planners*

Second Edition

THE COMPLETE ADULT
PSYCHOTHERAPY
Treatment Planner

A new, fully revised edition of the bestselling *The Complete Psychotherapy Treatment Planner*, this invaluable resource features:

- Treatment plan components for 39 behaviorally based problems—including five completely new problem sets
- A step-by-step guide to writing treatment plans
- Over 500 additional prewritten treatment goals, objectives, and interventions
- Handy workbook format with space to record your own treatment plan options
- Over 100,000 **Practice** *Planners* sold

Arthur E. Jongsma, Jr., and L. Mark Peterson

Practice *Planners*

Arthur E. Jongsma, Jr., Series Editor

Brief Therapy
HOMEWORK
PLANNER

- Contains 62 ready-to-copy homework assignments that can be used to facilitate brief individual therapy
- Homework assignments and exercises are keyed to over 30 behaviorally-based presenting problems from *The Complete Psychotherapy Treatment Planner*
- Assignments may be quickly customized using the enclosed disk
- Over 100,000 **Practice** *Planners* sold

Gary M. Schultheis

Practice *Planners*

The Clinical
DOCUMENTATION
SOURCEBOOK

Second Edition

A Comprehensive Collection of
Mental Health Practice
Forms, Handouts, and Records

FEATURES

- Contains ready-to-use forms for managing the mental health treatment process
- Covers every stage of the treatment process
- Includes customizable forms on disk
- Over 100,000 **Practice** *Planners* sold

Donald E. Wiger

Practice *Planners*

Arthur E. Jongsma, Jr., Series Editor

The Adult Psychotherapy
PROGRESS NOTES PLANNER

This time-saving resource:

- Outlines Progress notes components for 39 behaviorally-based problems
- Covers the gamut of practice outcomes for every intervention suggested in the best-selling *Complete Adult Psychotherapy Treatment Planner, 2nd Edition*
- Includes 1,000s of pre-written session and patient presentation descriptions
- Provides a handy workbook format with space to record your own progress-note sessions
- Over 150,000 **Practice** *Planners* sold

Arthur E. Jongsma, Jr.

Practice*Planners*

Treatment Planners cover all the necessary elements for developing formal treatment plans, including detailed problem definitions, long-term goals, short-term objectives, therapeutic interventions, and DSM-IV™ diagnoses.

❏ **The Complete Adult Psychotherapy Treatment Planner,** Second Edition
  0-471-31924-4 / $49.95

❏ **The Child Psychotherapy Treatment Planner,** Second Edition
  0-471-34764-7 / $49.95

❏ **The Adolescent Psychotherapy Treatment Planner,** Second Edition
  0-471-34766-3 / $49.95

❏ **The Addiction Treatment Planner,** Second Edition
  0-471-41814-5 / $49.95

❏ **The Couples Psychotherapy Treatment Planner**
  0-471-24711-1 / $49.95

❏ **The Group Therapy Treatment Planner**
  0-471-37449-0 / $49.95

❏ **The Family Therapy Treatment Planner**
  0-471-34768-X / $49.95

❏ **The Older Adult Psychotherapy Treatment Planner**
  0-471-29574-4 / $49.95

❏ **The Employee Assistance (EAP) Treatment Planner**
  0-471-24709-X / $49.95

❏ **The Gay and Lesbian Psychotherapy Treatment Planner**
  0-471-35080-X / $49.95

❏ **The Crisis Counseling and Traumatic Events Treatment Planner**
  0-471-39587-0 / $49.95

❏ **The Social Work and Human Services Treatment Planner**
  0-471-37741-4 / $49.95

❏ **The Continuum of Care Treatment Planner**
  0-471-19568-5 / $49.95

❏ **The Behavioral Medicine Treatment Planner**
  0-471-31923-6 / $49.95

❏ **The Mental Retardation and Developmental Disability Treatment Planner**
  0-471-38253-1 / $49.95

❏ **The Special Education Treatment Planner**
  0-471-38872-6 / $49.95

❏ **The Severe and Persistent Mental Illness Treatment Planner**
  0-471-35945-9 / $49.95

❏ **The Personality Disorders Treatment Planner**
  0-471-39403-3 / $49.95

❏ **The Rehabilitation Psychology Treatment Planner**
  0-471-35178-4 / $49.95

❏ **The Pastoral Counseling Treatment Planner**
  0-471-25416-9 / $49.95

❏ **The Juvenile Justice and Residential Care Treatment Planner**
  0-471-43320-9 / $49.95

❏ **The Psychiatric Evaluation & Psychopharmacology Treatment Planner**
  0-471-43322-5 / $49.95 (available 2/02)

❏ **The Adult Corrections Treatment Planner**
  0-471-20244-4 / $49.95 (available 6/02)

❏ **The School Counseling and School Social Work Treatment Planner**
  0-471-08496-4 / $49.95 (available 8/02)

Progress Notes Planners contain complete prewritten progress notes for each presenting problem in the companion Treatment Planners.

❏ **The Adult Psychotherapy Progress Notes Planner**
  0-471-34763-9 / $49.95

❏ **The Adolescent Psychotherapy Progress Notes Planner**
  0-471-38104-7 / $49.95

❏ **The Child Psychotherapy Progress Notes Planner**
  0-471-38102-0 / $49.95

❏ **The Addiction Progress Notes Planner**
  0-471-10330-6 / $49.95

Name_____

Affiliation_____

Address_____

City/State/Zip_____

Phone/Fax_____

E-mail_____

On the web: practiceplanners.wiley.com

To order, call 1-800-225-5945
(Please refer to promo #1-4019 when ordering.)
Or send this page with payment* to:
John Wiley & Sons, Inc., Attn: J. Knott
605 Third Avenue, New York, NY 10158-0012

❏ Check enclosed ❏ Visa ❏ MasterCard ❏ American Express

Card #_____

Expiration Date_____

Signature_____

*Please add your local sales tax to all orders.

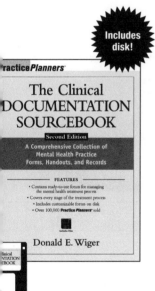

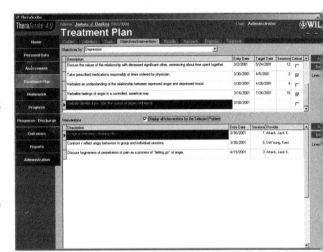

The Chemical Dependence Treatment Documentation Sourcebook

A Comprehensive Collection of Program Management Tools, Clinical Documentation, and Psychoeducational Materials for Substance Abuse Treatment Professionals

James R. Finley and Brenda S. Lenz

John Wiley & Sons, Inc.

New York • Chichester • Weinheim • Brisbane • Singapore • Toronto

This publication is designed to provide accurate and authoritative information in regard to the
subject matter covered. It is sold with the understanding that the publisher is not engaged in
rendering professional services. If legal, accounting, medical, psychological or any other expert
assistance is required, the services of a competent professional person should be sought.

Designations used by companies to distinguish their products are often claimed as trademarks.
In all instances where John Wiley & Sons, Inc. is aware of a claim, the product names appear in
initial capital or all capital letters. Readers, however, should contact the appropriate companies
for more complete information regarding trademarks and registration.

Library of Congress Cataloging-in-Publication Data:

Finley, James R., 1948–
    The chemical dependence treatment documentation sourcebook : a
comprehensive collection of program management tools, clinical
documentation, and psychoeducational materials for substance abuse
treatment professionals / James R. Finley and Brenda S. Lenz.
        p.   cm.
    Includes bibliographical references
    ISBN 0-471-31285-1 (pbk./disk)
    1. Substance abuse—Treatment—Forms.   I. Lenz, Brenda S.
II. Title.
RC564.15.F56   1998
616.86′06—dc21   98-22930

Printed in the United States of America.

10 9 8 7 6 5

Contents

Contents

Contents

Contents

Chapter 11   Other Mental Health Issues: Materials for Use in Psychoeducational Groups 11.1

Contents

This book is dedicated to our parents,
who came before us and have showed us the way in so many things;
to our children, who will follow after us and yet also have much to show us;
to our colleagues; and above all,
to the many clients with whom we have shared so many experiences,
who have given us so much,
and who will continue to do so in the years ahead.

Practice Planner Series Preface

The practice of psychotherapy has a dimension that did not exist 30, 20, or even 15 years ago—accountability. Treatment programs, public agencies, clinics, and even group and solo practitioners must now justify the treatment of patients to outside review entities that control the payment of fees. This development has resulted in an explosion of paperwork.

Clinicians must now document what has been done in treatment, what is planned for the future, and what the anticipated outcomes of the interventions are. The books and software in this Practice Planner series are designed to help practitioners fulfill these documentation requirements efficiently and professionally.

The Practice Planner series is growing rapidly. It now includes not only the original *Complete Psychotherapy Treatment Planner* and the *Child and Adolescent Psychotherapy Treatment Planner*, but also *Treatment Planners* targeted to specialty areas of practice, including: chemical dependency, the continuum of care, couples therapy, older adult treatment, employee assistance, pastoral counseling, and more.

In addition to the *Treatment Planners*, the series also includes *TheraScribe®: The Computerized Assistant to Psychotherapy Treatment Planning* and *TheraBiller™: The Computerized Mental Health Office Manager*, as well as adjunctive books, such as the *Brief Therapy, Chemical Dependence, Couples*, and *Child Homework Planners, The Psychotherapy Documentation Primer*, and *Clinical, Forensic, Child, Couples and Family*, and *Chemical Dependence Treatment Sourcebooks*—containing forms and resources to aid in mental health practice management. The goal of the series is to provide practitioners with the resources they need in order to provide high-quality care in the era of accountability—or, to put it simply, we seek to help you spend more time on patients and less on paperwork.

ARTHUR E. JONGSMA, JR.
Grand Rapids, Michigan

Preface

These are demanding times for substance abuse treatment professionals. Several trends are combining to make the challenges facing clinicians in this field more complex than they have ever been:

- Both the scope of the problem and the demand for solutions are greater than ever before. While some promising shifts are taking place, such as a downward trend in DWI arrests in most areas, on the whole America is experiencing a resurgence of addiction-related problems. The increased availability, lower prices, and higher potency of popular street drugs, together with other factors, appear to be fueling a rise in substance abuse and dependence. At the same time, the mass media devote more attention to drug-related crimes and related stories such as incidents involving celebrities than they have in the past.

- Prevailing concepts about how we should treat addiction and alcoholism have changed. Methods have become more sophisticated, drawing on multiple theoretical schools and orientations. Addiction is now seen as interwoven with other life issues, and many of the people we treat have more complex problems—multiple diagnoses, homelessness, and entanglement with the judicial system are commonplace. The days of simple, single-focus confrontational treatment are gone, and clinicians are expected to address a widening range of issues in the context of substance abuse treatment.

- Resources and standards are tighter. In the past, people diagnosed as dependent on alcohol or other drugs were often treated via lengthy stays in residential treatment programs, with relatively little scrutiny of how those programs worked or what results they produced. Today, with the growth of managed care, the drive for economy and efficiency in substance abuse and mental health treatment programs is creating an increasing demand for thorough and intensive outpatient addiction treatment programs as a shorter term and less expensive alternative to residential treatment. At the same time, a heightened focus on measurable outcomes means that those outpatient programs are being submitted to searching and skeptical examination of every aspect of their functioning, clinical and administrative. Accountability is a higher priority than ever before, and at times everyone from clients to employers to regulatory agencies to insurance companies and HMOs seems to be from Missouri, the "Show Me" state. Finally, more and more programs are competing for funding that is not growing in pace with the demand.

The result of this combination of trends is that as treatment providers, we are likely to be called upon to create new treatment programs or revise existing ones. When the call comes, we are expected to offer more broad-ranging treatment options, more thorough planning and documentation, and more efficient program management than ever before.

If this is a typical day, clinicians in dozens of places around the country are struggling with the challenges of creating these new programs, often on short notice and often with no previous experience or training in treatment program design or in program or personnel management. The tasks of establishing and running an addiction treatment program can be daunting. Many who are reading these words may be clinicians faced with this situation or one like it. Our reason for writing this book is to share lessons learned and tools we have found useful to help our peers achieve greater success faster, and with fewer growing pains along the way.

Based on our experience designing, building, and running chemical dependence treatment programs, we have chosen three key elements as our focus for this book:

1. *Sound program design* based on analysis of the community's needs, the available resources, and the goals to be achieved. Ideally, this addresses not only addictions but the deficits in life skills that are inseparable from chemical dependency and so often undermine the client's efforts at change.

2. *Clear and well-organized clinical documentation* enabling providers to keep comprehensive records of every phase of treatment while still having time to concentrate on therapy rather than paperwork.

3. *Dynamic and effective psychoeducational materials* addressing all aspects of the addictive lifestyle and, even more vital, teaching clients about healthy alternatives.

Like the *Clinical Documentation Sourcebook* by Dr. Donald Wiger (1997) and other books of its type, the *Chemical Dependence Treatment Documentation Sourcebook* provides you with practical tools you can start using immediately. We offer a clear and sequential framework to follow in thinking through and designing your program, and materials you can use to take it from concept to full operation. This is a flexible, à la carte offering—take what you need and use it as is or modify it as you see fit. Our aim is to save you time and to provide you with a flexible, comprehensive, and organized set of resources so that you can focus on carrying out your program and working with clients.

Our objective is to provide the most comprehensive collection of resources needed to build and run a chemical dependency treatment program in one place. Rather than merely provide guidance on program structure and administration, or useful clinical documentation, or ready-to-use psychoeducational materials, we are offering all of the above, providing resources that have not previously been combined in one offering and doing so in a way that allows you the flexibility to use them with a variety of settings, populations, and modes of treatment.

This book is divided into three sections. For the reader who is charged with the responsibility of designing and/or establishing a new chemical dependence treatment program, Chapters 1 and 2 are the place to start. For those whose task includes designing the program, Chapter 1 provides a framework and a list of key questions to guide the clinician in gathering all the necessary information and creating a program design. Chapter 2 continues the planning process (and is a logical place to start if your program design has already been determined). In this chapter, we offer a proven and effective project management and scheduling system to walk the program planner through the steps necessary to produce a timetable, a list of tasks, and a means of monitoring progress in getting your program up and running.

Chapters 3 through 7 are intended to be useful for those starting new programs and those working in established settings. These chapters provide clinical documentation designed with substance abuse treatment in mind. All forms included are reproduced on the accompanying computer diskette and can be reproduced as they are or modified as the user wishes using Microsoft Word, Corel WordPerfect, Lotus

Preface

WordPro, or other word processing software programs. For new programs, these forms may be adopted, modified as necessary, and put to immediate use. Where standing administrative procedures and documentation are in place, they may be used to either augment or replace portions of existing documentation wherever they offer improvements over forms in current use. These forms are divided into Chapters 3 through 7 by functional area. Chapter 8 addresses outcome measurements. Rather than creating new testing instruments, we have surveyed the field and offer the reader our suggestions regarding the process of choosing or creating those that will most effectively meet the needs of any specific program's population and goals.

Chapters 9 through 11 are for use in starting new programs and enriching existing ones. These chapters contains all the materials needed for over 24 psychoeducational presentations on chemical dependence and related topics. We urge readers to take what they want and adapt it as they see fit. All materials in these chapters are included on the companion diskette.

We hope this combination of materials is useful in a wide variety of settings, and we welcome any feedback readers may have to offer.

JAMES R. FINLEY, MA
BRENDA S. LENZ, MS

Chapter 1

Key Decisions

TARGET POPULATION

The first and most fundamental decisions to be made in planning a treatment program for chemical dependence are these: Who will this program serve, and what will the program do for them? Either we as the clinicians providing the treatment make these decisions, or someone else makes them for us. Of course, it is usually the case that we are told who we will treat and what problems we will address, which simplifies our task. Still, we may be originating or proposing a new program to address an unmet need or be called on to advise and guide those who are making these decisions, so this chapter is organized around the assumption that none of these decisions have been made yet.

The reality is that we serve both the individuals receiving treatment and those people or organizations who refer the clients to our programs and pay for that treatment. That being the case, we must consider the needs of both. In addition, there is a third group of stakeholders in the treatment process, namely, the family members, close friends, employers and coworkers, and other concerned people affected by the client's substance abuse and related problems. Because they are also affected, and because they have a powerful role to play in reinforcing or undermining our clients' success in treatment and afterward, we must also consider their wants and needs.

Answering the following questions is the first step in forming a clear program design.

1. What Population(s) Will This Program Treat?

Age group: _____ Early adolescent (12–15) _____ Late adolescent (16–17) _____ Any adolescent

_____ Young adult (18–35) _____ Any adult _____ Senior

Special populations: _____ Male only _____ Female only _____ Homeless _____ Veteran

_____ Gay/lesbian _____ Ethnicity: _____ _____ Language: _____

_____ From specific referral source: _____

Problem(s): _____ Alcohol dependent only _____ Other drug dependent only (drug: _____)

_____ Polysubstance dependent _____ Substance abuser *or* dependent

_____ Substance abuse only without dependence _____ Dual/multiple diagnosis

_____ Combination of substance abuse/dependence with other specific problem

(specify: _____)

2. What Will Be This Program's Goal(s) for Treatment Outcomes?

Re substance abuse: _____ Achieve and maintain abstinence _____ Maintain existing abstinence

_____ Avoid substance abuse/substance-related misconduct (not abstinence)

Re other problems: _____ Stop/avoid compulsive behavior other than substance abuse

_____ Stop/avoid criminal/antisocial behavior

_____ Other (specify: _____)

3. What Referral Sources Will This Program Serve, and What Are Their Desired Outcomes?

Referral sources	Desired outcomes
_____ Self-referrals	_____
_____ Courts/probation/parole	_____
_____ Other government agency	_____
_____ Government/private employee assistance programs (EAPs)	_____
_____ HMOs (specify: _____)	_____
_____ Other (specify: _____)	_____

4. What Significant Others will Participate in Treatment, and What Are Their Desired Outcomes?

Significant others	Desired outcomes
_____ Spouses/partners	_____
_____ Parents/siblings	_____
_____ Children	_____
_____ Other family _____	_____
_____ Employer/coworkers	_____
_____ Friends/other _____	_____

METHODS AND SERVICES TO BE PROVIDED

You have identified the population your program will treat as well as other stakeholders in the process; together with your staff, they make up the *who* of your program. You have chosen treatment goals or desired outcomes; those are the *what*. Next comes the *how*, the decisions you must make regarding specific services your program will provide. These choices will be based on a variety of factors. Again, we ask you to take some time to specify information that will help you determine the *how* of your program.

Theoretical Orientation

Your theoretical orientation, and that of your organization, will shape many of the choices you make in designing your chemical dependence treatment program. Do you subscribe to the disease model, or do you see substance abuse as strictly a behavioral issue? Do you practice a cognitive-behavioral, psychodynamic, humanistic, or eclectic approach to therapy? The answers to these and other questions will already have come into play, helping to determine how you defined your outcome goals for treatment. They will also drive many of your decisions regarding the specific types of services you include in your program design. It is wise to take a few moments and consider this question and also consider the outlooks of any other individual clinicians or organizations that will be involved in this program. Differing views in this area can be either a source of confusion and conflict that will destroy your program, or a source of strength, diversity, and versatility, depending on how they are handled. It is a good idea to resolve any questions or issues in advance in this area, determining where any potential conflicts exist and how you will handle them.

Services Needed

EFFICACY-BASED OPTIONS. What specific types of services appear most effective in working with your chosen population, based on your theoretical orientation, your own experience, and the evidence of other successful programs?

Check all that apply: _____ Psychoeducational group counseling _____ Psychoeducational homework
_____ Intensive group therapy _____ Individual counseling/therapy _____ Family therapy
_____ Psychiatric treatment, including psychoactive medications _____ Support group attendance
_____ Residential/inpatient treatment _____ Day treatment, including on-site schooling
_____ Use of methadone, antabuse, naltrexone, or other medications to curb substance abuse
_____ Other: _____

On a separate sheet of paper list all the items you checked, titling it Program Services.

PERCEIVED NEEDS.   What specific services do your clientele and your referral/funding sources tell you they want and need most? _____
_____
_____
_____

If any of these services are not on your Program Services list, add them to the list unless they are impossible for you to provide or you have other reasons not to provide them. Place a check mark next to any that are already on the list.

MARKET NICHES.   What relevant services are *not* currently available to this population in your community? To turn the question around: Of the services checked above, which are already being provided to this population, and by whom?

The fact that a service or combination of services is already provided does not rule it out as an option for your program, but if it is needed and not being provided, it is of more obvious value to the clientele, the referral sources, and the community. For example, the authors at one time chose to start an intensive outpatient program (IOP) in their community, partly because no IOP then existed there, leaving a gap between low-intensity psychoeducational groups and full-scale residential treatment. By choosing to design and launch an IOP, we knew we had a ready source of referrals that were not being served elsewhere; also, persuading the courts and other referral resources to use our program was made much simpler than it would have been had they been using an existing IOP elsewhere in the community.

In surveying existing programs to determine what is already being done, we suggest learning what types of services the following sources offer your chosen population.

Government programs (federal, state, county, municipality, including school systems):
Services offered: _____
_____

Private community mental health agencies, both nonprofit and for-profit:
Services offered: _____
_____

Colleges and universities (these often run free or low-cost clinics as training facilities):
Employee assistance programs (EAPs):
Services offered: _____
_____

Churches, charitable organizations:
Services offered: _____
_____

Support groups:
Services offered: _____
_____

GAPS IN EXISTING SERVICES.   Of the types of services you checked as being effective for your population and desired outcomes, which if any are not currently being provided in your community? Equally important, why not? Reasons might include prohibitive cost, lack of qualified personnel, or simply the fact that no one has previously identified the need and tried to provide the service. For each service you identify as not being provided, note the reasons for that service's absence, as best as you can determine those reasons:

Type of service   *Reason(s) not provided*

_____   _____

_____   _____

_____   _____

_____   _____

_____   _____

If the reasons that have prevented others from providing these services will also prevent your doing so, there is no point in considering them as components of your program. Cross these services out on your Program Services list if they were included there. However, if the reasons others do not provide these services are not barriers for you, these services may be the most obvious ones to include among the core components of your program. If this is the case, again make a check mark next to each item falling into this category. You may have two checks next to some items now.

FUTURE NEEDS.   Can you identify any substance abuse treatment needs that may not have been significant in the past but will be in the near future? These future needs could be the result of new trends in substance abuse, legislative mandates, demographic shifts, new developments in the field of substance abuse treatment, or other changes. Take a moment to consider and note here any potential future needs you anticipate developing during the next year or so:

_____

_____

_____

Again, place a check mark next to each item on this list where it appears on your Program Services list, or add it if it isn't included on that list yet.

What You Can Offer

The purpose of the preceding section was to identify services it would be most helpful for you to offer. It is also necessary to consider any restrictions under which you must work, either in terms of services you are required to provide or those you are forbidden or unable to provide. These mandates and restrictions may be imposed by legislative or regulatory bodies, by the referral/funding sources themselves, or by your own management. Practical considerations may also rule out your providing some services because you lack the staff, facilities, or other means to do so.

MANDATES AND RESTRICTIONS.   List here any authorities that impose specific requirements or prohibitions with which you must comply, and note what those mandates require or prohibit in your program.

Mandating authority   *Requirement or prohibition*

_____   _____

_____   _____

_____   _____

_____   _____

_____   _____

Now underline those items on your Program Services list that are required, and cross out any that are prohibited.

Finally, examine the items on the list that are not crossed out, and place an *X* next to any service that you cannot provide because you lack the staff or the resources to do so and cannot obtain them.

When you have done this, rewrite the list, putting the services listed in a new sequence. First come those that are underlined and have one or more check marks; then those that are underlined only; then those with one or more check marks, most to fewest; next, items that are not crossed out and have no check marks; last, leave a gap on the page and then list any items with an *X* next to them.

Your program design is coming together. Previously, you have identified the client population and referral/funding sources with whom you will work and what treatment goals you will seek to accomplish with them. Now you have identified a core set of services you will provide, namely, the items on the first part of your new list.

For the services on the second part of the list, those that would otherwise fit into your program but that you can't provide because you lack the means, you can seek to identify other treatment sources and attempt to obtain those services for your clients through those treatment sources. A common example is support group attendance; you may not be able to offer support group meetings within your program, but you can meet this need by directing your clients to attend meetings of Alcoholics Anonymous (AA), Narcotics Anonymous (NA), or other groups elsewhere in the community.

Next we will turn to a series of questions to complete the *how* of your program plan: staffing, budget, and logistical concerns.

Staffing

Qualifications

The first question concerns the qualifications of your staff to provide the services you have listed. You must refer to government regulatory agencies, policies of referral sources, and sound professional judgment, and determine what credentials, training, and level of experience are needed to provide these services. If the clinicians available to staff your program have these requirements now, you need only be concerned with maintaining them. If not, you must either increase the level of qualification of your existing staff or hire additional clinicians with the qualifications you need.

Management support is critical in this area. If your management is dictating your program's structure to you, you must let them know of any shortfall in this area as early as you can. If you are proposing the program, be sure to include any additional training or new hires that will be needed as part of the information you present to management. You should also make sure management is aware of any ongoing costs for continuing training that this program necessitates.

Availability

If your organization has the qualified clinicians your program will need, you must make sure of their availability. Determine how many people will be required in what roles; be sure to allow for absences for training, vacations, illness, or other reasons.

If your organization has these qualified people now, they are probably already busy. Will their present duties become unnecessary, making them available for your program? If not, who will replace them in doing whatever they are doing now?

Equally important, are these individuals aware of what you are planning? Are they interested and willing to stop or cut back on what they are doing now to work in your program? If not, you will probably want to work with management to persuade them to join you. Their perception of your program may play a critical role in how they affect the clients you serve.

BUDGET

How much funding is available per client from your referral/funding sources and from any other sources? What will you charge per client? Will that pay for what you plan to do?

Your formulas for calculating this will vary from site to site, but some generalized formulas follow:

Personnel costs + Material and facilities costs + Administrative costs = Total costs

Total costs per month/Number of clients per month = Cost per client

For personnel costs, total the wages and benefits of each staff member providing services, then multiply by the amount of that staff member's work time devoted to this program. For example, suppose Therapist A earns $16 per hour in direct wages and another $5 per hour in benefits and administrative support, totaling $21 per hour; in a 40-hour work week, she spends 30 hours on this program. Personnel cost for Therapist A for this program is $630 per week.

For material and facilities costs and administrative costs, you will probably have to obtain figures from your organization's management personnel, based on calculating what portion of your physical facilities are used (both in square footage and in time), together with estimated costs for equipment depreciation, supplies used up, and a fair share of general administrative costs.

You are likely to find yourself working within tight constraints in terms of what you can spend on staffing, on program materials, and on the time in treatment for which referral sources are willing to pay.

For this reason, you may want to examine budget-stretching options. Some of these include making maximum use of group versus individual therapy (fortunately, group therapy is highly effective and often superior to individual therapy in dealing with substance abuse), the use of community support groups such as AA and NA to augment treatment, the use of interns and volunteer help if available, and the use of portions of existing programs. For example, in the IOP previously mentioned, the authors incorporated an existing relapse prevention program as one phase of the IOP after coordinating with the therapists running the existing program. The IOP clients were mingled with the existing client population of the relapse prevention program during that phase of their IOP treatment. Both programs benefited, and overall costs were kept down by avoiding redundancy.

LOGISTICS

Facilities and Equipment

You must determine where you will obtain the facilities and equipment your program's services will require. Typically, this will consist of rooms and furniture suitable for group or individual counseling, and electronic or audiovisual equipment, such as computers and printers, projectors and screens, TVs and VCRs, cassette tape players, copying machines, whiteboards and markers, use of telephone lines, storage of client case files, and so on. The checklist that follows is provided for your convenience:

Have	Need	N/A	
___	___	___	Group rooms with furniture
___	___	___	Individual counseling session rooms with furniture
___	___	___	Telephones
___	___	___	Computers & printers
___	___	___	Secure storage for client records
___	___	___	First-aid kit/supplies
___	___	___	AV equipment: projector(s) and screen(s)
___	___	___	AV equipment: TV(s) and VCR(s)
___	___	___	AV equipment: Video camera(s)

Have	Need	N/A	
____	____	____	AV equipment: cassette tape recorder(s)/player(s)
____	____	____	AV equipment: whiteboard/chalkboard and markers/chalk
____	____	____	AV equipment: copying machine(s)
____	____	____	Other: _____

Program Materials

You will also need to plan for program materials. These include those items bought or produced once and used indefinitely, such as videotapes, audiotapes, transparencies, and lesson plans, and items that must be regularly replaced, such as folders, handouts, workbooks, pens, pencils, and scratch paper.

Transportation

Depending on your situation, transportation may or may not be your responsibility. This can include both transportation to and from treatment for clients and their families and transportation to and from clients' homes for clinicians if in-home therapy is part of your program. If you are responsible for transportation, you must plan for the physical means—drivers, vehicles, fuel, maintenance, and time—and you must consider issues of safety and liability. If this is a new area for you, be sure to seek the guidance of someone who has managed this type of responsibility before.

Other Considerations

Finally, you may need to plan for other logistical considerations, depending on your program's structure. Some questions to consider:

Will you provide meals, snacks, coffee or tea, or other refreshments?

Will group outings for activities be part of your program?

If you direct participation in AA, NA, or other groups, will you provide transportation?

Will you include any organized activities that require any special equipment (i.e., athletics)?

Will you lend books or tapes to clients during their participation in your program?

SCREENING CLIENTS

It is wise and necessary to thoroughly educate your referral sources about the population your program will serve and the problems you will address. This will help them make the most effective use of your program, and it will go a long way to reduce inappropriate referrals. However, you will probably still see some referrals of clients who are inappropriate for your program, and it is vital to screen them out as early as possible. This is true for three reasons:

1. Placing a client in an inappropriate treatment setting may interfere with the safe and effective treatment of other clients in your program.

2. Inappropriate treatment is unlikely to benefit a client, and this may lead to a false perception on the part of referral sources that your program is not effective.

3. Last but most important, it is possible that inappropriate treatment could cause a client emotional or psychological harm under some circumstances, such as triggering a decompensation or other extreme reaction without having sufficient or adequately trained and experienced staff on hand to deal with the consequences for that client or others.

You will want to answer the following questions in screening clients to make sure they are appropriate referrals for your program:

- Does this client fall within the population this program is designed to serve (i.e., does he or she have the type of substance abuse problem this program is structured to address)?

- Does this client have coexisting problems that will interfere with treatment?

- Does this client possess the necessary competencies, motivation, and level of functioning to participate and succeed in this program? (Many clients, especially those who are referred involuntarily, will not be motivated for treatment when they start a program, but they must be willing to attend and participate at the minimum required level.)

- Does this client come from an appropriate referral source (some sources insist on exclusivity and will not share a program with other referral sources)? If this program is designed for clients who enter treatment voluntarily, is this client here of his or her own free will?

ADMINISTRATION AND PROGRAM MANAGEMENT

Clinicians are often tasked not only with designing new programs, but with managing them as well. At first glance, it may seem that this calls for an entirely different set of skills and knowledge from that required of a clinician. This perception is misleading, however. To the typical counselor or therapist who feels he or she has no background in program management, we pose this question: How much time do you spend on case management—on coordinating and working with other therapists, psychiatrists, other physicians, psychologists, case managers, school staff, EAP personnel, referral sources, utilization review staff, family members, probation and parole officers, Child Protective Services staff, and so on? If the answer is "a lot of time," we suggest that you are already a program manager, for you have been managing essentially one-client programs. The main difference is scale, not the type or difficulty of the management tasks involved. In this section, we list a number of areas where coordination is frequently necessary, together with questions it will be helpful to answer in advance as part of your program design.

Coordination/Integration with Other Treatment/Support Sources

CONCURRENT THERAPY/COUNSELING FROM OTHER SOURCES. Often, clients receive multiple types of services simultaneously from different providers. These other providers may be within your own organization or external to it. Your substance abuse treatment program design should include procedures and documentation for coordinating with providers of the following:

- Psychiatric treatment.

- Case management services.

- Mandated education/counseling.

- Psychological testing.

- Family counseling for other family members.

CLIENT ACTIVITIES OTHER THAN THERAPY. Your clients may also be participating in other activities that, though not considered therapy per se, will interact significantly with your work. Chemically dependent clients will often be involved with Alcoholics Anonymous, Narcotics Anonymous, Cocaine Anonymous, or other support groups. They may also be involved with non-drug-oriented support groups such as Parents Anonymous or Overeaters Anonymous or a wide variety of church groups. It is helpful to find out as much as possible about these other programs and integrate the help and support your client gets there with your own treatment program. At a minimum, you will need to find out about such activities and the role the client perceives them as playing in his or her life, lest you find yourself working at cross-purposes with a support group without realizing it.

Clinical Supervision

You may be the clinical supervisor overseeing the treatment taking place in your program, or you may need to obtain supervision for yourself and other clinicians working with your program clients, or both situations may coexist. Regardless, clinical supervision is a critical element in your program, for reasons of both accountability and sound clinical practice. Make sure this is clearly addressed and provided for in your program design, including the following:

- Qualifications and credentials required for clinical supervisors.

- Schedule and number of hours of supervision per week for each clinician.

- Nature of supervision (individual or group).

- Subjects discussed during supervision sessions.

- Documentation used to record supervision.

Coordination with Courts, Agencies, and Other Referral/Funding Sources

Again, this will be familiar ground for most experienced clinicians; new tasks may involve establishing procedures and documentation for significant events. It is wise to ensure that your substance abuse treatment program planning addresses the following matters in detail before you open the doors to your first referrals:

- Intake and orientation procedures, documentation, and materials.

- Follow-on referrals for successful clients, including standards defining success in treatment.

- Procedures defining plans for continuing care, aftercare, etc., for successful clients.

- Clinical and administrative procedures and documentation for treatment failure, including standards defining what constitutes failure, early interventions, warnings/counselings, staffings, notifications to referral sources, measures short of dropping clients from treatment, and criteria for readmission.

Monitoring and Measurement of Progress and Outcomes

With time, this can become one of your strongest means of identifying potential program improvements and of validating and selling your program to referral sources, as well as defending it against challenges by utilization management and review personnel. You may have the opportunity to affiliate your program with a new or ongoing research program, probably through a university or government agency interested in substance abuse issues; this is a potential source of funding and referrals. If you are able to affiliate with a research program, the people in that program will select the testing instruments and procedures used to measure outcomes in your treatment program.

If this is not the case, our recommendation is that you select existing, proven testing instruments, and plan a rigorous outcomes measurement program to be carried out from the beginning of your treatment program's existence. We address this topic in more detail in Chapter 8.

Incorporation/Termination of Previously Existing Programs

As mentioned earlier, you may be able to provide a better substance abuse treatment program at a lower cost either by absorbing existing programs, as they are or with modifications, or by routing your clients into those existing programs as part of their treatment while leaving those external programs otherwise unchanged. Any such use of existing programs should be carefully addressed in your treatment program design, with an explanation of the benefits of using existing resources in this manner.

Program Maintenance

Every component of your substance abuse treatment program will need to be replaced sooner or later, from staff (even yourself!) to facilities to referral sources. To be complete, your treatment program design must address this issue, including the following areas:

- Personnel turnover and replacement training: Identify how replacement personnel will be found, what training they will need, how long this process will take, and how staffing shortages will be handled in the meantime.

- Replacement of consumable materials and depreciated facilities: This item needs to be included in the budget submitted with the initial program proposal, as it is information that management needs to make fully informed decisions about this program.

Procedures for Modifying the Program as Needed after Its Establishment

Along with turnover, it is a certainty that this substance abuse treatment program will be changed and revised over time, for a variety of reasons. In some cases, staff will find that parts of the plan that seemed sound are impractical or ineffective; in other cases, the requirements of the clients or the referral sources will change, advances in the clinical knowledge available in the field may prompt improvements, or government regulations and management policies may change.

It will serve you well in the long run if you have procedures established to identify and quantify needed changes and to plan smooth transitions while implementing program changes once they are decided upon. This will include notification of and coordination with referral sources; it may require obtaining their permission and/or modifying contracts before changes can be made.

PUTTING IT ALL TOGETHER

25 Questions to Answer before Proceeding

1. What client population(s) will we serve?
2. What referral sources will we serve?
3. What role, if any, will family, friends, coworkers, and others play in treatment?

4. What current and future substance-abuse-related problem(s) and need(s) will we address?

5. Who will pay for treatment?

6. How long will it take and how much will it cost per client?

7. How will we do it: What specific types of services will we provide? Describe a typical course of treatment, including intake and orientation.

8. What elements of this treatment program are mandated by legislative or regulatory bodies, and how do they monitor compliance?

9. Who will provide each aspect or component of the treatment?

10. What qualifications, credentials, and experience are required for each aspect or component of the treatment provided?

11. What additional training, if any, will these providers need, and where and how will they get that training?

12. What resources will we need (staffing, facilities, time, equipment, materials, transportation, etc.)?

13. Of those resources, what do we have now?

14. What resources do we still need to obtain, and how and where will we get them?

15. Who will provide clinical supervision for the clinicians working in the program? What is the schedule for clinical supervision?

16. Whose help and cooperation will we need from outside this program?

17. How will we measure our progress and success or failure, as a program and for each client?

18. To whom will we need to report results?

19. What problems do we anticipate, and how will we solve them?

20. What will happen after treatment with clients whose therapy is successful?

21. What will happen with clients who fail to achieve treatment goals?

22. What are we doing now that we will change or stop doing, and how will we take care of the people using those services?

23. When will we have to have this program up and running?

24. How will we maintain the program once it is operational? How will we replace staff who leave? materials and equipment that are used up?

25. What will be our system for identifying, planning, and implementing needed changes and desired improvements?

Program Design Briefing/Proposal Worksheet

1. Population to be treated: _____

2. Referral source(s): _____

3. Exclusion factors (ineligible clients): _____

4. Problems to be addressed: _____

5. Theoretical orientation: _____

6. Desired treatment outcome(s): _____

7. Program structure choices: _____

      Structure: _____ multiphase   _____ single-phase

      Setting/level of intensity: _____ residential   _____ day treatment

                                 _____ intensive outpatient   _____ low-intensity outpatient

                                 _____ in-home   _____ on-site

                                 _____ combination in-home and on-site

      Mode(s) of treatment: _____ CD education group   _____ other education group

                                 _____ process/intensive group   _____ multifamily group

                                 _____ couple/family therapy   _____ individual therapy

                                 _____ support group (AA, etc.)   _____ intervention

                                 _____ other   _____ combination

8. Community resources and/or existing programs to be used: _____
_____

9. Strengths/unique advantages of this treatment program design: _____
_____

10. Duration of treatment: _____
_____

11. Clinicians providing treatment: _____
_____

12. Where treatment will be provided: _____
_____

13. Estimated cost per client of treatment: _____
_____

14. Fee charged per client: _____
_____

15. Program's estimated start-up date: _____
_____

Chapter 2

Basic Steps in Establishing a Chemical Dependence Treatment Program

PROJECT MANAGEMENT 101

The initial stages of establishing a chemical dependence treatment program involve tasks and decisions that, for the most part, call for us to function more as managers than as clinicians. Although clinical judgment will be involved in many of the choices that shape your program design, others will be determined by your budget, staffing, and other available resources. Furthermore, once you have a clear idea of what your treatment program will look like, the process of organizing and carrying out both clinical and management decisions will be a management-oriented process.

At this point, many therapists, counselors, social workers, and other clinicians claim that they have no training or experience, and very little interest, in being managers. Our aim with this chapter is not to transform you into an MBA-wielding management specialist; it is to give you useful tools to organize and schedule the start-up of your new chemical dependence treatment program.

The information in this chapter is intended to walk you through the steps necessary to get your program up and running, using four basic project management techniques we selected from the many available based on ease of learning and use. Specifically, the first method we cover is one with which many clinicians are already familiar: the brainstorming technique for generating as many ideas as possible about the topic under consideration. The second project management tool we discuss is the critical path method for placing the actions you will need to take in their necessary sequence. Third is the reverse scheduling technique, another approach with which many readers will be familiar; this is a simple way to devise a realistic time line for your program start-up, or for any other complex enterprise you may undertake. Finally, we present the structured team walk-through, useful for catching omissions and schedule conflicts and correcting them at their most harmless stage, before your plan is completed.

You may already be familiar with these methods or with others you prefer to use instead. If so, feel free to skim through this chapter, picking out and adapting whatever pieces of the processes you find useful.

BRAINSTORMING

First and foremost, anyone responsible for planning the establishment of a new program or project must have as complete a list as possible of required tasks to use as a starting point. To produce a comprehensive Things To Do list for your program's creation and start-up, we recommend a technique you may have taught clients: the brainstorming method for generating ideas. We suggest you do this as a group activity, if possible, though it will also serve your purpose if you are working alone at this stage.

If you are working with a group, try to recruit others who fit into one or more of the following categories:

- Those people who will form the staff of your new chemical dependence program.

- Representatives of organizations you hope will be your program's referral sources; if possible, the actual individuals with whom you will be coordinating referrals.

- Individuals who have participated in the start-up of other treatment programs (if you know someone who has been involved in a program start-up that experienced many problems, their experience and perspective may be especially useful!).

- People who have worked in the type of program you plan to establish.

- People with experience organizing, starting, and/or managing any complex group activity.

- People who are strongly detail-oriented, "left-brain" thinkers.

- People who are strongly creative, imaginative, "right-brain" thinkers.

Once you have identified the people who will be members of your brainstorming group, coordinate with them to schedule a meeting at a convenient time and place; allow at least three hours for the meeting. When you set up this meeting, arrange to be free of distracting interruptions and set the stage to create a relaxed, informal atmosphere.

When your group is assembled and you have gone through the process of introducing members and explaining why you asked each to help, explain the choices you have made regarding the structure of your chemical dependence treatment program. Essentially, this will consist of your answers to the list of questions at the end of Chapter 1. Then, unless everyone present is already experienced with this technique, explain the brainstorming process to your team.

Your initial group objective is to generate as many ideas as possible without considering whether they are practical or realistic. In this case, the ideas will specify tasks that need to be done in the course of starting this new treatment program. With one person acting as a recorder and writing down the team members' ideas (we suggest that the person who organizes the meeting do this), the members of the team begin suggesting tasks as fast as they can think of them, without worrying about putting them in sequence or about whether everything makes sense. At this stage, ask that no one comment on any idea mentioned, just keep tossing out new thoughts as fast as they are conceived. Also ask members to avoid censoring their own ideas, that is, leaving any thought unmentioned because it sounds silly or off-target. We recommend that the recorder write the ideas on transparency sheets and project them on an overhead projector. This may help generate more new thoughts. We further recommend bringing a cassette tape recorder and blank tape and recording the session. Often, several people may speak at once or they may throw out new ideas too fast for the recorder to capture them all in writing. The tape recorder comes in handy because it enables you to continue the brainstorming session rather than stopping to go back and repeat what has been said; you can then review the tape afterward and catch any ideas that didn't get written down when they were voiced.

Keep your brainstorming session going until everyone present has run out of inspiration; then, if necessary, review the cassette tape and make sure all ideas mentioned are written down. This may trigger a few more thoughts from members of your group; add these to the list as well. Once you have a long list, let the group take a break while you make copies for all group members of the transparency sheets on which their thoughts are written.

When your brainstorming group reconvenes, distribute copies of the idea list they generated, then discuss each item in turn. This is the time to start thinking analytically and logically. Without belittling any ideas or their originators, your group will examine each proposed task and answer the following questions:

- Will this task indeed be necessary for the successful start-up and operation of this program?

- Who are all the people who will have to carry out this task?

- What resources will the person(s) responsible need to carry out this task? These include:

- Other people's participation.

- Information.

- Money.

- Facilities.

- Transportation.

- Equipment.

- Telecommunications resources (i.e., telephone, e-mail, Internet access).

- Documentation, references, or other written/audiovisual materials.

- Anything else identified by your group as needed.

- How long will this task take from beginning to end?

When you are finished, you should have a lengthy list of tasks to be accomplished, with each task annotated to reflect who will carry it out and the resources they will need to do so, as well as the amount of time necessary. Again, make copies of this list and distribute them to the members of the brainstorming group. Thank them for their time and help, and ask them to contact you and pass on any additional thoughts they have after the group adjourns. Finally, if possible, ask them if they are willing to help you again at the fourth stage of the planning process by participating in a structured walk-through, and schedule a follow-up meeting at a later date for that purpose, again allowing at least three hours.

This technique accomplishes several valuable things for the clinician planning a new program:

- It provides multiple perspectives, each person bringing his or her own experience, skills, knowledge of the situation, and thinking style.

- Because at least some members of the group are likely to be among the people responsible for carrying out the tasks identified, it is a proactive early step in gaining their informed consensus and cooperation, inviting them to think of themselves as your partners and supporters from the beginning of your new program's design, keeping the key individuals concerned with your project informed, and identifying problems or conflicts as early as possible.

- It gives others an increased awareness of the magnitude of the job you are undertaking, which may smooth the way if you need to cut back on other work activities to accommodate the demands of this process.

Once your Things To Do list is created, your next job is to place all the tasks on the list in sequence. Specifically, you are looking for things that must happen before or after other things on the list. For example, if one of your identified tasks is to conduct presentations to educate referral sources about the new program, necessary tasks before this can be done would include developing informational handouts and presentation materials, identifying specific individuals who will act as referral sources, contacting them, and scheduling meetings to make your presentations.

As you scan your list of tasks, many of these sequences will be obvious, and some new tasks will probably occur to you and need to be added. Using a word processing program with cut-and-paste capabilities to rearrange your list and add items as needed will make this part of the planning process much easier.

You will find some tasks, and some sequences of tasks, that can be carried out concurrently. For example, the following subgroups of tasks can probably be executed simultaneously:

- Arranging for facilities, transportation, and equipment.

- Obtaining or creating psychoeducational and program information materials.

- Identifying and contacting referral sources.

- Identifying and orienting program staff.

You can place these items side by side on your list to show that they can happen simultaneously. You will probably find it easier to work with your list if you record sequences that can happen at the same time as other sequences in parallel columns when you create your master list. If you are using a word processing program that gives you the capability of organizing a portion of a page in columns, this process is simplified.

An important note: After you put items side by side, either single tasks or columns showing sequences of things that must be done, it is important to think about the resources needed to accomplish these side-by-side tasks. If they require the same people or the same resources, it may be impossible to carry them out at the same time. It is critical to check for duplications of this kind, lest you set up a bottleneck in your plan by scheduling key people, equipment, or facilities to be in use for more than one task at once. When such conflicts exist, there are two ways to handle them: Where possible, obtain additional resources (someone else to carry out a task, additional transportation, alternative facilities, etc.) so that both activities can take place at once; where additional resources are unavailable, look to see which task or sequence of tasks if postponed is most likely to cause unwanted delays, probably because of other tasks that follow after it is completed, and schedule that task or sequence to be done first.

When you are finished, you will have a master list of tasks, in the order in which they must be accomplished, possibly including parallel columns showing groups of items to be done simultaneously with other groups. An example is provided at the end of this chapter.

THE CRITICAL PATH

Once you are satisfied that you have identified the tasks that must be accomplished, placed them in proper sequence, and eliminated any possible conflicts created by scheduling the same people or resources for more than one task at the same time, the next step is to convert the list into a graphic picture called a *bubble chain diagram.* Essentially, your top-to-bottom list is turned into a left-to-right chain of circles connected by lines. Each task is shown as a circle or bubble, with sequences running from left to right. Tasks that can be carried out simultaneously are shown as parallel lines of bubbles. Leave room in each circle for the following information: the name of the task; the time needed to carry out the task; starting and ending dates and times for the task (these are left blank at this point).

You may choose to list key people and resources in each circle as well, but this can make your circles so large, or your diagram so visually cluttered, as to make this technique hard to use.

An easy alternative way to show additional information in the bubble chain diagram is to draw the circles in different colors, with each color representing a key person (when more than one person is involved, this can be shown by drawing the circles in multiple colors), and using different colors for the information written inside the circles, with each color representing a key resource. Figure 2.1 presents an example of a bubble chain or critical path diagram.

Once your bubble chain diagram is finished, it becomes easy to identify the *critical path.* This is the strand running through your entire chain of events in which the required times for events that must happen in sequence adds up to the longest total time. Any delay

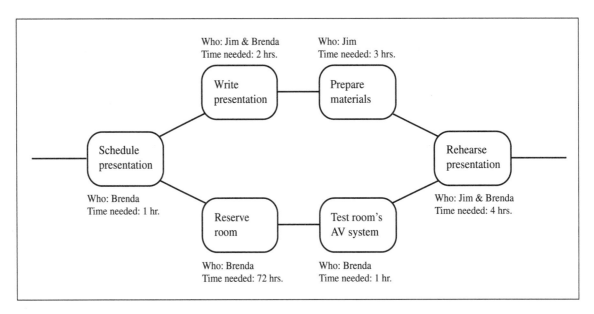

Figure 2.1 In this example, the critical path diagram is in mid-development and shows a temporary branching. Jim and Brenda are preparing to make a presentation to a group of prospective referral sources. Two sequences of actions are shown taking place simultaneously and coming back together at the time of the presentation rehearsal. Because the lower branch will take more time due to the 72 hours needed to reserve a room, the critical path would lie along that branch; i.e., time slippage there will set the whole project back, whereas the top branch has room for some slack. They will have over 72 hours between scheduling the presentation and the rehearsal due to the reservation delay, but the tasks on the upper branch only take a total of 5 hours, leaving over 67 hours of possible slack without delaying the rehearsal.

beyond the allotted amount of time for any of these tasks will delay the completion of the whole project, hence the name critical path.

To identify this critical path, work your way along the line of bubbles, adding up the times required for the tasks in the bubbles to find the total time for the whole sequence of events. Where the bubble chain branches into parallel lines showing tasks to be done simultaneously, one of these parallel lines will take longer than the other(s) running beside it. This line which requires the most time is part of your critical path. The other branches running beside it, which will take less time to complete, are places where you can afford some slack and slippage in your schedule without your whole project necessarily being held up as a result. Figure 2.1 includes an example of this.

REVERSE SCHEDULING

Now you are ready to move on to the third step in this planning process, the reverse scheduling technique. Again, many people will find this to be a method they have been using for much of their lives. To complete this step, begin at the end of the completed bubble chain, the last circle or bubble on the critical path. You will recall that each bubble contains a place to enter the starting and ending dates and times for the task listed in that bubble. Enter your completion deadline—the date and time at which you must be finished with this entire process—as the ending date and time for that bubble. Use the amount of time required to count back and figure out the starting time for the same bubble.

Then take the starting time you just entered for the last bubble and copy it into the second-to-last bubble as the ending time for that bubble. This is the last possible time you can complete that task to start the next on time. Again, use the time required for the task in this bubble to calculate the required starting date and time and fill it in.

Work your way back along the critical path to the beginning in this manner. When you have finished the critical path, fill in the starting and ending dates and times for the circles on the branches of the chain that are not parts of the critical path.

After completing this process, you can look at the starting date and time for the first task and see when you must begin your project to finish by your stated deadline. If you find that you are already past this starting date and time for the first task, your deadline is impossible to meet unless you can cut the time required to accomplish tasks somewhere along the critical path or find ways to simultaneously carry out tasks you have shown as happening in sequence. If your deadline is indeed impossible to meet, the sooner you inform all the people concerned, the better.

After completing this reverse scheduling process, you can go back to the master list of tasks and add the start and completion dates and times for each task.

Next, as a further cross-check to avoid schedule conflicts when you put your plan into action, make a separate schedule for each key person and each key resource, showing what that person will be doing and how that resource will be used from beginning to end of your program's start-up. A calendar software program will come in handy for this.

STRUCTURED WALK-THROUGH

Now you are ready to reconvene the planning group that helped you with the brainstorming session earlier. As preparation, make copies of several documents for all the people who will attend the walk-through meeting:

- The final version of the master task list, showing the following information for each task:

  - The name of the task.

  - The person(s) who will execute the task.

  - The resources needed to execute the task.

  - The amount of time needed.

  - The starting and ending dates and times.

- The individual schedules for all key people and resources.

- The completed bubble chain diagram including the critical path.

The work to be done at this meeting is, as the term walk-through implies, to visualize carrying out the plan from beginning to end, step by step. It seems to work best to begin by reviewing the master task list and the individual schedules, briefly examining each item and soliciting comments about any problems or questions seen by anyone present, and either resolving them on the spot if possible or noting that the plan needs more work in those areas if no immediate fixes are apparent.

Once this is done, your group will turn to the bubble path diagram. Ask all attendees to mentally place themselves in the position of the person(s) putting this plan into action and, beginning with the first circle, envision carrying the task out, asking themselves whether the information in the circle is valid. The following questions are useful:

- Are there any key people who will be involved in the task who are not listed?

- Will additional important resources be needed?

- Is the time allotted either insufficient or excessive?

- Are there any missing tasks or steps between the previous circle and this one?

Once the group has worked its way from beginning to end of the bubble chain diagram, adding and amending if necessary, the walk-through is complete.

It may be that the clinician at this stage finds substantial revisions to be made to the master task list, the individual schedules, and the bubble chain diagram. If so, this is neither unusual nor a cause for discouragement. It is normal for revision to be needed at this stage, and it is far less costly in time, money, and stress to spot problems and correct them at this point than later on while you are acting on this plan.

If significant revisions are to be made, you may want to either convene one more meeting of your planning group to review the final product, or ask them to review it individually and give you their final feedback.

The end result of all this is that you will have an impressively coherent, practical, and well-thought-out plan. Changes and adjustments will still become necessary as you proceed with building your program, but you will have kept unpleasant surprises to a minimum.

This process may sound incredibly tedious and laborious, and in many ways it can feel that way while one is going through it. However, if your program start-up is typical, the tedium and labor involved in exhaustive planning will save you from significant amounts of stress and frustration, accompanied by even greater amounts of labor, while you do the work. Additional benefits include the following:

- Your plan will serve as a detailed record of your efforts.

- This plan will be useful as a starting point and source documentation for similar projects in the future.

- The people with whom you work will be favorably impressed by your skill, versatility, and attention to detail.

- These techniques, once learned, can be applied to a wide variety of other complex endeavors, ranging from building a house to having a baby.

High-Visibility Planning Considerations

Following are some specific tasks and elements of the planning process that have great impact on the success or failure of the entire plan. It is wise to pay special attention in these areas.

Presentations

When you are selling your ideas to management and referral/funding sources, it is important to review your presentation in advance with these ideas in mind:

- Have you stayed focused on *their* interests rather than yours? Their interest is in how your program will help them do their jobs and serve their needs.

- Have you anticipated questions and objections and worked out good answers and solutions ahead of time (if you can't come up with a good answer or solution for an objection, your plan needs to be revised until you can)? It is a big help to get outsiders who haven't been part of the planning process, but who are knowledgeable about this type of program, to critique your plan and presentation and find as many flaws as they can, so you can fix them before your real audience sees the presentation.

- Have you planned to involve your audience in your presentation—do you use participatory questioning? Do you draw as many connections as you can between what you are proposing and what they are doing already? Do you point out ways your program will solve problems that are causing them difficulty?

Coordination

It pays to accomplish tasks involving getting information, authorizations, agreements, and assistance from people or agencies outside your immediate planning group (or yourself if you *are* the planning group) as early in the process as practical, and to get in contact with those people or agencies even before that. You want to let them know what's coming, sound them out to make sure you'll have their support when you need it, and get their input and ideas for possible improvements.

Reinventing the Wheel

Establishing a program is a lot of work. If you are typical, at this point you may be feeling overwhelmed by the scale and detail of the plan you must carry out. You will benefit if you avoid doing more than you have to.

Where you can use existing resources ethically, legally, and without compromising the quality of your program, do so. These resources may be documentation, psychoeducational materials, or even whole programs you can incorporate as subprograms. For example, as mentioned in Chapter 1, in one program the authors established, rather than build a key phase from scratch we included an already existing relapse prevention group as a step-down phase in the larger program, adding our program clientele to the existing population of that group (after careful coordination with the therapists running the existing group!). This saved us the time and effort we would have put into creating a schedule and psychoeducational materials for 10 group sessions on relapse prevention. This can also gain your program additional active support by validating and increasing the usefulness of the work others have done, thereby recruiting them as stakeholders.

This chapter has presented a detailed set of techniques to enable you to systematically plan the start-up of the chemical dependence treatment program you designed in Chapter 1. Again, these techniques are ones we chose because they are relatively easy to learn and because they produce solid results when properly applied. They are not the only methods that work, and if you are familiar with other approaches that you would rather use, by all means substitute whatever works for you for what we have suggested here. Our aim is to expand your toolkit and to save you time and effort, and we urge you to read and use this chapter with that aim in mind.

In Chapters 3–7 of this volume, we continue this process by providing clinical documentation for your use according to your own needs, existing resources, and convenience. Chapters 9–11 conclude by providing psychoeducational teaching materials suitable for adaptation or use as is in conducting presentations on a variety of topics focused directly on substance abuse and on related life issues.

Chapter 3

Precontact: Referral Forms and Procedures

This chapter includes blank forms to be used to communicate with external sources and clients referred for services. You may want to provide blank forms to those agencies from whom you receive referrals to make the referral process consistent and timely.

Only four forms are included because in most cases, external referral sources will be doing most of the paperwork and will use their own forms. In addition, the precontact stage is a brief portion of the process of entering treatment, with the bulk of the paperwork involved in bringing a client into your program taking place in the pretreatment intake and evaluation process, which is covered in Chapter 4. The following forms are included in this chapter:

Appointment Notification/Confirmation Letter

Referral and Treatment Compliance Follow-Up Letter

Thank You for Your Referral

Referral for Additional Services

Appointment Notification/Confirmation Letter

Date: ____/____/____

Dear: _____

You have been referred to, or have chosen to receive services from, our agency. You were referred by: _____. Your first appointment is scheduled for the following date and time:

Date: ____/____/____   Day: _____   Time: _____ AM/PM

You will be seeing: _____

If you are unable to keep this appointment, please call this agency in advance by calling the following number: _____.

• You can expect the first appointment to take approximately _____, as we will need to complete forms and gather additional information to best serve you. This will also allow time to answer any questions you may have.

• In order to complete this initial appointment in a timely fashion, please bring the following information and/or documentation with you: _____

_____

_____

_____

• This will help us work with you in determining insurance coverage, fees for services, and/or who will be billed.

• The fee for your first visit will be $ _____. This agency's policy on payment is

_____

_____

However, payment for services is the client's responsibility regardless of what arrangements have been made with other payers.

I look forward to meeting with you!

Sincerely,

Name: _____

Title: _____

Referral and Treatment Compliance Follow-Up Letter

Date: ____/____/____

To: _____

Client Name: _____ Case #/ID #: _____

Referral / Treatment Status

( ) Client met with our intake worker, clinician, doctor on: ____/____/____.

( ) Client failed to attend screening/intake appointment dated: ____/____/____.

( ) Client is scheduled to attend the following ____ Individual ____ Marital/Family ____ Group counseling/therapy program _____ starting ____/____/____.

( ) Client failed to attend his/her scheduled session on ____/____/____.

( ) Client has failed to schedule an appointment as of this date.

( ) Client enrolled but failed to complete the following program:_____
Reason for failure: _____

( ) Client attended sessions but has not fulfilled financial requirements.

( ) Client completed screening/intake but failed to enroll in the program.

( ) Client previously noncompliant but currently attending sessions.

( ) Client satisfactorily completed required sessions and other tasks/activities and received a certificate of completion dated: ____/____/____.

( ) Client has been contacted and has declined services at this time (reason(s) given if any):
_____

( ) Client has been referred for additional services to: _____

Additional Comments: _____
_____
_____
_____

Signature of Staff Member Completing Form: _____ Date: ____/____/____

Name/Title of Staff Member Completing Form: _____

Thank You for Your Referral!

To: _____ Agency/School/Company: _____

We have processed your referral of _____ , Case #: _____,

for services at this program/agency. Date Referral Received ____/____/____

Current Status

( ) We have been unable to contact the above named person with the information provided to us.

( ) The client has scheduled an appointment on ____/____/____ at _____ AM/PM
with _____ for the purpose of _____.

( ) The referred person has been enrolled in the following ___ Individual ___ Marital/Family
___ Group counseling/therapy program. His/her tentative start date is ____/____/____.

( ) The referred person has declined services (reason(s) given if any): _____
_____.

( ) We apologize for not being able to provide services at this time. We have placed this person on
a waiting list and will notify both you and him/her when we are able to provide services. We
estimate that this will be on about ____/____/____.

( ) Additional comments: _____
_____.

We will provide you with a Referral and Treatment Compliance Follow-Up Letter to advise you
of any significant events in this client's treatment. Please contact us if you need additional
information, or if you have any additional information that may assist us in providing services. Your
referral is important to us!

Signed: _____ Name/Title: _____

Program/Service: _____ Phone: _____ Fax: _____

Referral for Additional Services

Client Name: _____ Case #: _____ Date: ____/____/____

Referral Source/Contact: _____

Client Address: _____ Client/Sponsor ID# / SSN #: _____

_____ Agency Address: _____

Client Phone: (H) _____ _____

(W) _____ Agency Phone: _____ Fax: _____

Parent/Guardian: _____ Agency Contact Person: _____

Emergency Contact Name/Phone: _____

Preferred Focus of Treatment: _____

_____

Service(s)/Program(s) Requested:

(   ) Individual counseling   (   ) Case management

(   ) Family counseling   (   ) Psychological testing

(   ) Group counseling   (   ) Psychiatric assessment

(   ) Substance abuse counseling   (   ) Medication monitoring

(   ) Medical examination _____

(   ) Other: _____

Appointment(s) Will Be Scheduled by:

(   ) Client   (   ) Clinician   (   ) Customer service rep.   (   ) Other: _____

Insurance Information:

Insurance Company: ____ Blue Cross/Blue Shield ____ CHAMPUS/TriCare ____ Medicare
____ Aetna ____ Cigna ____ Premier ____ Health Partners
____ Other: _____

Policy #: _____ Enrollment/Plan/Group Number: _____ Effective Date: ____/____/____

Signature of Staff Member Completing Form: _____ Date: ____/____/____

Name/Title of Staff Member Completing Form: _____

Chapter 4

Intake and Assessment Forms and Procedures

Because substance abuse treatment is often combined with treatment for other comorbid issues, the documentation in this chapter provides a framework for a generalized intake and assessment process with special attention to substance abuse issues. We have incorporated documentation of other issues with the idea that the clinician can use some of these forms *in place of,* rather than *in addition to,* existing documentation that does not address drug and alcohol abuse issues as effectively as needed for a substance abuse treatment program. This is done with the aim of helping clinicians keep their paperwork load manageable, and with an eye toward making this volume comprehensive and useful. The following forms are included in this chapter:

Initial Client Information

Therapist Clinical Assessment Form

Substance Dependence/Abuse Assessment

Confidential Brief Health Information Form

Consent for Treatment

Release of Information

Confidentiality in Therapy

Client Rights Form

Financial Information Form

Payment Agreement for Services

Initial Client Information

Name: _____   Birth date: ____/____/____

Address: _____   Today's Date: ____/____/____

_____   Phone: (H) _____

Employer: _____   Phone: (W) _____

Address: _____   SSN: _____

Family Information

Marital status: _____ Married _____ Yrs _____ Never married _____ Separated

_____ Divorced _____ Yrs _____ Widowed _____ Yrs

Children (Names and ages): _____

_____

Household: ___Live alone ____ Live w. partner and/or children ____ Live w. parents/other family

____ Homeless ____ Live w. roommate(s)/other ____ Group home/residential treatment center

____ Incarcerated

Will family or others participate in your counseling? _____ If so, who will participate?

Name:_____ Relationship: _____

Name:_____ Relationship: _____

Work/Education Information

Profession/type(s) of work: _____

Years in current field of work: _____ Years in other fields: _____ Years formal education: _____

Work/education goals: _____

Medical and Other Information

Please list any medical problem you are being treated for: _____

Please list any medications you take: _____

In case of a medical or other emergency, please tell us who you would like us to call:

Name: _____ Phone: _____

Address: _____ Relationship _____

Substance Abuse Information

Do you feel you have a drug or alcohol problem? _____ If yes, why? _____

What is your drug of choice (the drug, including alcohol, you use most often)? _____

How often have you used this drug in the past? _____ How much do you usually use? _____

When was the first time you used it? _____ When was the last time you used this drug? _____

What is the longest you have voluntarily gone without this drug? _____ Why? _____

What other drugs have you used in the past 6 months? _____

Please briefly describe the drug or alcohol related event that caused you to come to treatment: _____

_____

Counseling Information

Reason for coming to counseling/desired services: _____

Have you been in treatment or counseling before? _____ If so, please give us the following information:

Purpose/Issues: Name of Counselor: When & for How Long: Results:

_____   _____   _____   _____

What are your goals for the outcome of counseling? Please describe how you hope your life will be

different:_____

Therapist Clinical Assessment Form

1. Identifying Data:

Name: _____ Date of Birth: ____/____/____ Date of Assessment: ____/____/____

Gender: M _____ F _____ Client ID/Case File #: _____ Primary Language: _____

Source of Information:

Client: _____ Spouse/Partner (Name): _____ Parent/Guardian (Name): _____

Referring Agency Staff Member (Name/Title): _____

Other (Name/Relationship) _____

2. Presenting Problem and History:

Presenting Problem/Reason for Referral/Behavioral Symptoms (onset, frequency, duration):

_____

_____

Mental Health Treatment History (inpatient/outpatient, including date, duration, and outcome):

Date	Location	Problem	Treatment Provider's Name	Duration	Outcome
_____	_____	_____	_____	_____	_____
_____	_____	_____	_____	_____	_____
_____	_____	_____	_____	_____	_____

Family Mental Health Treatment History:

Family Member	Date	Location	Problem	Duration	Outcome
_____	_____	_____	_____	_____	_____
_____	_____	_____	_____	_____	_____
_____	_____	_____	_____	_____	_____

Family History (family of origin, current family constellation, patterns in family relationships):

Genograms:

Family of Origin   Current Family Constellation

_____   _____

Social History/Issues:

Sexual: Gender identity: _____ Currently sexually active? _____ Age of first sexual experience? _____
Sexual issues or problems: _____

Spiritual: Faith group, if any: _____ Active in religious/spiritual activities? _____
Spiritual issues or problems: _____

Housing: Describe current living situation: _____
Housing issues or problems relevant to treatment: _____

Cultural/leisure/recreational: Ethnocultural heritage/identity: _____
Hobbies/activities: _____
Cultural issues or problems relevant to treatment: _____

Social/support resources: Resources in use: _____
Needs, issues, or problems in this area relevant to treatment: _____
_____

Relationships: Marital status: _____ Previous marriages: _____
Other significant relationships: _____

Educational/Vocational/Financial/Military History:

Educational: Years of education: _____ Current/past educational issues or problems: _____
_____

Vocational: Current employment status: _____ Job satisfaction level: _____
Current & past jobs: _____
_____

Vocational issues or problems relevant to treatment: _____
_____

Financial issues or problems relevant to treatment: _____
_____

Military history: Ever in service? _____ Years served: _____ How did service end? _____
Nature of primary duties: _____ Feelings about service experience: _____
Combat experience, esp. any trauma: _____
Issues or problems related to military service: _____
_____

Developmental History (Unusual events during pregnancy/childbirth, developmental delays/milestones, speech and language development, special skills/talents):
_____
_____

Legal History (current status and past legal involvement, incl. civil cases, divorce/separation/custody issues): _____
_____
_____

For DUI, BAC at arrest: _____ Other substance-related arrest(s) (specify): _____
_____

Abuse History (abuse past and present, whether reported and outcome, age at time of abuse, identity of perpetrator(s), client's role as victim/perpetrator/witness):
_____
_____

Substance Abuse History:

	Age at First Use	Pattern of Use	Frequency of Use	Route of Administration	Date of Last Use	Current Use?
Alcohol	_____	_____	_____	_____	_____	_____
Amphetamine	_____	_____	_____	_____	_____	_____
Methamphetamine	_____	_____	_____	_____	_____	_____
Cocaine/Crack	_____	_____	_____	_____	_____	_____
Heroin	_____	_____	_____	_____	_____	_____
Other IV drug use	_____	_____	_____	_____	_____	_____
Hallucinogens	_____	_____	_____	_____	_____	_____
Cannabis	_____	_____	_____	_____	_____	_____
Methadone	_____	_____	_____	_____	_____	_____
Barbiturates	_____	_____	_____	_____	_____	_____
Inhalants	_____	_____	_____	_____	_____	_____
Steroids	_____	_____	_____	_____	_____	_____
Nicotine	_____	_____	_____	_____	_____	_____
Caffeine	_____	_____	_____	_____	_____	_____
Other rx meds	_____	_____	_____	_____	_____	_____
Other	_____	_____	_____	_____	_____	_____

Drug of choice: _____ Most frequent time of use: _____ Morning use? _____

Use to relax or help sleep? _____ Use to relieve pain/discomfort or feel better? _____

Most frequent setting for use (time, place, people): _____

Briefly list experiences of: DTs? _____ Seizures? _____

Tolerance? _____ Withdrawal? _____ Blackouts/memory loss? _____

Vocational/educational/familial/legal/economical changes related to use? _____
_____

Longest and last period of voluntary abstinence Longest: _____ Last: _____

Family history of substance abuse (which members) _____

Has anyone told you they were concerned about your drinking/drug use or asked you to stop
(who/when)? _____ Have you attended AA/NA (when)? _____

Willing to attend AA/NA? _____ Currently attending AA/NA? _____ How often? _____

Have an AA/NA sponsor? _____ Home group? _____ Willing to work with a sponsor? _____

Do you think your drinking/drug use is a problem (if so, why)? _____
_____
_____

Other current/past compulsive/addictive behaviors (gambling, eating, sex, work, caffeine/nicotine,
exercise, etc.): _____
_____

Mental Status:

General appearance: Neat _____ Disheveled _____ Formal _____ Casual _____ Seductive _____

Comments: _____
_____

Orientation: Identity _____ Time _____ Place _____ Activity _____

Comments: _____
_____

Behavior: Impulse control adequate _____ inadequate _____ Describe: _____
_____

Motor activity: Normal ____ Hyperactive/Agitated ____ Restless ____ Passive/Hypoactive ____
Posturing ____ Tics/Ritualistic actions (including vocal) ____ Rigid ____ Comments: _____
_____

Mood: Appropriate _____ Relaxed _____ Anxious/Fearful _____ Angry _____ Euphoric _____
Guarded _____ Suspicious _____ Sad/Tearful _____ Depressed _____ Withdrawn _____
Labile _____ Apathetic/Indifferent _____ Manic _____ Comments: _____
_____

Affect: Consistent with mood/activity ____ Dissonant with mood/Activity ____ Labile ____
Blunted _____ Flat ____ Constricted _____ Comments: _____
_____

Speech: Coherent ____ Incoherent _____ Pressured ____ Halting _____ Idiosyncratic _____
Quantity ____ Volume _____ Speed ____ Impediment _____ Comments: _____
_____

Self-concept: Adequate/Satisfactory ____ Inadequate/Poor _____ Unrealistic ____ Comments:
_____

Thought process: Associations logical _____ Loose ____ Tangential/Incomprehensible _____
Content realistic ____ Obsessive/Ruminative ____ Delusional ____ Grandiose _____
Phobic _____ Concentration good _____ Fair _____ Poor _____ Inconsistent _____
Comments: _____

Judgment: Unimpaired _____ Uncertain ____ Impaired ____ Comments: _____
_____

Perception: Normal _____ Hallucinations (auditory, visual, tactile, olfactory, taste) _____
Illusions _____ Comments: _____
_____

Memory: Recent: intact __ not intact __ selective ___ Remote: intact __ not intact __ selective ___
Comments: _____
_____

Insight into situation: Unimpaired ____ Limited ____ Absent ____ Distorted/delusional ____
Comments: _____
_____

Suicidal potential: Current ideation ____ Current intent ____ Has plan ____ Has means ____
Lethality of plan/Means ____ Prior threats/Gestures/Attempts ____
Willing to contract against self-harm? _____ Comments: _____
_____

Homicidal potential: Current ideation ____ Current intent ___ Has plan ___ Has means ____
Prior threats/Gestures/Attempts at homicide/Serious harm to others ___
Willing to contract against harming other(s)? ___ Comments: _____
_____
_____

3. Assessment Summary and Recommendations:

DSM-IV Diagnostic Codes:

Axis I: _____ _____   _____ _____

_____ _____   _____ _____

Axis II: _____ _____   _____ _____

_____ _____   _____ _____

Axis III: _____ _____   _____ _____

_____ _____   _____ _____

Axis IV: _____ _____   _____ _____

_____ _____   _____ _____

Axis V: GAF   Current: _____   Past year: _____

Recommendations for treatment and referral(s): _____

_____

Client's desired outcome of treatment: _____

_____

Client's motivation for change: _____

_____

Client's strengths/resources: _____

_____

Client's limitations/obstacles: _____

_____

Other assessments indicated? None indicated _____
        Psychiatric Evaluation _____   Specific areas to evaluate: _____
        Psychological Testing _____   Specific tests/Types of test: _____
        Medical Evaluation   _____   Specific areas to evaluate: _____
        Depression Inventory _____   Other: _____

Documentation to be obtained:

Medical: _____

_____

School: _____

_____

Other agencies/Treatment facilities: _____

_____

_____

Other needed resources or services (legal, medical, financial, social, support groups, etc.):

_____

_____

Assessor's Name/Title: _____ Signature: _____ Date: ____/____/____

Client/Guardian's Name: _____ Signature: _____Date: ____/____/____

Substance Dependence Assessment

DSM-IV Dependency Symptoms (as shown by . . .)	Drug of Choice #1	Drug of Choice #2	Drug of Choice #3	Other Drug(s)
Dx of dependency requires 3 or more symptoms as patterns over 12-month period				
Tolerance:				
Withdrawal:				
Loss of control: Uses more/for longer than intended:				
Persistent desire/efforts to cut down or control use:				
Substantial time devoted to use:				
Important activities given up or reduced due to use:				
Use despite knowledge of adverse physical or psychological consequences:				
TOTAL (3 or more?)				

Substance Abuse Assessment

DSM-IV Substance Drug(s) Abuse Symptoms (as shown by . . .)	Drug of Choice #1	Drug of Choice #2	Drug of Choice #3	Other Drug(s)
Failure in major role obligations:				
Use in hazardous situations:				
Legal problems related to use:				
Continued use despite adverse results:				
One or more?				

DSM-IV Diagnostic Criteria Met

Substance Dependence: 3 or more of 7 symptoms present as patterns over a 12-month period

303.90 Alcohol dependence _____	Additional Specifiers:
304.40 Amphetamine dependence _____	With physiological dependence _____
304.30 Cannabis dependence _____	(tolerance and/or withdrawal seen)
304.20 Cocaine dependence _____	Without physiological dependence _____
304.50 Hallucinogen dependence _____	(no tolerance or withdrawal)
304.60 Inhalant dependence _____	Early full remission _____
305.10 Nicotine dependence _____	(No dependence/abuse criteria for 1–12 mo.)
304.00 Opioid dependence _____	Early partial remission
304.90 Phencyclidine dependence _____	(1/more dependence/abuse criteria for 1–12 mo.)
304.10 Sedative, Hypnotic, or	Sustained full remission _____
Anxiolytic dependence _____	(no dependence/abuse criteria 12 mo/more)
304.80 Polysubstance dependence _____	Sustained partial remission _____
304.90 Other (or unknown)	(1/more dependence/abuse criteria 12 mo/more)
substance dependence	On agonist therapy _____
	In a controlled environment _____

Substance Abuse: 1 or more of 4 symptoms recurring within a 12-month period without meeting criteria for substance dependence

305.00 Alcohol abuse _____	305.50 Opioid abuse _____
305.70 Amphetamine abuse _____	305.90 Phencyclidine abuse _____
305.20 Cannabis abuse _____	305.40 Sedative, Hypnotic, or
305.60 Cocaine abuse _____	Anxiolytic abuse _____
305.30 Hallucinogen abuse _____	305.90 Other (or unknown)
305.90 Inhalant abuse _____	substance abuse _____

Dimensions:	Substance Abuse Psychoed. Group	Dependence/ Relapse Prev. Psychoed. Group	Intensive Out-Patient Program	Residential Tx Program
Substance Abuse/Depend	Dx of subst. abuse vs. dependence	Dx of substance dependence	Dx of substance dependence	Dx of substance dependence
Suicidal/ Homicidal	No serious danger to self or others	No serious danger to self or others	No serious danger to self or others	Significant danger to self or others
Medical Issues	Nothing interfering with treatment	Nothing interfering with treatment	Nothing interfering with treatment	Needs 24-hr med. care/monitoring
Mental Status	Not significantly impaired, capable of insight	Not significantly impaired, capable of insight	No more than moderately impaired	Significant/ disabling cognitive impairment
Emotional Status	Low/moderate stress/anxiety/ depression, good rehab potential with minimal support	Low/moderate stress/anxiety/ depression, good rehab potential with minimal support	Moderate/high stress/anxiety/ depression, poor rehab potential without daily support	High stress/ anxiety/ depression, unable to manage in outpatient setting
Program Acceptance	Wants help/ change, willing to cooperate with treatment	Wants help/ change, willing to cooperate with treatment	Requires frequent/ daily monitoring for tx compliance	Requires constant monitoring for tx compliance
Relapse Potential	Good potential to stop abuse with psychoed treatment	Good potential to abstain/avoid relapse with psychoed treatment	Relapse risk high without intensive treatment program	Relapse likely without controlled environment
Environmental Stressors	Daily environment supports recovery/ treatment goals	Daily environment supports recovery/ treatment goals	Daily environment indifferent/hostile to recovery/ treatment	Daily environment hostile to recovery/ treatment
Coping Skills/ Support Network	Adequate coping skills/support network	Adequate coping skills/support network	Marginal coping skills/support network	Ineffective coping skills/support network
Commitment to Recovery	At least moderate commitment to recovery	At least moderate commitment to recovery	Ambivalent/ apathetic/mildly to moderately resistant	Actively resistant to treatment/ recovery

(Table heading: Substance Abuse Treatment/Education Programs — Treatment Placement Matrix)

1. For each dimension in left column, choose the phrase to its right that best describes the person being evaluated. Put a check or a brief comment in that box. Where two or more columns have the same phrase, use the box farthest to the left.

2. Once all rows are checked refer the client to treatment in the type of program identified with the marked column farthest to the right. If any boxes are marked under <u>Residential</u>, refer to residential treatment; if the farthest-right box marked is under <u>Intensive Outpatient</u>, refer to an intensive outpatient program, etc.

Other Indicators Often Connected to Substance Abuse

1. Blackouts (gaps in memory): ___ Y ___ N   If Y, about how many times? ____
    Describe most recent blackout experience:_____
    _____
    _____
    _____

2. Repeated falls, fights, work/sports injuries, etc.: ___ Y ___ N   If Y, about how many times? ____
    Describe most recent occurrence: _____
    _____
    _____
    _____

3. Substance-related hallucinations/delusional episodes: ____ Y ____ N If Y, describe: _____
    _____
    _____
    _____

4. Negative changes in social circle/recreational activities: ___ Y ____ N If Y, describe: _____
    _____
    _____
    _____

5. Repeated STDs: ____ Y ____ N If Y, how many? _____

6. Looks older than actual age: ____ Y ____ N

7. Relationship problems/domestic violence: _____ Y ____ N If Y, describe: _____
    _____
    _____
    _____

8. Financial difficulties: ____ Y ____ N

9. Frequent job changes: ____ Y ____ N

10. Frequent geo. moves: ____ Y ____ N

11. Frequent minor legal infractions: ___ Y ___ N

12. Family history of substance abuse problems: _____ Y ____ N If Y, describe: _____
    _____
    _____
    _____

    Treatment Referral Based on Diagnostic Criteria, Treatment Placement Matrix, and Other Indicators:

    No substance abuse treatment needed   _____   Intensive outpatient program   _____
    Outpatient abuse/dependence psychoed grp. _____   Residential treatment program _____
    Outpatient dependence/relapse prev. grp.   _____   Other: _____

    Therapist Name: _____ Signature: _____ Date: ___/___/___

Confidential Brief Health Information Form

Name: _____   Birth Date: ____/____/____
Address: _____   Phone: (H) _____
          _____   SSN: _____
Primary Care Physician: _____   Phone: _____
Today's Date: ____/____/____

List any health problems or concerns you now have:

Type of problem/concern:	How long:	Under a doctor's care? (Y/N, name of doctor):
_____	_____	____ _____
_____	_____	____ _____
_____	_____	____ _____
_____	_____	____ _____

How would you describe your general health at this time? _____

When and where was your most recent physical exam? _____

Did the results of that exam show that you had any medical problems at that time? _____
If yes, what were they? _____
_____
_____

Please list any times you have been hospitalized or had surgery:

When:	Name and location of hospital, reason you were hospitalized:	Type of surgery/other treatment & outcome:	Present status:
____/____/____	_____	_____	_____
____/____/____	_____	_____	_____
____/____/____	_____	_____	_____

Please list other major illnesses or injuries you have had, especially injuries to head/neck/spine:

When:	Type of illness or injury:	Treatment & outcome:	Present status:
____/____/____	_____	_____	_____
____/____/____	_____	_____	_____
____/____/____	_____	_____	_____

Please list any current medications, and also any medications you have taken in the past year (either prescribed or over the counter) and the reasons you are or were taking them:

Type of medication:	Reason taken:	Any complications or side effects:
_____	_____	_____
_____	_____	_____
_____	_____	_____
_____	_____	_____

Do you now have, or have you ever had, seizures or convulsions? _____ If yes, when, and what condition caused them? _____
_____
_____

Do you have any allergies? _____ If yes, what are they? _____
_____
_____

Please describe your family history of illness or diseases (any major illness experienced by a parent or sibling and any illness that seems to run in your family):

Who: Type of illness: Treatment &outcome: Present status:

_____   _____   _____   _____
_____   _____   _____   _____
_____   _____   _____   _____
_____   _____   _____   _____

For Women Only:
At what age did you start to menstruate? _____ Do you now have, or have you had, any problems
with your menstrual period? _____ If yes, please describe these problems:_____
_____
_____

Have you had any:
Pregnancies?   _____   If yes, how many?   _____   When? _____
Miscarriages?   _____   If yes, how many?   _____   When? _____
Abortions?   _____   If yes, how many?   _____   When? _____
Menopausal symptoms or treatment? _____ If yes, when? _____
_____
_____

For Men Only:
Do you now have, or have you had, problems with your prostate, difficult or painful urination, or
impotence? _____ If yes, please describe these problems: _____
_____
_____

For Children (only if your child is the primary client for this therapy):
What immunizations has your child received (you may provide a copy of his or her shot record if that is
easier)?
When: Type of immunization: Any problems or side effects:
____/____/____   _____   _____
____/____/____   _____   _____
____/____/____   _____   _____
____/____/____   _____   _____

Lifestyle/Health Habits:
On average, how many hours of sleep do you get? _____ Do you have problems with sleep? If yes,
what kind of sleep problems do you have? _____
_____
_____

Do you exercise regularly? _____ If yes, how often and for how long? _____
In what kinds of exercise or physical activities do you participate? _____
_____
_____

How is your appetite? _____ Do you have any problems with your appetite? _____
If yes, what kind of problems are they? _____
_____
_____

Have you recently gained or lost a significant amount of weight (for most adults, more than 20 pounds in 6 months — if you are smaller than average, a lesser amount may be significant for you)? _____
If yes, please describe this weight gain/loss and what you believe is the reason: _____
_____
_____
_____
_____

How much coffee, tea, cola, or other substance containing caffeine do you consume each day? _____
_____
_____
_____

Do you smoke or use chewing tobacco or snuff? _____ If yes, how much? _____
Are you a former tobacco user who has quit? _____ If yes, when did you quit? _____
Please indicate which of the following drugs you have used, if any:

	Age at First Use	How Often You Usually Use(d)	How Much You Usually Use(d)	Method(s) of Use	How Long Since Last Use
Alcohol	_____	_____	_____	_____	_____
Methamphetamine	_____	_____	_____	_____	_____
Amphetamines ("speed")	_____	_____	_____	_____	_____
Barbiturates ("downers")	_____	_____	_____	_____	_____
Cocaine (powder)	_____	_____	_____	_____	_____
Cocaine (crack)	_____	_____	_____	_____	_____
Hallucinogens (LSD, etc)	_____	_____	_____	_____	_____
Heroin	_____	_____	_____	_____	_____
Methadone	_____	_____	_____	_____	_____
Morphine	_____	_____	_____	_____	_____
Opium	_____	_____	_____	_____	_____
Inhalants	_____	_____	_____	_____	_____
Marijuana/Hashish	_____	_____	_____	_____	_____
PCP ("Angel dust")	_____	_____	_____	_____	_____
Steroids	_____	_____	_____	_____	_____

Client/Guardian's Name: _____ Signature: _____ Date: _____/_____/_____
Staff Member Name: _____ Signature: _____ Date: _____/_____/_____

Consent for Treatment

1. I have been fully informed of my rights as a client of this agency, the extent and limits of confidentiality in therapy, and the goals associated with this therapy. With that knowledge, I request and consent to receive therapy from qualified personnel of this agency. Initials: _____

2. I understand that the staff of this agency may not disclose information about my therapy to anyone outside this agency without my written consent, except as required by law to comply with a court order, to prevent suicide/self-harm or harm to others, or to stop or prevent abuse of a child, senior, or disabled person. However, I also understand that my participation in treatment may require my written consent to allow staff of this agency to provide some information about my therapy to a referring agency and/or an insurance company or other payer, and that if this is the case, the form provided for my written consent for this disclosure will state what specific types of information will be disclosed. Initials: _____

3. I understand that my therapist may work with me at this agency, in my home, or in other settings based on his/her professional judgement. I further understand that my therapy may involve my participation in individual, couple, family, and/or group counseling, and may involve homework assignments for me to do outside of therapy sessions. I agree to participate actively in my therapy, to cooperate with my therapist, and to complete required homework assignments or other activities included in my therapy. Initials: _____

4. I understand that if I participate in group counseling, a condition of my doing so is that I protect the privacy and confidentiality of other participants. I agree that if I participate in group counseling, I will not disclose information about the identity, words, or actions of other group counseling participants to anyone outside the therapy group. Initials: _____

5. I understand that my therapy may include my attendance at meetings of independent self-help support groups including Alcoholics Anonymous, Narcotics Anonymous, and/or other programs. I agree to participate in such programs if assigned and to abide by the practices of those programs regarding protecting the privacy and anonymity of other program participants. Initials: _____

Client/Guardian's Name: _____ Signature: _____ Date: ____/____/____

Agency Representative Name: _____ Signature: _____ Date: ____/____/____

Release of Information

I, _____ , hereby authorize the release and disclosure of the following clinical and/or therapeutic records for the following purpose(s):

[ ] Authorization to release information regarding counseling and therapy care and treatment.

[ ] Authorization to release information held under the Drug Office and Treatment Act of 1972 (PL-92255) and the Comprehensive Alcohol Abuse and Alcoholism Prevention Treatment and Rehabilitation Act Amendments of 1974.

[ ] Authorization to release information related to Human Immunodeficiency Virus (HIV) and Acquired Immune Deficiency Syndrome (AIDS).

Please release authorized information between (your agency name here) and:

_____

_____

_____

_____

_____

Specific information to be released (client's initials to approve release):

_____ Assessments and evaluations   _____ Psychosocial history

_____ Continued care & treatment   _____ Discharge summary

Correspondence (specify): _____

Other (specify): _____

_____

Purpose(s) for which information is to be released: _____

_____

_____

_____

_____

_____

Revocation/Expiration: This Release of Information is subject to revocation by the under-signed at any time except to the extent that information has already been disclosed based on authorization contained herein. Unless further limited by a date stated here, _____ , this Release of Information will automatically expire after a period of 180 days from the date signed. I have the right to receive a copy of this Release of Information upon my request.

Client/Guardian's Name: _____ Signature: _____ Date: ____/____/____

Therapist Name: _____ Signature: _____ Date: ____/____/____

Confidentiality in Therapy

Before you tell your therapist about yourself, you have the right to know what information can and cannot be kept confidential. Please read this and initial each item only if you understand and agree to the conditions described. If there is anything you don't understand, your therapist will explain it in more detail.

General Extent and Limits of Confidentiality

The laws and ethics governing therapy require that therapists keep all information about clients confidential except for certain types of information and situations. Those exceptions are:

1. *Client's desire:* If you want your therapist or this agency to give information about your case to anyone outside this agency, you must sign a Release of Information giving written permission for this disclosure.

> *Acknowledgment:* **I understand that if I want my therapist or this agency to give information about my case to any outside person or agency, I must sign a Release of Information. Initials: _____**

2. *Safety:*

a. *Risk of self-harm:* If your words or behavior convince your therapist that you are likely to harm yourself, either deliberately or because you are unable to keep yourself safe, your therapist must do whatever he or she can to prevent you from being harmed. This means the therapist must take action up to and including hospitalizing you with or without your consent. If this situation comes up, your therapist will discuss it with you before taking action unless it appears that this would be unsafe or immediate action is needed to keep you from being harmed.

b. *Risk of harm to others:* If you threaten serious harm to another person, your therapist must try to protect that person. He or she would report your threat to the police, warn the threatened person, and try to prevent you from carrying out your threat. If this situation comes up, your therapist will discuss it with you before taking action unless it appears that this would be unsafe or immediate action is needed to keep you from acting on your threat.

> *Acknowledgment:* **I understand that if my therapist believes there is a serious risk that I will hurt or kill myself or another person, my therapist is legally required to report this, warn the endangered person if someone other than myself, and take whatever action seems needed in his or her professional judgement to prevent harm to myself or others. Initials: _____**

c. *Emergencies:* In an emergency when your health or your life is endangered, your therapist must provide medical personnel or other professionals any information about you that is needed to protect your life, but only information that is needed for that purpose. If possible your therapist would discuss it with you and get your permission first. If not, he or she would talk with you about it afterward.

> *Acknowledgment:* **I understand that in an emergency when my health or life is in danger, my therapist must give other professionals any information about me that is needed to protect my life. Initials: _____**

3. *Abuse:* If your therapist obtains information leading him or her to believe or suspect that someone is abusing a child, a senior citizen, or a disabled person, the therapist must report this to a state agency. To "abuse" means to neglect, hurt, or sexually molest another person. The therapist cannot investigate and decide whether abuse is taking place: if the suspicion is there, the therapist must report it. The state agency will investigate. If you are involved in a situation of this kind, you should discuss it with a lawyer before telling your therapist anything about it unless you are willing to have the therapist make such a report. If this situation comes up, your therapist will discuss it with you if possible before making a report.

Acknowledgment: **I understand that if my therapist believes or suspects that a child, a senior citizen, or a disabled person is being abused or neglected, my therapist must report this to a state agency who will then investigate the situation. Initials: _____**

4. *Therapy of children, families, and couples:*

a. *Children and adolescents:* It is the policy of this agency, when a therapist treats children and adolescents, to ask their parents or guardians to agree that most details of what their children or adolescents tell the therapist will be treated as confidential. However, parents or guardians do have the right to *general* information about how therapy is going. The therapist may also have to tell parents or guardians about information if their children or others are in any danger. If this situation comes up, the therapist will discuss it with the child or adolescent first before talking to the parents or guardians.

Acknowledgment: **I understand that if my child or adolescent is in therapy, the therapist will give me as the parent or guardian only general information about therapy, except that the therapist will tell me if he or she finds out from my child or adolescent that they or others are in danger. Initials: _____**

b. *Families:* At the start of family therapy all participants must have a clear understanding of any limits on confidentiality that may exist. The family must also specify which members of the family must sign Release of Information forms if necessary for the records of family therapy.

Acknowledgment: **I understand that in family therapy, all members of the family must understand the limits of confidentiality and must agree on which family members will have the power to sign Release of Information forms authorizing disclosure of information about the family's history or treatment.**
Initials: _____ Initials: _____ Initials: _____ Initials: _____ Initials: _____ Initials: _____

c. *Couples:* If one member of a couple tells a therapist something the other member does not know, and not knowing this could harm him or her, the therapist cannot promise to keep it confidential from the other person. If this occurs the therapist will discuss it with you before doing anything else.

Acknowledgment: **I understand that if I am in couples therapy and tell the therapist something my partner does not know, and not knowing this could harm my partner, the therapist and this agency cannot promise to keep that information confidential from my partner. Initials: _____ Initials: _____**

5. *Group therapy:* In group therapy, the other members of the group are not therapists. They are not bound by the ethical rules and laws governing therapists. To avoid problems in this area, it is this agency's policy to ask all members of therapy groups to agree to protect one another's confidentiality, and to remove from the group any member who does violate another member's confidentiality. Still, this agency cannot be responsible for such disclosures by other clients, and it may be better for you to discuss information you feel must be legally protected in an individual session with your therapist than in a therapy group session.

> *Acknowledgment:* **I understand that in group therapy, I do not have the same degree of confidentiality in group sessions that I have in individual sessions with my therapist, and that other group members are not therapists and are not bound by the ethical rules and laws governing therapists. Initials: _____**

6. *Professional consultation:* Your therapist may consult with a clinical supervisor or another colleague about your treatment. The other therapist must give you the same confidentiality as your therapist.

If this fellow therapist is employed at this agency, no written authorization from you is required. If your therapist discusses your case with a professional outside this agency, such as a therapist who treated you in the past, he or she must get your written permission (a Release of Information form) first. If another professional asks your therapist for information about you during or after your treatment, your therapist cannot provide any information unless that other professional provides a Release of Information which you have signed authorizing your therapist to provide that information.

> *Acknowledgment:* **I understand that my therapist may discuss my history and treatment with other therapists for professional purposes, and that if these other therapists are not employed at this same agency my therapist must get my specific written permission in advance. Initials: _____**

7. *Legal proceedings:* If a judge orders your therapist to provide information about your history or your treatment, the therapist must do so.

> *Acknowledgment:* **I understand that if ordered by a judge, my therapist must give the court whatever information about my case the judge rules to be necessary. Initials: _____**

8. *Debt collections:* If you fail to pay for services as agreed, and other methods of resolving the problem fail, this agency may have to use a collection agency or other legal means to collect the fees you owe. The only information the agency would disclose for this purpose would be your name and address, the dates you received services, and the amount of your unpaid balance.

> *Acknowledgment:* **I understand that if I fail to meet my financial obligation to this agency and it becomes necessary to use legal means to collect my fees, the agency may disclose my name, address, dates of services, and balance due for this purpose. Initials: _____**

9. *Recording therapy:* This agency will not record therapy sessions on audiotape or videotape without your written permission. If you give permission for such recording, you have the right to know who will see or hear the recording, for what purpose(s) it will be used, and when it will be erased or destroyed.

> *Acknowledgment:* **I understand that my therapy will not be recorded on audiotape or videotape without my written permission. Initials: _____**

10. *Referring agencies and conditions of treatment:* If you have been involuntarily referred for treatment by a court or a government agency such as a probation department or Child Protective Services, your treatment may include requirements that you comply with conditions including reporting of information about your therapy to the agency that referred you for treatment, or reporting to that agency if you appear to have violated laws regarding substance abuse or agency rules regarding satisfactory participation in this program. If such reporting requirements exist, your therapist will tell you about them before you start therapy, and will notify you when making any such required reports.

Acknowledgment: **I understand that if I have been involuntarily referred for treatment by a court or government agency, the conditions of my therapy may include mandatory reporting to the referring authority about my therapy and/or any violations I commit of laws regarding substance abuse or of agency rules regarding my conduct while in this program. Initials: _____**

11. *Independent disclosure by client:* Any information that you yourself share outside of therapy, willingly and publicly, will not be considered protected or confidential by a court.

Acknowledgment: **I understand that if I myself willingly and publicly disclose information about my therapy, that information is no longer confidential or legally protected. Initials: _____**

Our signatures here show that we have read, understand, and agree to the conditions presented above.

Client Name(s): _____ Date: ____/____/____

Signature: _____

Parent/Guardian Name: _____ Date: ____/____/____

Signature: _____

Therapist Name: _____ Date: ____/____/____

Signature: _____

Client Rights Form

1. I understand that I have the right to decide not to enter therapy (although depending on my situation there may be legal or other consequences for not entering or completing therapy), not to participate in any particular type of therapy, and to terminate therapy at any time. If I wish to terminate therapy here and continue therapy elsewhere, I will be given a list of providers with whom I can continue. Initials: _____

2. I understand that I have the right to a safe environment during therapy, free from physical, sexual, and emotional abuse. Initials: _____

3. I understand that I have the right to complete and accurate information about my treatment plan, goals, methods, potential risks and benefits, and progress. Initials: _____

4. I understand that I have the right to information about the professional capabilities and limitations of any clinician(s) involved in my therapy, including their certification/ licensure, education and training, experience, specialization, and supervision. I have the right to be treated only by persons who are trained and qualified to provide the treatment I receive. Initials: _____

5. I understand that I have the right to written information about fees, payment methods, co-payments, length and duration of sessions and treatment. Initials: _____

6. I understand that my confidentiality will be protected, and information regarding my treatment will not be disclosed to any person or agency without my written permission except under circumstances where the law requires such information to be disclosed. I understand that I have the right to know the limits of confidentiality, the situations in which the therapist or agency is legally required to disclose information about my case to outside agencies, and the types of information which must be disclosed. Initials: _____

7. I understand that I have the right to know if my therapist will discuss my case with supervisors or peers. I understand that no portion of my therapy may be recorded in audio or video form without my informed written consent, and that if I consent to have any portion of my therapy recorded I have the right to know who will see or hear the recording(s), for what purpose(s) the recording(s) will be used, and when and how the recording(s) will be erased or destroyed. Initials: _____

8. I understand that I have the right to request a summary of my treatment, including diagnosis, progress in treatment, prognosis, and discharge status. Initials: _____

9. I understand that I have the right to request the release of my clinical information to any agency or person I choose. Initials: _____

Client/Guardian's Name: _____ Signature: _____ Date: ____/____/____

Therapist Name: _____ Signature: _____ Date: ____/____/____

Financial Information Form

Client's Name: _____ Date: ____/____/____ Case File #: _____
Address: _____ Phone: _____ Work Phone: _____
_____ SSN: _____ Date of Birth: ____/____/____
Name of Employer: _____
Address of Employer: _____ Position/Title: _____
_____ Supervisor: _____

Do you have health insurance coverage?   Yes _____   No _____
Do you intend to use it to pay for services?   Yes _____   No _____
If no, how do you intend to pay for services? _____
_____

If yes, please complete the following:

Insurance Information:

Insurance Company: ____ Blue Cross/Blue Shield   ____ CHAMPUS/TriCare   ____ Medicare
____ Aetna   ____ Cigna   ____ Premier   ____ Health Partners
____ Other: _____

Policy #: _____ Enrollment/plan/group number: _____ Effective date: ____/____/____
Calendar year deductible: $ _____   Deductible year starts: _____
Deductible met for year? Yes _____   No _____
Co-payment required: Is outpatient group therapy covered? Yes _____   No _____

Must referrals be made by a primary care physician or other gatekeeper? Yes _____   No _____
Any exclusions or limitations affecting this therapy, including number of sessions, types of therapy
excluded from coverage, monetary caps, conditions not covered: _____
_____

Name of policyholder, if different from client: _____
Client's relationship to policyholder: _____

Provider's address: _____   Provider's phone: _____
_____
_____

Pre-approval or pre-authorization required? Yes _____   No _____
Pre-approval for specific provider? Yes _____   No _____
Pre-approval authorization number: _____
Number/Type sessions pre-approved: _____

I grant this agency permission to release any information obtained during assessments or treatment
which is necessary to support insurance claims for my/our treatment. I understand that I am responsible
for all charges, regardless of insurance coverage.

Client/Guardian's Name: _____ Signature: _____ Date: ____/____/____

Payment Agreement for Services

I, _____ , request that the therapist/agency named above provide professional services to me and I agree to pay fee(s) of:

$ _____ per session for individual therapy.

$ _____ per session for family/marital therapy.

$ _____ per session for group therapy.

I agree that I am responsible for the charges for services provided by this therapist to me, although other insurance carriers may make payments on my account. I understand insurance deductibles, co-payments, or full-fee for services are due at time of services.

I further guarantee that charges for services provided will be paid upon receipt of billing statements from (this therapist/agency) and that the balance will be paid in full unless special arrangements are made for alternative payment scheduling. If such alternative arrangements are made, I guarantee that payment will be made in compliance with those arrangements.

I understand that this office will bill insurance companies and other third party payers, but cannot guarantee such benefits, and is not responsible for collection of such payments.

I have read the client's rights form and reviewed the fee schedule. In signing this form, I understand my rights as a client at this agency and responsibilities for payment.

Client/Guardian's Name: _____ Signature: _____ Date: ____/____/____

Therapist/Agency Representative: _____ Date: ____/____/____

Chapter 5

Treatment: Counseling and Therapy Forms and Procedures

The forms in this chapter include those needed to document contact with the client once treatment has begun. These include forms whose functions are directive, such as treatment planning documents and a behavioral contract, and those used to record actual progress in therapy. The following forms are included in this chapter:

Behavioral Contract

Master Treatment Plan

Treatment Plan Update/Revision Form

Group Therapy Progress Note

Individual/Family Session Progress Note

Self-Help Program Meeting Review/Critique Form

Behavioral Contract

Name of client: _____ Client ID #: _____ Date of birth: ____/____/____

Clinician: _____ Treatment Program: _____ Date of contract: ____/____/____

I, _____ , understand and agree to comply with the following treatment recommendations. I understand that I must follow these conditions in order to remain in my treatment program. In signing this contract, I agree to meet the following conditions:

_____ 1. I will remain free from all mind altering substances unless prescribed by a doctor, and if I am taking any prescribed medications I will take them in the way the doctor instructs me.

_____ 2. I will attend all my therapy sessions on time with one absence allowed for an emergency.

_____ 3. I will attend _____ support group meetings per week and document my attendance.

_____ 4. I will get a support group sponsor and meet with him/her _____ times each week, and if requested will have my sponsor talk with my therapist to confirm I am doing this.

_____ 5. I will call the crisis line, my therapist, or 911 if I feel I might kill or hurt myself or someone else (or this local emergency number _____).

_____ 6. Other condition: _____

_____ 7. Other condition: _____

I am committing myself to honoring this contract for the following time period:
from ____/____/____ to ____/____/____ , or until a specific event takes place as follows: _____
_____

I understand that if I do not comply with these requirements, the consequences will be as follows:
_____
_____

I understand that I will retain a copy of this contract and a copy will be kept by the program staff.

Client/Guardian's Name: _____ Signature: _____ Date: ____/____/____

Staff's Name: _____ Signature: _____ Date: ____/____/____

Master Treatment Plan

Identification Data

Client Name: _____ Admit Date: ____/____/____ Clinician: _____

Client ID#: _____ Age: _____ Gender: _____ Birth Date: ___/___/___

Initial Sessions Authorized: _____ Anticipated Length of Treatment: _____

Status upon Admission: _____ Vol _____ Invol (DTS ____ DTO _____) _____ Mandatory

Treatment Modality(ies): ____ Indiv/Fam ____ Psychoed. Group ____ Aftercare ____ Psychiatric

_____ Intensive Outpatient _____ Day Treatment _____ Residential _____ Other: _____

Problem List

Problem #1: _____

      Review Date: ____/____/____ Status: ___ Resolved ___ Improved ___ Unchanged ___ Worse

Problem #2: _____

      Review Date: ____/____/____ Status: ___ Resolved ___ Improved ___ Unchanged ___ Worse

Problem #3: _____

      Review Date: ____/____/____ Status: ___ Resolved ___ Improved ___ Unchanged ___ Worse

DSM-IV Diagnostic Impression

	Code	Description with Qualifiers
Axis I:	_____	_____
	_____	_____
	_____	_____
Axis II:	_____	_____
	_____	_____
	_____	_____
Axis III:	_____	_____
	_____	_____
	_____	_____
Axis IV:	_____	_____
	_____	_____
	_____	_____

Axis V: Current functioning: _____

           Past year functioning: _____

Primary Diagnosis: _____ Manifested by: _____

_____

Client Strengths: _____

_____

Potential Obstacles to Treatment: _____

_____

_____

Treatment Goals and Interventions

Overall/Long-Term Goal #1 (Related to Problem # _____):

      Target date: ____/____/____ Date resolved: ____/____/____

Measurable Objective 1.A: _____

Intervention 1.A.1: _____

Frequency: _____ Start date: ____/____/____ Completion date: ____/____/____

Intervention 1.A.2: _____

Frequency: _____ Start date: ____/____/____ Completion date: ____/____/____

Intervention 1.A.3: _____

Frequency: _____ Start date: ____/____/____ Completion date: ____/____/____

Measurable Objective 1.B: _____

Intervention 1.B.1: _____

Frequency: _____ Start date: ____/____/____ Completion date: ____/____/____

Intervention 1.B.2: _____

Frequency: _____ Start date: ____/____/____ Completion date: ____/____/____

Intervention 1.B.3: _____

Frequency: _____ Start date: ____/____/____ Completion date: ____/____/____

Measurable Objective 1.C: _____

Intervention 1.C.1: _____

Frequency: _____ Start date: ____/____/____ Completion date: ____/____/____

Intervention 1.C.2: _____

Frequency: _____ Start date: ____/____/____ Completion date: ____/____/____

Intervention 1.C.3: _____

Frequency: _____ Start date: ____/____/____ Completion date: ____/____/____

Overall/Long-Term Goal #2 (Related to Problem # _____):

      Target date: ____/____/____ Date resolved: ____/____/____

Measurable Objective 2.A: _____

Intervention 2.A.1: _____

Frequency: _____ Start date: ____/____/____ Completion date: ____/____/____

Intervention 2.A.2: _____

Frequency: _____ Start date: ____/____/____ Completion date: ____/____/____

Intervention 2.A.3: _____

Frequency: _____ Start date: ____/____/____ Completion date: ____/____/____

Measurable Objective 2.B: _____

Intervention 2.B.1: _____

Frequency: _____ Start date: ____/____/____ Completion date: ____/____/____

Intervention 2.B.2: _____

Frequency: _____ Start date: ____/____/____ Completion date: ____/____/____

Intervention 2.B.3: _____

Frequency: _____ Start date: ____/____/____ Completion date: ____/____/____

Measurable Objective 2.C: _____

Intervention 2.C.1: _____

Frequency: _____ Start date: ____/____/____ Completion date: ____/____/____

Intervention 2.C.2: _____

Frequency: _____ Start date: ____/____/____ Completion date: ____/____/____

Intervention 2.C.3: _____

Frequency: _____ Start date: ____/____/____ Completion date: ____/____/____

Overall/Long-Term Goal #3 (Related to Problem # _____):

     Target date: ____/____/____ Date resolved: ____/____/____

Measurable Objective 3.A: _____

Intervention 3.A.1: _____

Frequency: _____ Start date: ____/____/____ Completion date: ___/___/____

Intervention 3.A.2: _____

Frequency: _____ Start date: ____/____/____ Completion date: ___/___/____

Intervention 3.A.3: _____

Frequency: _____ Start date: ____/____/____ Completion date: ___/___/____

Measurable Objective 3.B: _____

Intervention 3.B.1: _____

Frequency: _____ Start date: ____/____/____ Completion date: ___/___/____

Intervention 3.B.2: _____

Frequency: _____ Start date: ____/____/____ Completion date: ___/___/____

Intervention 3.B.3: _____

Frequency: _____ Start date: ____/____/____ Completion date: ___/___/____

Measurable Objective 3.C: _____

Intervention 3.C.1: _____

Frequency: _____ Start date: ____/____/____ Completion date: ___/___/____

Intervention 3.C.2: _____

Frequency: _____ Start date: ____/____/____ Completion date: ___/___/____

Intervention 3.C.3: _____

Frequency: _____ Start date: ____/____/____ Completion date: ___/___/____

Discharge Plan

Projected Date for Resolution of Problems: ____/____/____ Projected No. of Sessions Required: ____

Criteria for Discharge from Treatment: _____
_____
_____
_____

Aftercare Plan: _____
_____
_____
_____

Comments: _____
_____
_____
_____

My/our signature(s) here indicate(s) that I/we have participated in designing this treatment plan, understand it, and accept responsibility to carry out my/our portion(s) of this plan.

Client/Guardian's Name: _____ Signature: _____ Date: ____/____/____

Program staff's Name: _____ Signature: _____ Date: ____/____/____

Treatment Plan Update/Revision Form

Client Name: _____ Client ID#: _____ Clinician Name: _____

Date Master Treatment Plan Formulated: ___/____/____   Date of Revision: ___/____/____

Updates/Revisions to Problem List

New Problem: Problem # ____ Description/Status: _____
_____

Revision of Existing Problem # ____ Current Description/Status: _____
_____

Updates/Revisions to Diagnosis

	DSM-IV Code	Description	Manifested by:
New Primary Diagnosis:	_____	_____	_____
New Additional Diagnosis:	_____	_____	_____

Updates/Revisions to Goals, Objectives, and/or Interventions

New Goal: Goal # ____ Related to Problem # ___ Description of Goal: _____
_____

Revision of Goal # ____ Goal as Revised: _____
_____

Revision of Goal # ____ Goal as Revised: _____
_____

New Objective: Objective # ____ Related to Goal # ____ Description of Objective: _____
_____

Revision of Objective # ____ Objective as Revised: _____
_____

Revision of Objective # ____ Objective as Revised: _____
_____

New Intervention: Intervention # ____ Related to Objective # ____ Description of Intervention: _____
_____
   Frequency: _____ Start Date: ___/____/____ Completion Date: ___/____/____
Revision of Intervention # ____ Intervention as Revised: _____
   Frequency: _____ Start Date: ___/____/____ Completion Date: ___/____/____
Revision of Intervention # ____ Intervention as Revised: _____
   Frequency: _____ Start Date: ___/____/____ Completion Date: ___/____/____

Other Update/Revision

_____
_____

My/our signature(s) here indicate(s) that I/we have participated in this treatment plan update/revision, understand it, and accept responsibility to carry out my/our portion(s) of this updated/revised plan.

Client/Guardian's Name: _____ Signature: _____ Date: ___/____/____

Program staff's Name: _____ Signature: _____ Date: ___/____/____

Group Therapy Progress Note

Client Name: _____ Client ID#:: _____ Birth Date:____/____/____

Program: _____ Session Date: ____/____/____ Session #: ____

Topic: _____ Length of Session: _____

Format: _____ Didactic _____ Process _____ Guided Discussion _____ Other: _____

Training Aids: _____ Videotape _____ Audiotape _____ Written Material _____ Transparencies
_____ Other: _____

Problem & Objective of Session: _____

Level of Participation: _____ Active _____ Moderate _____ Minimal _____ Absent

Data (self-report, observations, interventions, current issues/stressors, functional impairment, group
behavior, motivation, progress): _____
_____
_____
_____
_____
_____
_____
_____
_____
_____

Assessment (progress, evaluation of intervention, obstacles or barriers): _____
_____
_____
_____
_____
_____
_____
_____
_____

Plan (tasks to be completed between sessions, objectives for next session, changes, recommendations,
sessions remaining, date of next session, plan for termination): _____
_____
_____
_____
_____
_____
_____
_____
_____

Clinician's Name: _____ Signature: _____ Date: ____/____/____

Individual/Family Session Progress Note

Client Name: _____ Client ID#:: _____ Birth Date:____/____/____

Program: _____ Session Date: ____/____/____ Session #: _____

Present in Session: _____ Length of Session: _____

Modality of Treatment: _____

Problem: _____

Objectives of Session: _____

Data (self-report, observations, interventions, current issues/stressors, functional impairment, interpersonal behavior, motivation, progress): _____

_____
_____
_____
_____
_____
_____
_____
_____
_____

Assessment (progress, evaluation of intervention, obstacles or barriers): _____

_____
_____
_____
_____
_____
_____
_____
_____
_____

Plan (tasks to be completed between sessions, objectives for next session, changes, recommendations, sessions remaining, date of next session, plan for termination): _____

_____
_____
_____
_____
_____
_____
_____
_____

Clinician Name: _____ Signature: _____ Date: ____/____/____

Self-Help Program Meeting Review/Critique Form

Directions: DO NOT TAKE THIS FORM WITH YOU TO THE MEETING, and please do not write information that would violate anyone's anonymity or confidentiality!

1. Meeting Information:
   Group Name:_____
   Program (AA, NA, etc.): _____ Location: _____ Date/Time:_____
   Meeting format: _____ Tag/Open sharing _____ Speaker _____ Book/Step study
   Other (please describe): _____
   _____ All-male or all-female _____ Mixed   Number of people present: _____

2. What was the main topic of the meeting?_____

3. What were your general thoughts and feelings on that topic? _____
   _____
   _____
   _____
   _____

4. In what ways could you relate to the experiences and feelings shared by others at this meeting? Were you unable to relate to some people, and if so what was the difference between them and you that made you unable to relate? _____
   _____
   _____
   _____
   _____

5. What other thoughts and feelings did this meeting cause you to have? _____
   _____
   _____
   _____
   _____

6. How many people at the meeting did you know? _____

7. Please state your level of participation in this meeting: _____
   _____
   _____
   _____
   _____

8. What did you gain from this meeting? _____
   _____
   _____
   _____

Chapter 6

Treatment: Program Administration Forms and Procedures

This chapter includes forms to assist clinicians and other staff members with program administration. These forms are designed to assist with correspondence and communication with referral sources, among agency program staff, and among others within the agency. This chapter also includes forms to be used upon termination and discharge.

The following forms are included in this chapter:

Client Encounter Summary

Monthly Progress Note/Report

Self-Help Program Attendance Verification Form

Extended Services Request Form

Notification of Failure to Attend Treatment Appointment

Program Attendance/Completion Information

Attendance/Completion Information: Intensive Outpatient Program

Certificate of Completion

Program/Services Discharge Summary

Client Encounter Summary

Client Name: _____ Client ID#: _____ Program: _____

Date/ Time	Time Spent	Intake	Assess	Indiv. Session	Family Session	Group Session	Phone Call	Corre- spond.	Staffing/ Meeting	Off-site/ In-home	Other	Staff Initials

Monthly Progress Note/Report

Client Name: _____ Client ID#: _____ Program: _____

Treatment Agency: _____ Referral Source: _____

Admission Date: ____/____/____ Projected Discharge Date: ____/____/____

Date of Report: ____/____/____ Reporting Period: ____/____/____ to ____/____/____

Type/Level of Care: _____ Length of Treatment: _____

Program Attendance

	Ind./Family Sessions		Group Sessions	
	Attended	Missed	Attended	Missed
Sessions this period:	_____	_____	_____	_____
Sessions to date:	_____	_____	_____	_____

_____ Satisfactory

   (Meets program requirements)

_____ Unsatisfactory

Dates of attendance: _____

Dates of excused absences: _____

Dates of unexcused absences: _____

Degree of participation/involvement: ___ Active ____ Minimal ____ Inactive/passive ___ Absent

Support Group Attendance

	AA/NA		Other: _____	
	Attended	Missed	Attended	Missed
Sessions this period:	_____	_____	_____	_____
Sessions to date:	_____	_____	_____	_____

_____ Satisfactory

   (Meets program requirements)

_____ Unsatisfactory

Dates of attendance: _____

Dates of excused absences: _____

Dates of unexcused absences: _____

Degree of participation/involvement: ___ Active ____ Minimal ____ Inactive/Passive ___ Absent

Compliance with Other Treatment Program Requirements

Maintaining chemical abstinence/sobriety: ____ Yes ____ No ___ Questionable   # of UAs/Other

Abstinence from other compulsive behavior:____ Yes ____ No ___ Questionable   tests this period:

   (if being addressed in treatment)   _____

Any substance relapses? ____ Yes ____ No   Comments: _____

_____

Any other compulsive behavior relapses? ____ Yes ____ No   Comments: _____

_____

Working with support program sponsor: ____ Yes ____ No   Comments: _____

_____

Attending support program home group: ____ Yes ____ No   Comments: _____

_____

Other program requirements satisfied: ____ Yes ____ No   Comments: _____

_____

Treatment goals/objectives revised this period? ____ Yes ____ No   If yes, changes made: _____

_____

Overall Progress toward Treatment Goals/Objectives

_____ Excellent _____ Satisfactory _____ Fair _____ Marginal _____ Unsatisfactory

Comments: _____

_____

_____

_____

_____

_____

____ Services continued ____ Terminated: Discharge date: ____/____/____ Reason: _____

Comments/recommendations (suggested treatment plan revisions, concerns, etc.): _____

_____

_____

_____

_____

_____

_____

Client/Guardian's Name: _____ Signature: _____ Date: ____/____/____

Self-Help Program Attendance Verification Form

Date	Time From/To	Program	Group Name	Meeting Location	Signature of Chairperson

Extended Services Request Form

Provider Information	Client Information
Agency Name: _____	Name:_____
Address: _____	DOB: ____/____/____ SSN: _____
Phone: _____ Fax: _____	Address: _____
Contact Person: _____	_____
Initial Date of Service: ____/____/____	Phone: H: _____ W: _____

Requesting Service Dates: ____/____/____ through ____/____/____

Primary Diagnosis (DSM-IV code): _____ Description: _____

Secondary Diagnosis: _____ Description: _____

Type(s) of services requested: _____

Number of units/hours utilized: _____ Number of additional units/hrs. requested: _____

Treatment interventions utilized: _____

Substance abuse history: _____
_____

Other mental health history: _____
_____

Presenting symptoms: _____
_____

Current mental status: _____
_____

Current stressors/functional impairments as result of this disorder: _____
_____

Summary of client progress in treatment; current status in treatment: _____
_____

Documentation of client effort/motivation in treatment: _____
_____

Prognosis with explanation: _____
_____

Other services client is receiving for this disorder (include any medications): _____
_____

Revisions to current treatment plan: _____
_____

Discharge criteria and aftercare/relapse prevention plan: _____
_____

Clinician Name/Title: _____ Signature: _____ Date: ____/____/____

Notification of Failure to Attend Treatment Appointment

Date: _____/_____/_____

Dear _____ :

This letter is being sent as I am concerned that:

_____ you _____ the following person, for whom you are the legal guardian: _____
has failed to keep the following treatment appointment(s):

Date(s):   Nature of Appointment(s):

_____/_____/_____   _____

_____/_____/_____   _____

_____/_____/_____   _____

_____ The following referring agency staff is/are being notified, as required by the conditions
of this referral: _____ Probation/Parole Officer   _____ Child Protective Services Caseworker
             _____ Other: _____

Please contact this agency at (Phone _____) to reschedule the appointment(s)
missed. If you are unable to attend consistently or no longer desire services for yourself and/or your
family, and wish me to make a referral for treatment elsewhere, please contact me immediately.
If I do not hear from you by (Date _____/_____/_____), this agency will close your file and make any
required notifications that you are no longer in treatment here at that time.

Sincerely,

cc:

Program Attendance/Completion Information

Client Name: _____   Case/File ID#: _____

Name/Type of Program   Duration

_____   _____ Hrs   _____ Pre-Test Score   _____ Post-Test Score
(CD/DWI Education)

_____   _____ Hrs   _____ Pre-Test Score   _____ Post-Test Score
(Relapse Prevention)

Group/Individual Session Attendance

Session 1 (___ hours) Date: ____/____/____   Session 2 (___ hours) Date: ____/____/____

Session 3 (___ hours) Date: ____/____/____   Session 4 (___ hours) Date: ____/____/____

Session 5 (___ hours) Date: ____/____/____   Session 6 (___ hours) Date: ____/____/____

Session 7 (___ hours) Date: ____/____/____   Session 8 (___ hours) Date: ____/____/____

Session 9 (___ hours) Date: ____/____/____   Session 10 (___ hours) Date: ____/____/____

Session 11 (___ hours) Date: ____/____/____   Session 12 (___ hours) Date: ____/____/____

Session 13 (___ hours) Date: ____/____/____   Session 14 (___ hours) Date: ____/____/____

Session 15 (___ hours) Date: ____/____/____   Session 16 (___ hours) Date: ____/____/____

Session 17 (___ hours) Date: ____/____/____   Session 18 (___ hours) Date: ____/____/____

Session 19 (___ hours) Date: ____/____/____   Session 20 (___ hours) Date: ____/____/____

Assignments acceptable and completed on time: _____ Yes   _____ No

Appropriate participation in treatment: _____ Yes   _____ No

Treatment goals met: _____ Yes   _____ No

Exit session note (participation/prognosis): _____
_____
_____

Referred to: _____ Aftercare/Further therapy   _____ Support group meetings
              _____ Back to referring authority _____ Other: _____

Completion certificate issued: ____ Yes: Dated: ____/____/____   _____ No: Reason: _____
_____
_____

Clinician Name/Title: _____ Date: ____/____/____

Signature: _____

Attendance/Completion Information

Client Name: _____   Case/File ID#: _____

Intensive Outpatient Program

WEEK ONE	WEEK TWO	WEEK THREE	WEEK FOUR
Homework	*Homework*	*Homework*	*Homework*
Assign 1 ____	Assign 1 ____	Assign 1 ____	Assign 1 ____
Assign 2 ____	Assign 2 ____	Assign 2 ____	Assign 2 ____
Assign 3 ____	Assign 3 ____	Assign 3 ____	Assign 3 ____
Classes	*Classes*	*Classes*	*Classes*
Topic 1 ____	Topic 1 ____	Topic 1 ____	Topic 1 ____
Topic 2 ____	Topic 2 ____	Topic 2 ____	Topic 2 ____
Topic 3 ____	Topic 3 ____	Topic 3 ____	Topic 3 ____
Topic 4 ____	Topic 4 ____	Topic 4 ____	Topic 4 ____
Topic 5 ____	Topic 5 ____	Topic 5 ____	Topic 5 ____

Assignments acceptable and completed on time: _____ Yes _____ No

Appropriate participation in treatment: _____ Yes _____ No

Treatment goals met: _____ Yes _____ No

Exit session note (participation/prognosis): _____

_____

_____

_____

_____

Referred to: _____ IOP Phase II   _____ IOP Phase III   _____ Aftercare/Further therapy

_____ Support group meetings   _____ Back to referring authority

_____ Other: _____

Completion certificate issued: ____ Yes: Dated: ____/____/____   ____ No: Reason: _____

_____

_____

_____

_____

Clinician Name/Title: _____   Date: ____/____/____

Signature: _____

CERTIFICATE OF COMPLETION

This is to certify that

_____

has completed all activities and requirements included in the

Program Title

Conducted at

Name of Agency

Having participated in (# of hours of program) of

Group Therapy and Education

on Chemical Dependence and Related Issues

Date: ____/____/____   **Client ID#:** _____   **Staff Signature:** _____

Program/Services Discharge Summary

Date of Report: _____/_____/_____

Client Name: _____ Client ID#: _____ Program: _____

Treatment Agency: _____ Referral Source: _____

Program Admission Date: _____/_____/_____ Program Discharge Date: _____/_____/_____

Type/Level of Care: _____ Length of Treatment: _____ Number of Sessions: _____

Initial reason for treatment: _____

Admitting Diagnosis   (DSM -IV Codes):

Axis I: _____   Axis II: _____   Axis III: _____   Axis IV: _____   Axis V: _____

_____   _____   _____   _____   _____

_____   _____   _____   _____   _____

Primary diagnosis manifested by: _____

Discharge Diagnosis   (DSM -IV Codes):

Axis I: _____   Axis II: _____   Axis III: _____   Axis IV: _____   Axis V: _____

_____   _____   _____   _____   _____

_____   _____   _____   _____   _____

Reason for Discharge

_____ Treatment plan objectives attained   _____ Moved out of area

_____ Closure against staff advice   _____ Client withdrew

_____ Lack of attendance/contact   _____ Client deceased

_____ Client referred elsewhere   _____ Incarceration

_____ Non-compliance with program rules   _____ Other: _____

Services Provided

_____ Individual   _____ Inpatient   _____ Psychoeducational group

_____ Family   _____ In-home   _____ Intensive/outpatient

_____ Intensive group   _____ Other: _____

Problem Resolution

Status	Problem: _____	Problem: _____	Problem: _____
Resolved	_____	_____	_____
Improved	_____	_____	_____
Same	_____	_____	_____
Problem worse	_____	_____	_____
Unable to determine	_____	_____	_____

Discharge Summary (significant findings, status at discharge, recommendations or referrals for further treatment, aftercare plan): _____

_____

_____

Clinician Name/Title: _____ Signature: _____ Date: _____/_____/_____

Supervisor Name/Title: _____ Signature: _____ Date: _____/_____/_____

Chapter 7

Treatment: Special Situations

This chapter includes blank forms to be used to document special or critical situations that have not been covered in previous chapters and, in some cases, are more likely to arise in the course of substance abuse treatment than in most other types of therapy. In this type of program, you will see a high proportion of involuntary clients from a variety of referral sources. They may need additional specialized services, or you may want or be required to communicate with their referral sources. Also, reflecting the seriousness of the problems being addressed, chemically dependent clients are also more likely than many other categories of people to undergo crises during treatment.

Additionally, the field of alcohol and other drug abuse treatment is being enriched and broadened by the development of new and innovative treatments, such as acupuncture techniques specialized for treating addictions; thus, one form allows clients to consent to specialized procedures. In particular, drawing on one of the authors' training in Eye Movement Desensitization and Reprocessing (EMDR), three forms are included for use with this form of therapy, which is growing in popularity and provides a specific protocol for treatment of substance abuse problems. (Note: As with any specialized therapy technique, EMDR should be used only by clinicians with the necessary training. There are special cautions and considerations involved in treating chemical dependence using EMDR.)

The following forms are included in this chapter:

Contract Against Suicide, Self-Harm, or Harm to Others

Consent for Specialized Technique/Procedure

Request/Referral for Specialized Service

Eye Movement Desensitization and Reprocessing (EMDR)

Eye Movement Desensitization and Reprocessing (EMDR) Consent for Treatment

Eye Movement Desensitization and Reprocessing (EMDR) Session Progress Note

Contract Against Suicide, Self-Harm, or Harm to Others

I, _____ , **agree to the following:**

1. I understand that my therapist has a legal, ethical, and professional obligation to take all practicable and reasonable measures she/he considers necessary to ensure my safety from suicide and/or self-harm. I agree that this is in my best interests and that I will cooperate with my therapist by providing honest information about any thoughts, desires, or impulses I have to hurt or kill myself. **Initials:** _____

2. I agree not to act on any thoughts, desires, or impulses I may have to hurt or kill myself between _____ and _____ . **Initials:** _____
                 (date/time or event)   (date/time or event)

3. If, at any time, I feel unable to resist any thoughts, desires, or impulses I may have to hurt or kill myself, I agree that rather than act to hurt or kill myself I will do the following:
   a. Call my therapist at _____ (office) or _____ (pager). If I am unable to reach my therapist, I will:
   b. Call the Suicide/Crisis Hotline at _____ . If I am unable to reach the Hotline, I will:
   c. Call 911.
   d. _____ **Initials:** _____

4. If, after talking with my therapist and/or a Suicide/Crisis Hotline worker I still feel unable to resist any thoughts, desires, or impulses I may have to hurt or kill myself, I agree that rather than act to hurt or kill myself I will call 911 and tell the 911 operator that I am thinking or hurting or killing myself, or I will physically go to the Emergency Room at _____ and tell the staff there that I am thinking or hurting or killing myself. **Initials:** _____

5. I agree that I will either keep this contract with me or where I can quickly get to it at all times while it is in force, or that I will copy down these telephone numbers and keep them with me while this contract is in force. **Initials:** _____

Client/Guardian's Name: _____ Date: ____/____/____

Signature: _____

Therapist Name: _____ Date: ____/____/____

Signature: _____

Consent for Specialized Technique/Procedure

Client Name: _____ Client ID#: _____ Program: _____

Date: ____/____/____ Clinician Name and Title: _____

Treatment Modality Suggested: _____

Treatment Diagnosis: DSM-IV Code: _____ Description: _____

Manifested by: _____

Treatment goals/objectives and rationale for specialized therapy: (see attached treatment plan/ progress notes) _____
_____
_____
_____

Clinician's credentials, qualifications, and experience related to this treatment procedure: _____
_____
_____
_____

Number of sessions recommended: _____   Target completion date: ____/____/____

1. I understand that I have the right to information about the professional capabilities, specialization, education and training, certification/licensure, and experience of the above named clinician related to his/her providing this treatment technique. **Client Initials:** _____

2. In signing this consent, I am stating that I understand and agree to the treatment I will receive, and that the benefits and risks of this procedure have been explained to me. I understand that I may terminate or withdraw from this treatment at any time. **Client Initials:** _____

Client Name: _____ Date: ____/____/____

Signature: _____

Clinician Name: _____ Date: ____/____/____

Signature: _____

Clinical Supervisor Name/Title: _____ Date: ____/____/____

Signature: _____

Request/Referral for Specialized Service

(If going to an individual/organization outside the parent agency, this form must be accompanied by a Release of Information.)

Client Name: _____ Client ID #: _____ Date of Birth ____/____/____

Client's Treatment Program: _____ Date of Referral: ____/____/____

Referred by:	Referred to:

Clinician: _____   Clinician: _____

Agency: _____   Agency: _____

Address: _____   Address: _____

_____   _____

Phone: _____   Phone: _____

Fax: _____   Fax: _____

Responsible for Payment: _____

Client receiving services for: _____

Service Requested

_____ *Urine analysis or other drug testing:* Specify if other than UA: _____

Please test for use of: _____   _____   _____

_____   _____   _____

Please submit results to: _____

Date tested: ____/____/____

_____ *Other lab work:* Test for: _____

Please submit results to: _____

Date tested: ____/____/____

_____ *Medical exam:* Examine for: _____

Please submit report to: _____

Symptoms: _____

Date of exam: ____/____/____

_____ *Psychological exam/testing:* Examine/test for: _____

Please submit report to: _____

Reason for referral: _____

Date of exam/test: ____/____/____

Psychiatric Evaluation: Evaluate for: _____

Please submit report to: _____

Reason for referral: _____

Date of evaluation: ____/____/____

Other specialized service: Service requested: _____

Please submit results to: _____

Reason for referral: _____

Date of service: ____/____/____

Recommendations by specialized service provider based on findings: _____

_____

_____

_____

_____

_____

_____

_____

_____

_____

_____

_____

_____

Service Provider's Name/Title: _____ Date: ____/____/____

Signature: _____

Eye Movement Desensitization and Reprocessing (EMDR)

You have been given this handout because the professional(s) treating you believe you might benefit from receiving a specialized type of therapy called Eye Movement Desensitization and Reprocessing, or EMDR. Before you can decide whether to participate in this treatment, you must understand what is being offered and what you are being asked to. The purpose of this handout is to explain EMDR and answer the questions people often ask about it. If you don't understand the information in this handout or if you have questions that aren't answered here, you should talk to the therapist or other professional who is suggesting this therapy for you and get the information you need to make a fully informed decision.

What EMDR Is

EMDR is a method of therapy that is highly effective at providing relief to people suffering from a variety of emotional problems. In particular, EMDR can be useful in treatment of substance abuse problems, though as you will read later in this handout there are some addictive problems for which it is not advised, and in any case special preparation is required.

EMDR's approach is based on the idea that our brains and nervous systems have ways of remembering and handling experiences that are both physical and mental. In other words, some parts of a memory are the physical images, sounds, and feelings stored in our brains and nervous systems, and along with those physical parts, the memories also include the thoughts and emotions connected with them, both what we felt and thought when the experience happened and what we think and feel about it now.

Normally, as time goes by our brains and nervous systems are able to "process" these physical sensations, thoughts, and feelings so that they become merely memories. The emotional pain and distress fade, so we are able to remember without feeling as strongly upset as we did when the event happened and while it was fresh in our minds. This "processing" of experiences appears to have a physical element to it, often involving rapid eye movements such as we have when we are dreaming. Many researchers believe that when we dream, we are processing experiences in the way described above.

It seems that painful memories sometimes get "stuck" and don't finish being processed, so that they stay as fresh and painful as if they had just happened, sometimes for years or decades. This may happen because the experience is so intense that it overwhelms the processing system's ability to handle it. It leaves the person who has had such an experience feeling that he or she can't get over it. This is sometimes recognized by diagnostic terms such as Post-Traumatic Stress Disorder, and at other times may just be indicated by the client's continuing to feel emotional pain that does not diminish with time.

EMDR uses guided eye movements or other rhythmic sensory activities such as listening to finger-snaps or feeling taps on a person's hands, combined with training in relaxation and stress management and other mental and emotional therapy, to "unstick" the processing mechanism and let the painful experiences shift from being fresh and painful to being memories that no longer cause intense upset -- one way to describe it would be to say that on a mental and emotional level, it changes them from unhealed wounds to faded scars.

The process of EMDR is a multistep method. The therapist begins by collecting life history information from the client and evaluating his or her personality, situation, and problems to see whether this therapy is a good idea for this person. If it appears to be a suitable therapy, the therapist explains what is involved in detail, so that the client can decide whether to participate in EMDR. If EMDR looks appropriate and the client, after learning about it, wants to receive the therapy, the therapist prepares him or her by teaching relaxation and stress management methods and having the client practice them, as well as helping the client expand and reinforce his or her emotional support network and resources. Once the client is prepared, typically after devoting at least one entire therapy session and the time between that and the next session to the teaching and support reinforcement mentioned above, the therapist goes on to do a current assessment of the type and degree of distress the client is suffering. This is based on the client's descriptions of his or her thoughts and feelings and on detailed self-rating scales. These three steps (history, preparation, and assessment) take place before the EMDR-specific treatment techniques are used.

The EMDR-unique treatment begins with *desensitization*. This is the first time the therapist actually uses the eye movement or other nervous-system-stimulation techniques; this triggers an "unsticking" and acceleration of the brain and nervous system's physical processing of the painful experiences. This typically takes one or two sessions, sometimes more, and results in a significant lessening of distress. One experience or issue is addressed at a time, and for each one, desensitization is followed by an *installation* phase in which a supportive, positive way of thinking and feeling about the experience is reinforced as a replacement for the old painful and negative thoughts and feelings. This takes place during the same session, immediately after completion of desensitization for each experience or issue. Installation is not done until desensitization is complete — if desensitization takes more than one session, the therapist works with the client at the end of each incomplete session to help them see the progress made so far, to make sure they are not in a crisis, and to help them make maximum use of their support system and resources.

Two concluding phases following installation in the processing of each painful memory are the *body scan*, seeking lingering physical signs that the trauma is not fully processed (if such signs are found, the therapist returns to the desensitization phase and finishes the work on that issue); and the *closure* phase, in which the therapist continues the support and education process and gets the client's renewed promise to use his or her support resources including the therapist as needed between sessions.

At the next session, the therapist conducts the final phase, *reevaluation*. In this phase the client and therapist check for signs that the trauma(s) processed at the previous session have not been fully dealt with. If there are signs that the client is still experiencing effects of unresolved trauma, they return to the desensitization phase to help the client complete processing of that experience or issue.

What EMDR Is Not

EMDR is not hypnosis. It is not NeuroLinguistic Programming, another therapy that combines physical, mental, and emotional techniques. EMDR is not a blanket solution for all problems or all people, nor is it a simple technique to be used without careful preparation and follow-up.

What EMDR Will Do

For many people, EMDR will do the following:

* Give quick and substantial relief and peace of mind from emotional suffering stemming from experiences they "can't get over," whether those are very recent or decades in the past; typically this relief will generalize to the aftereffects of other, similar experiences.

* Help achieve new understanding and insights about the meanings of experiences, and connections between those experiences and patterns of thought and behavior in their lives.

* Help change patterns of substance abuse in which a person automatically turns to a chemical to achieve a desired feeling or state of mind, reorienting these impulses or cravings toward healthy substitutes.

* Sometimes, EMDR helps people regain memories in greater detail or fill in gaps in their memories—it is important to note that there is no guarantee that any memory "recovered" in this way is true or accurate; often these memories seem to be more symbolic than literally true.

* Other times, EMDR leads to the forgetting of disturbing details in traumatic memories, although there is only one recorded case of a memory disappearing completely.

* Increase the feeling of having control over one's own destiny and actions that is sometimes lost as a result of suffering emotional trauma.

What EMDR Won't Do

EMDR will **NOT** typically do some things:

* It will not cause painful memories to completely disappear.

* It will not guarantee that memories will return, or that they will be true and accurate if they do.

* It will not get rid of anxiety or distress that is appropriate and suitable to the present situation; for example, if a person is currently in danger, it will not make them feel safe.

* It will not make memories worse or more painful.

Cautions

The following cautions must be considered in deciding whether to participate in EMDR:

* While a specialized EMDR protocol for substance abuse is useful in treating such problems, people with active chemical dependencies, or who are in recovery but do not have strong recovery programs and support systems, may be prone to relapse during or after EMDR therapy unless they receive proper preparation. Some report that they have no craving to use drugs or drink after treatment, but others have had strong cravings. If you have had a drinking or drug problem in the past but you are now clean and sober, before you receive EMDR therapy, you should make sure you have people available to help you through any cravings that might otherwise influence you to start drinking or using again.

In particular, people who have recently (within 6 months) become clean and sober after long-term use of stimulant drugs such as methamphetamine, other amphetamines, or cocaine, may have extreme and intense reactions that are too much for them to cope with, and may need to be hospitalized. If you have this kind of history, you need to talk with your therapist about this before deciding on EMDR.

* People who are not physically able to tolerate high stress for short periods may not be good candidates for EMDR, as it can be physically very taxing.

* Therapists preparing to use EMDR should not only be trained in this method, they should be prepared by training and experience to help clients through the extreme emotions some people experience during EMDR. These may include rage, panic, intense grief, or re-experiencing disturbing physical sensations that were part of the original traumatic experiences. Only a trained therapist should use EMDR, for the safety of the person receiving the therapy, and it should be done only in a setting where any help and support that might be needed is available.

* Therapists should also be generally qualified to work with the specific types of issues and clients they use EMDR to treat. For example, a therapist who had insufficient experience or training to treat a person suffering from Posttraumatic Stress Disorder without EMDR should not attempt to treat that person for that problem with EMDR.

* EMDR should be used only in a situation where the client:
— feels extremely safe and comfortable with the therapist;
— will be totally honest about what he or she is experiencing during and after therapy; and
— will follow through on promises to call on the therapist or other supportive people if he or she experiences emotional disturbances after a therapy session.

* EMDR can be used with people of any age. Standard procedures are modified for children.

* For clients who have limited coping skills and/or emotional support resources, it is vital to strengthen their abilities and strengths in these areas before proceeding with EMDR treatment. The therapist plays a key role in this strengthening and reinforcing period by teaching them ways to relax and cope with stress and by helping them increase their support network. This support network may include family members, close friends, the therapist, and organized support groups.

We have given you a lot of basic information about EMDR in this fact sheet, but many people have more questions that are not answered here. Please take your time reading this, then ask your therapist about any other questions that you have, to help you in deciding whether or not you feel this treatment is for you. Eye Movement Desensitization and Reprocessing is a powerful and effective therapy method that has been very helpful to many people. We hope that if you decide to participate in EMDR therapy, it is equally helpful for you.

Questions/Notes

Eye Movement Desensitization and Reprocessing (EMDR) Consent for Treatment

Client Name: _____ Client ID#: _____ Program: _____

Date: ____/____/____ Clinician Name and Title: _____

Treatment Diagnosis: DSM-IV Code: _____ Description: _____

Manifested by: _____

Treatment goals/objectives and rationale for use of EMDR: (see attached treatment plan/progress notes)

_____

_____

Clinician's credentials, qualifications, and experience related to use of EMDR to treat this

disorder/problem: _____

_____

Number of sessions recommended: _____ Target completion date: ____/____/____

1. I understand that I have the right to information about what is involved in EMDR therapy. I have been given written information and have discussed this with my therapist, and I understand the potential benefits and hazards of this therapy. Specifically, I understand the following:

- EMDR may provide me substantial relief for the problem(s) it is used to treat, but it is not always effective and may not provide any benefit. **Client Initials:** _____
- I may experience strong cravings or urges to use or drink during or after EMDR therapy, and I will call on my therapist or others to help me cope with these cravings if I experience them and cannot be sure I can maintain my abstinence alone. **Client Initials:** _____
- I may experience intense and disturbing emotions, thoughts, mental images, or dreams during or after EMDR therapy, although these are normal and temporary and will typically pass fairly quickly. I will call on my therapist or others to help me cope with these things if I experience them and cannot be sure I can cope with them alone. **Client Initials:** _____
- During or after EMDR therapy, I may remember events and experiences I had not previously recalled. I understand that like dreams, these memories may be symbolic rather than literally true. The fact that I remember an event with EMDR does not mean it happened as I remember it. **Client Initials:** _____

2. I understand that I have the right to information about the professional capabilities, specialization, education and training, certification/licensure, and experience of the above named clinician related to his/her using EMDR to treat my disorder/problem. **Client Initials:** _____

3. In signing this consent, I am stating that I understand and agree to the EMDR treatment I will receive. I understand that I may terminate or withdraw from EMDR treatment at any time. **Client Initials:** _____

Client/Guardian's Name: _____ Signature: _____ Date: ____/____/____

Clinician Name: _____ Signature: _____ Date: ____/____/____

Clinical Supervisor Name/Title: _____ Date: ____/____/____

Signature: _____

Eye Movement Desensitization and Reprocessing (EMDR) Session Progress Note

Client Name: _____ Client ID #: _____ Date of Birth ____/____/____

Program: _____ Session Date: ____/____/____ Session #: _____

Present in Session: _____ Length of Session: _____

Problem: _____

Objectives of Session: _____

Data:

1. Starting stimulus type: ___ Eye movement ___ Horizontal ___ Vertical ___ Diagonal
    ___ Tones ___ Hand taps ___ Combined eye movement/tones.

2. Distancing metaphor: _____

3. Cue word for safe/peaceful place visualization: _____

4. Presenting issue/memory: _____

5. Picture: Mental image representative of the issue/memory: _____

6. Negative cognition: Client's negative self-belief in connection with the presenting issue or memory: _____
    _____
    _____

7. Positive cognition: Positive self-belief client seeks to substitute for negative self-belief: _____
    _____
    _____

8. Validity of Cognition (VOC) check: Client's starting rating of positive cognition on VOC scale (1-7): _____
    _____

9. Emotion/feeling associated with issue/memory: _____
    _____

10. Subjective Units of Disturbance (SUD) check: Client's starting rating of the degree of disturbance at these emotions or feelings using the SUDs scale (0-10): _____

11. Location: Client's perception of physical locus of the emotion or feeling: _____
    _____
    _____

12. Desensitization phase: ____ Complete ____ Incomplete Ending VOC _____ Ending SUD ____

Summary of events during desensitization phase: _____
_____
_____
_____
_____
_____
_____
_____

13. Installation done: ____ Yes ____ No (if incomplete)   Ending VOC _____
    Body scan clear: ____ Yes ____ No

14. Incomplete session closure: ____ Relaxation exercise(s) ____ Discuss with client
    ____ Reinforcement of progress

15. Closure/debrief: ____ Discuss with client ____ Renew agreement to use support system

Additional comments/observations during session: _____
_____
_____
_____
_____
_____
_____
_____

Assessment (progress, evaluation of intervention, obstacles or barriers): _____
_____
_____
_____
_____
_____
_____

Plan (tasks to be completed between sessions, objectives for next session, changes, recommendations,
sessions remaining, date of next session, plan for termination): _____
_____
_____
_____
_____
_____
_____

Clinician Name: _____ Signature: _____ Date: ____/____/____

Chapter 8

Outcomes Measurement

Often thought of as synonymous with utilization review or utilization management, outcomes measurement is related to these functions but differs from them in important ways. As a clinician working in a substance abuse treatment program, measuring outcomes is important both for refining and improving your program and for being able to demonstrate its effectiveness to your management, referral sources, and regulatory agencies.

This chapter provides basic information about outcomes measurement and outlines considerations you may want to consider in doing outcomes measurement within your program or treatment facility. Further, it offers a preview of some uses of the pretest and posttest forms included with the psychoeducational presentation materials in Chapters 9–11 of this manual. Included at the end of this chapter are sample forms to be used for tracking outcome evaluation findings and a consent form for outcomes measurement. Finally, although we are not including any specific outcome measurement instruments in this volume, we offer pointers directing clinicians to existing tests and surveys that have been validated by rigorous experimentation and extensive use, and which are widely known and accepted in the addictions treatment field.

DEFINITIONS

Outcome evaluation is *utilizing instruments designed specifically to assess the end result of treatment.* The basic purpose of outcome measurement is to find out whether, as a result of treatment exposure, an observable, measurable behavior change has occurred. This may be an increase in client knowledge, a change toward healthier life functioning, or a change in problematic (in this case, substance abusing) behaviors. Various outcomes measurement instruments measure changes either after therapy or during the course of treatment. Typically, by asking specific behavioral questions, instruments yield information used to assess and quantify changes. Changes can then be compared among different treatment approaches or between a given approach and no treatment.

METHODS

What Is Measured

The key question when choosing items to measure is *validity,* or relevance: How closely does the thing we are examining, counting, and so on, correspond with the life change we seek in the client? The aims of your program, that is, what changes you are trying to bring about, will direct you in your choice of assessment instruments. For substance abuse treatment programs, relevant outcomes can be evaluated in the following areas:

- Changes in substance abusing behavior, short-term and long-term.
- Changes in symptom frequency.
- Changes in symptom severity.
- Changes in other compulsive behaviors.
- Health-related changes.
- Clinical status as a result of treatment, including changes in other mental health conditions.
- Client satisfaction.
- Changes in marital/intimate relationship status.
- Changes in patterns of interaction with significant others and family members.
- Changes in patterns of interaction with the legal system (DWIs, etc.).
- Changes in work interactions (absenteeism, performance ratings, etc.).
- Level of participation in healthy recreational activities.
- Level of participation in religious/spiritual activities.

How Measurements Are Made

Here, the key question is *reliability:* Does this test, question, or method of observation measure what it is supposed to measure, accurately and consistently? Does it give the same results when different evaluators apply it to the same client or situation? Does a given type of client or group achieve the same results with repeated testings? Some outcomes measurements rely on reports from the client or others, whereas other measures use objective data collected from direct observation or from sources such as schools, the legal system, or objective measures of work performance. Specific methods for collecting data include the following:

- Narrative self-report by client.

- Narrative reports by significant others or family members.

- Completion of questionnaires, surveys, and other paper testing instruments by client and/or others.

- Clinical observation.

- Medical examinations and tests.

- Psychiatric evaluation.

- Psychological evaluation and testing.

- Collection of data from the legal system, employers, and other sources.

USING EXISTING INSTRUMENTS.   The use of established testing instruments has several advantages:

Easy to obtain: They have already been developed and are widely available.

Validity: It would be impossible for an individual to replicate the testing that has gone into validating any of the major established research instruments.

Credibility: Because of their known validity and widespread use, established instruments are respected and their results are more readily accepted than would be the case with a testing instrument you had created yourself.

Cross-comparison: Because standardized tests are in use by other treatment programs, if you also use them it is easier to compare your results with those of other clinicians in other programs.

CREATING YOUR OWN INSTRUMENTS.   There is also much to be said for developing your own data collection instruments:

Cost: Some standardized tests are expensive, whereas if you develop your own, you don't have to pay anyone a fee to use it.

Precision: By designing your own instrument, you can zero in on exactly the information you want to obtain and can customize questions and measures to your community and conditions. It may be difficult to find a standardized test that answers just the questions that are important to you, your regulators, your referral sources, and your clients.

Speed: Some standardized tests can be scored on site by your own clinical staff, but others must be sent away for scoring, meaning that you may wait weeks for results. If you build your own, you can score it right away if you wish.

When Measurements Are Made

Another vital element of designing an outcomes measurement system is obtaining data at the appropriate times to answer the questions your measures are designed to answer. There are four critical points in time when outcome measurements may be administered.

PRETREATMENT.   Obviously, studying the client during and after treatment can yield data about change only if a starting baseline has been established. For this reason, collect starting data on your clients as part of the intake process. To measure learning in a class or psychoeducational group, a pretest is needed to see how much clients know before the information is presented to them. Without a pretest, results from posttests can be wildly misleading; a person who knows a subject can sleep through a class and make a perfect score on the posttest, leading the instructor to think the student has done a fine job when no learning at all took place. By the same token, a posttest with half the answers wrong might represent a large improvement.

DURING TREATMENT.   Collecting data at various points in the treatment process will give you insight into the relative effectiveness of different components of your treatment program and may help you justify either including certain elements or making your program a given duration. Conversely, if you discover that beyond some point in midtreatment, the improvements your clients experience drop off, you may be able to shorten some part of your program without lessening its effectiveness.

AT COMPLETION OF TREATMENT.   It may seem a truism, but the only way you can tell whether a client has succeeded in achieving treatment goals is to ask or evaluate and find out. When we have clients submit to drug testing, count the AA meetings they attend, and check their answers on posttests after psychoeducational presentations, we are doing outcomes measurement.

POSTTREATMENT FOLLOW-UP.   Because the ultimate goal of therapy is to restore people to satisfactory functioning on a long-term basis, it is important to measure the durability of the changes achieved. Specifically in the realm of substance abuse treatment, the first six months posttreatment are critical, as this is the time when the most relapses seem to occur.

PURPOSES AND USES OF OUTCOMES MEASUREMENT

Outcomes measurement is becoming increasingly significant in the arena of alcohol and other drug abuse treatment. At times, outcome evaluation is mandated by legislation, third-party payers, or accrediting bodies as funding appropriation is tied to objective data about client improvement. Further, there now exists demand and pressure for high-quality services by providers, quality demonstrated by outcome data.

As a result of these trends, you are likely to face demands that you include outcomes measurements in your program design and apply the results gained in decision making in clinical practice, program design, administration, and marketing.

Clinical Practice

Decisions in this area include specific choices of treatment goals, objectives, and interventions, as well as general decisions regarding theoretical orientation and philosophy. Outcomes measurement results are also incorporated into specific interventions, such as showing clients the difference in their own levels of functioning as a result of treatment.

Program Design

The decisions made in Chapter 1 are often assisted, or driven, by outcomes measurement results. For example, a body of outcomes research showing that people suffering from paranoid schizophrenia do not benefit from a certain type of group therapy would cause a clinician to steer clear of including such group work in designing a program for a dually diagnosed population containing a large percentage of schizophrenics. Many other examples will suggest themselves as you work through the program design process.

Program Administration

In this area, outcomes measurements can drive decisions about program policies. For example, studies showing that many addicts and alcoholics successfully complete treatment and achieve lasting recovery after one or more relapses early in therapy could be crucial in shaping policies on dealing with relapsing clients.

Marketing

The most effective way to persuade referral sources to send clients to your program is to show them convincing results. Because you can't have results for a program that has not yet started, you will have to rely on data from similar programs in the planning and start-up phase.

PRACTICAL CONSIDERATIONS

You will do outcomes measurement as part of your program; there is no way to avoid it. So, the questions you must answer are What will you measure, and how? The following factors are important on a pragmatic level; they will determine what is possible and practical for you to do in this area.

Training of Assessors

Do not choose a testing methodology that requires training that your staff do not have and cannot get easily. In many cases, certain measures can only be used with extensive specialized training, as in the case of the many tests that can be legally administered only by a licensed psychologist.

Personnel Turnover

If you anticipate a high rate of turnover, do not rely on a measurement program that requires continuity of individual staff members over long periods.

Time and Resources Available for Testing

Most self-administered standardized tests can be supervised by and scored by office or clinic staff in relatively brief time periods. However, cost is also a factor; potential users should confirm whether fees are involved before using any standardized measure, as some are quite expensive. It is also important to remember legal issues in regard to copyright protection of any standardized instrument.

Similar to the checklist of program design questions in Chapter 1, here is a list of questions, ten this time, to guide you in planning your approach to outcomes evaluation:

1. What population do you serve? Does the screening instrument chosen or designed fit the individuals you are assessing?

2. Will you use standardized instruments or create your own? Remember the benefits and drawbacks of each.

3. What variables do you want to measure? This will influence selection, timing, and frequency of assessments. Do you want to assess only changes in drug consumption patterns, or are you also concerned with related life problems and functional impairments?

4. How much funding do you have for testing, if any? What are the costs in direct fees, required training, and staff time for any instruments you are considering using?

5. Who will administer and score the instruments? What training and qualifications do they have?

6. Will the same individuals perform initial baseline testing and follow-ups?

7. What are your intervals of evaluation during treatment and/or posttreatment?

8. What change do you expect to induce in clients through your treatment interventions? How will you know whether that change has occurred?

9. What type of instrument do you want to use? Will you use self-report instruments or clinical observation instruments?

10. What will you do with the results? Will you share them with clients, make changes to existing program elements, design new treatment components, use data to explain

and justify your program to management and administration, and/or use the data for marketing?

RESOURCES

Government Resources

A wide and useful variety of publications and other resources related to substance abuse treatment outcomes measurement are available from the federal government, many at no cost to the user.

The best federal source of information and literature on this topic is the National Clearinghouse for Alcohol and Drug Information (NCADI), P.O. Box 2345, Rockville, MD, 20847-2345, with a toll-free telephone number (800-729-6686) and a World Wide Web site (http://www.health.org) for ease of use in requesting materials. The NCADI will send you a catalogue from which you can select and request materials by mail, telephone, or Internet. By submitting a form included in the catalogue, you can be placed on a mailing list to receive updated information as new materials become available in your areas of interest.

A related source, whose publications can be obtained through the NCADI, is the Substance Abuse and Mental Health Services Administration (SAMHSA) Rockwall, IL, 5600 Fishers Lane, Rockville, MD 20857. Of particular value and interest to clinicians building treatment programs is the Treatment Improvement Protocol (TIP) series of publications. TIP 14, *Developing State Outcomes Monitoring Systems for Alcohol and Other Drug Abuse Treatment,* bears directly on the subject of this chapter. The other TIP publications also relate to substance abuse research issues and program design, many of them addressing specific client populations and/or treatment issues.

Other Sources

Turning to private sources of instruments and information, a number of useful books are widely available and are included in the recommended reading list at the end of this manual.

Books that will be useful in establishing this part of your program include the volume by Dr. Lewis R. Aiken (1997), *Questionnaires and Inventories: Surveying Opinions and Assessing Personality,* which offers excellent and comprehensive instruction on the art and science of developing assessment instruments.

A second helpful book, this one focusing on the use of outcomes measurement in working with managed care, is *The Measurement and Management of Clinical Outcomes in Mental Health,* by Howard, Lish, Lyons, and O'Mahoney (1997). This includes a chapter on using outcomes in substance abuse treatment and lists and discusses a number of popular standardized instruments.

Rounding out this short and by no means inclusive list of recommendations, you may want to add one or both volumes of *Measures for Clinical Practice* by Corcoran and Fischer (1994) to your professional library. Volume 1 discusses measures for use with adults, and Volume 2 deals with assessments of couples, families, and children.

Forms Included in This Chapter

We include two forms for use in integrating outcomes measurements into your substance abuse treatment program:

Outcomes Measurement Tracking Form

Consent for Participation in Outcomes Assessment

Outcomes Measurement Tracking Form

Client Name: _____ Client ID#: _____ Program: _____

Treatment Agency: _____ Program Admission Date: _____/_____/_____

Reason for Admission: _____ Therapist/Clinician: _____

Admitting Diagnosis (DSM-IV Codes):

Axis I: _____ Axis II: _____ Axis III: _____ Axis IV: _____ Axis V: _____

_____ _____ _____ _____ _____

_____ _____ _____ _____ _____

Primary diagnosis manifested by: _____

	Baseline Measurement Date: __/__/__	Treatment Measurement #1 Date: __/__/__	Treatment Measurement #2 Date: __/__/__	Treatment Measurement #3 Date: __/__/__	Treatment Measurement #4 Date: __/__/__
Assessment Tool #1: _____					
Assessment Tool #2: _____					
Assessment Tool #3: _____					
Assessment Tool #4: _____					

Number of Sessions

_____ Individual _____ Inpatient _____ Psychoeducational group

_____ Family _____ In-home _____ Intensive/outpatient

_____ Intensive group _____ Other: _____

Date Tx completed: ___/____/____ Discharge Diagnosis (DSM -IV Codes)

Axis I: _____ Axis II: _____ Axis III: _____ Axis IV: _____ Axis V: _____

_____ _____ _____ _____ _____

_____ _____ _____ _____ _____

Status at discharge: _____

Additional comments: _____

_____

_____

_____

Clinician Name/Title: _____ Signature: _____ Date ____/____/____

Supervisor Name/Title: _____ Signature: _____ Date ____/____/____

Consent for Participation in Outcomes Assessment

At different times in the course of your treatment we may be asking you to complete certain questionnaires, interviews, tests, or other measurements. These are designed to help us evaluate and improve your treatment plan, progress in treatment, and/or any changes to your plan or referrals to other providers we may need to make. The information we collect will be kept confidential, like the rest of the information in your file at this agency. We will inform you about any decisions or changes that are based on the information we collect in this way. We may also contact you to ask for feedback some time after you have completed treatment with us. This is also to evaluate our program by measuring the long-term benefits we are able to provide our clients. We thank you for your cooperation in this effort.

Please fill out the following form so that we can contact you more easily for this follow-up evaluation and do so in a way that avoids inconveniencing you:

Do you have a phone at home? _____ Phone Number: _____

Do you have a work phone where we may contact you? _____ Phone Number: _____

Do you have an e-mail address where we may contact you? _____ E-mail: _____

What is your mailing address _____

Please indicate the way you would prefer we contact you. Check one or more:
_____ Telephone _____ E-Mail _____ Letter _____ In-person appointment
_____ Other: _____ Do you prefer that we contact you at _____ home or _____ work?

Is it okay to leave a message if you are not available?_____

Is there a time or day that it is more convenient for us to contact you? _____

I understand that all results of outcome measurement completed by _____
will be kept confidential at the level of individual identification and will be shared only with the treatment providers at the above mentioned clinic/agency who are involved with my treatment.

Client Signature: _____   Date: ____/____/____

Chapter 9

Addictions and Other Compulsive Behaviors

Materials for Use in Psychoeducational Groups

Although chemical dependency treatment programs may be based on a variety of theoretical orientations, nearly all include cognitive or cognitive-behavioral psychoeducational components. The materials included in this chapter consist of detailed facilitators' guides, participant handouts designed to facilitate note taking, and pre- and posttests to measure effectiveness of the sessions in which the materials are presented. These materials are designed to be used either in conjunction with other teaching aids such as transparencies, videotapes, and audiocassettes, or as stand-alone tools useful without additional aids. Drawing on educational learning theory, the use of visual training aids offers the ideal teaching approach by presenting information in visual (transparencies or other aids), auditory (the presenter's discussion of the material), and tactile/kinesthetic (the act of writing out key points of the information while filling in the blanks on the handouts) formats. These materials are also designed to offer maximum opportunity for group members to participate actively in the teaching and learning process, and to present material from a pragmatic, plain-English perspective to make it as accessible as possible to a broad range of participants.

Four topics regarding addiction and other compulsive behaviors are addressed in the materials included in this chapter:

Psychopharmacology, Part 1 (depressants, stimulants, narcotics, and cannabis)

Psychopharmacology, Part 2 (hallucinogens, inhalants, PCP, and anabolic steroids)

The Process of Addiction

The Process of Relapse

Facilitator's Guide
Facilitator's Guide **Psychopharmacology, Part 1**

INTRODUCTION

Subject and Why It Is Important

Ask for ideas about definition of psychoactive drug, write responses on the board or flip chart, and briefly discuss them. Provide a dictionary definition: a psychoactive drug is one "influencing the mind or mental processes" (a massive unabridged dictionary makes a good visual aid at this point). Invite group members to offer ideas about what this type of influence could be, write their answers on the board or flip chart, and briefly discuss. Possibilities include:

1. Changing of the user's mood
2. Distortion of perceptions of time, space, and the meanings of events
3. Actual speeding up or slowing down—physically, mentally, and emotionally
4. Changes to the user's judgment and control of inhibitions
5. Changes to the user's ability to think logically and interpret events accurately
6. Changes to the user's level of motivation to achieve goals

Point out that this presentation is about these kinds of changes, about how psychoactive drugs affect the human brain, nervous system, and other parts of the body; ask if any member of the group is unaffected and unconcerned by these types of changes in his or her own brain, nervous system, and body.

Class Policies

Explain to participants that they will be evaluated on their accomplishment of these goals.

LEARNING GOALS Upon completion of this class, participants should demonstrate understanding of ways psychoactive drugs can affect users by listing, without notes or references, at least four types of psychoactive effects such drugs may have.

Upon completion of this class, participants should demonstrate with an accuracy rate of at least 80% knowledge of general categories of psychoactive drugs and effects common to each category by matching, without notes or references, psychoactive effects with the categories of drugs producing those effects.

QUESTIONS As the instructor, you may ask participants to hold their questions until the end or ask them at any time during class. If participation is a high priority, we recommend allowing questions at any time; if brevity is more important, it works better to hold questions until the end.

PRETEST/POSTTEST Pass out the pretest if you choose to use it, asking participants to fill out and turn in their answer sheets without putting names on them; tell them the posttest will be given at the end of class.

Background and Lead-In

Ask the discussion question, How long have human beings been using psychoactive drugs, and what were some of the earliest drugs? *Answer:* Since prehistory, people have used drugs. Drugs in use for thousands of years (in other words, since before the modern pharmaceutical industry and synthetic drugs) include:

1. Depressants (alcohol, both fermented and distilled)
2. Stimulants (coca, caffeine, nicotine, sugar, etc.)
3. Cannabis (marijuana, hashish)
4. Narcotics (opium and derivatives)
5. Hallucinogens (psilocybin, peyote, mescaline, ergot)

Discuss the question, What additional types of drugs are now in use—in other words, "modern" drugs? *Answer:* More drugs in each of the categories above (even hash oil in the case of cannabis), plus inhalants, phencyclidine polychloride (PCP), and anabolic steroids.

Ask, *Why* do people use drugs? *Answer:* For many reasons, including:

- For effect—the drug's action is pleasant or useful (this includes medical use); it allows people to temporarily feel more pleasure, less pain or discomfort, or both.
- For social/popularity reasons—people use drugs to fit in with their friends, as a shared pleasurable activity, or to show off.
- Cultural and religious customs—religious practices in many faiths include the ritualized use of psychoactive chemicals; examples range from the communion wine in many Christian services to the use of ganja (marijuana) in some Caribbean religious practices such as those of the Rastifarians and the use of organic hallucinogens in some Native American rites.

Ask the discussion question, When and why does drug use become a problem instead of a good thing? Write down and briefly discuss answers. Offer one answer: Drug use becomes a problem when the drug has negative effects that outweigh the benefits of the positive effects but a person keeps using it anyway. Ask for input and briefly discuss what types of negative effects users might experience.

TYPES OF DRUGS AND THEIR EFFECTS

Depressants

Ask students to list depressants. Answers include:

1. Barbiturates (Seconal, Nembutal, Amytal, Phenobarbital, etc.)
2. Alcohol

Effects of depressants may last anywhere from 1 to 16 hours, depending on method of use and type and amount of drug, and may include:

Positive Effects:	Negative Effects:
Calming effect: reduced fear, anxiety, anger*	Drowsiness*
Increased feeling of well-being*	Disorientation*
Increased confidence*	Impaired motor coordination*
Sleep-inducing*	Impaired judgment*
Reduced physical pain/discomfort*	Blackouts
	Nausea and vomiting with minor overdose
	Unconsciousness/coma/death with large overdose*
	Carcinogenic*
	Birth defects*
	Tolerance and withdrawal with chronic use*
	Physical and psychological addiction*

* These effects, positive and negative, are also often seen in users of other classes of drugs.

Stimulants

Ask students to list stimulants. Answers include:

1. Cocaine (including powder cocaine, crack, and basuco, which is incompletely processed cocaine often contaminated with gasoline or other petroleum products)
2. Amphetamines, including methamphetamine ("ice," "crystal," "meth," "critty," and other street names)
3. Caffeine
4. Nicotine

Effects of stimulants may last anywhere from 30 minutes to 20 hours, depending on method of use and type and amount of drug, and may include:

Positive Effects:	Negative Effects:
Increased energy, speed, strength	Anxiety, irritability, and paranoia
Increased alertness and concentration	Tremors (shakes)*
Increased feeling of well-being*	Insomnia
Increased sexual desire	Poor nutrition*
Faster reaction time	Headaches
Increased confidence*	Impaired judgment*
Euphoria*	Problems with divided attention
Decreased appetite, weight loss	Elevated pulse, breathing, temperature, blood pressure
Decreased need for sleep	
Local anaesthetic (cocaine and derivatives)— medical uses	Hallucinations with overdose/prolonged use
	Convulsions/seizures/stroke with overdose*
Vasoconstrictor—medical uses	Tolerance and withdrawal with chronic use*
	Physical and psychological addiction*

* These effects, positive and negative, are also often seen in users of other classes of drugs.

Cannabis

Ask students to list cannabis-containing drugs. Answers include: marijuana, hashish, and hash oil. All contain up to 426 separate chemicals, with delta-9-tetrahydrocannibinol (THC) being the main active ingredient. Effects of cannabis drugs may last anywhere from 2 to 16 hours, depending on method of use and type and amount of drug, and may include:

Positive Effects:

May act either as a stimulant or depressant

Calming effect: reduced fear, anxiety, anger*

Treatment for glaucoma: reduces intraocular fluid pressure

Reduction of physical pain, discomfort, and nausea*

Euphoria*

Increased sense of well-being*

Increased confidence*

Negative Effects:

Dry mouth, red eyes, decreased body temperature

Reduced muscular strength

Weakened immune system

Drowsiness*

Disorientation*

Dulled senses*

Impaired coordination, time/space perception

Impaired judgment*

Impaired short-term memory

Impaired concentration, reduced ability to do complex tasks

Paranoia*

Carcinogenic*

Birth defects*

Sex hormone imbalance with prolonged use*

Damage to lungs, throat with prolonged use*

Psychological addiction with prolonged use*

* These effects, positive and negative, are also often seen in users of other classes of drugs.

Narcotics

Ask students to list narcotics. Answers include:

Opium

Morphine

Heroin

Methadone

Codeine

Demerol

Percodan

Effects of narcotics may last anywhere from 4 to 24 hours, depending on method of use and type and amount of drug, and may include:

Positive Effects:	Negative Effects:
Reduction of pain/discomfort*	Drowsiness*
Euphoria*	Disorientation*
Increased sense of well-being*	Dulled senses
Calming effect: reduced fear, anxiety, anger*	Impaired motor coordination*
Sleep-inducing*	Impaired judgment*
	Unconsciousness/convulsions/coma/death with overdose*
	Tolerance and withdrawal with chronic use*
	Physical and psychological addiction

* These effects, positive and negative, are also often seen in users of other classes of drugs.

CONCLUSION

Recapitulate the following key points:

1. Psychoactive drugs are chemicals that have any of these effects:
    * Changing of moods
    * Distortion of perception
    * Speeding up or slowing down
    * Changes to judgment or control of inhibitions
    * Changes to ability to think logically and interpret events accurately
    * Changes to levels of motivation to achieve goals

2. Since prehistory, people have used drugs, including:
    * Stimulants
    * Depressants
    * Narcotics
    * Cannabis
    * Hallucinogens

    More recently, new drugs have been added in each of these categories, and the additional categories of inhalants, PCP, and steroids have been added.

3. Reasons people use drugs include:
    * For effect
    * Social/popularity reasons
    * Cultural and religious customs

4. Drug use becomes a problem when negative effects outweigh the benefits.

5. This presentation has offered information about four categories of drugs—depressants, stimulants, cannabis, and narcotics. The other categories—hallucinogens, inhalants, PCP, and steroids—are covered in a different presentation.

REVIEW OF LEARNING GOALS AND POSTTEST

1. Demonstrate understanding of ways psychoactive drugs can affect users
2. Demonstrate knowledge of general categories of psychoactive drugs and effects

QUESTIONS/DISCUSSION BEFORE POSTTEST

ADMINISTER POSTTEST

QUESTIONS/DISCUSSION AFTER POSTTEST

1. Definition of a psychoactive drug: A chemical that has one or more of the following effects:

   a. Changing of _____

   b. Distortion of _____

   c. _____ up or down _____

   d. Changes to _____ or control of _____

   e. Changes to ability to _____ and _____

   f. Changes to levels _____ to _____

2. People have been using psychoactive drugs for how long? _____

3. Categories of drugs people used before modern times include: _____
_____
_____

4. Additional types of drugs now in use include: _____
_____
_____

5. Reasons people use drugs are: _____
_____
_____

6. Drug use becomes a problem when: _____
_____
_____

7. Depressants: Drugs in this category include: _____
_____

Effects may last _____ . Positive and negative effects can include:

<u>Positive</u>   <u>Negative</u>

8. Stimulants: Drugs in this category include: _____
_____
_____

Effects may last _____. Positive and negative effects can include:

<u>Positive</u>   <u>Negative</u>

9. Cannabis: Drugs in this category include: _____
_____
_____

Effects may last _____. Positive and negative effects can include:

<u>Positive</u>   <u>Negative</u>

10. Narcotics: Drugs in this category include: _____
_____
_____

Effects may last _____. Positive and negative effects can include:

<u>Positive</u>   <u>Negative</u>

Name: _____   Date: ____/____/____

1. Definition: Name up to six effects a chemical would have to cause in a person using it for that chemical to be called a "psychoactive drug."

_____   _____

_____   _____

_____   _____

2. People have been using psychoactive drugs for about how long? _____

3. Name up to three reasons people use psychoactive drugs: _____

_____

_____

4. In your opinion, when does use of psychoactive drugs become a problem for a person? _____

_____

_____

5. Name up to four categories or classes of psychoactive drugs, and list at least two effects of drugs in each category or class.

Category/Class: Effects:

_____   _____

               _____

_____   _____

               _____

_____   _____

               _____

_____   _____

               _____

6. Matching: Match the drugs with the correct descriptions:

a. Caffeine _____	1)	Created as "nonaddictive" morphine substitute
b. Alcohol _____	2)	Alkaloid stimulant found in "crack"
c. Cocaine _____	3)	Stimulant found in tobacco products
d. Phenobarbital _____	4)	Most widely abused depressant drug
e. Nicotine _____	5)	Tar level several times higher than tobacco
f. Opium _____	6)	Widely use/abused legal stimulant
g. Marijuana _____	7)	Synthetic depressant
h. Methamphetamine _____	8)	Cannabis form with highest THC levels
i. Heroin _____	9)	Addictive organic narcotic
j. Hash oil _____	10)	Synthetic stimulant

Name: _____   Date: _____/_____/_____

INTRODUCTION

Subject and Why It Is Important to This Group

Remind group that this is a continuation of Part 1, covering additional categories of drugs not discussed in detail in that presentation.

Review the definition of a psychoactive drug as one that "influences the mind or mental processes" in ways including the following:

- Changing of the user's mood
- Distortion of perceptions of time, space, and the meanings of events
- Actual speeding up or slowing down — physical, mental, and emotional
- Changes to the user's judgement and control of inhibitions
- Changes to the user's ability to think clearly
- Changes to the user's level of motivation to achieve goals

Review reasons people use drugs:

- For effect
- Social reasons
- Religious or cultural reasons

Review idea that drug use becomes a problem when the drug has negative effects that outweigh the benefits *but a person keeps using it anyway.*

Ask group to reflect on the first presentation and name ways they can use the information provided.

Class Policies

Explain to participants that they will be evaluated on their accomplishment of these goals.

LEARNING GOAL Upon completion of this class, participants should demonstrate with an accuracy rate of at least 80% knowledge of the four types or categories of psychoactive drugs discussed in this presentation and some effects common to each category by matching, without notes or references, psychoactive effects with the categories of drugs producing those effects.

QUESTIONS As the instructor, you may ask participants to hold questions until the end or ask them during class. If participation is a high priority, we recommend allowing questions any time; if brevity is more important, it works better to hold questions until the end.

PRETEST Pass out the pretest if you choose to use it, asking participants to fill out and turn in their answer sheets without putting names on them; tell them the posttest will be given at the end of class.

Background/Review and Lead-In

Ask the discussion question, How did the coming of modern times and the Industrial Revolution change the reasons and ways people use psychoactive drugs? *Answer:* The reasons didn't change much—people still use drugs for effect, because they like the way the drugs make them feel or the things the drugs allow them to do. The old categories and drugs have remained in use:

- Depressants (alcohol, both fermented and distilled, and now barbiturates and other synthetic depressants)
- Stimulants (coca, caffeine, nicotine, sugar, etc., with the addition of amphetamines including methamphetamine and other synthetic stimulants)
- Cannabis (marijuana, hashish, and now also hash oil)
- Narcotics (opium and derivatives, with the modern additions of heroin and a wide range of synthetic narcotics including codeine, Demerol, Percodan, and others)
- Hallucinogens (psilocybin, peyote, mescaline, ergot, plus a number of synthetics, with LSD being the most widely known and used)

    Some new categories have been added:

- Inhalants—drugs used in gas or vapor form
- Phencyclidine polychloride, or PCP—a complex drug with wide-ranging effects that may vary from person to person and time to time
- Anabolic steroids—synthetic imitations of natural body chemicals related to physical growth and development of sexual characteristics for both genders

TYPES OF DRUGS AND THEIR EFFECTS

Hallucinogens

Ask students to list hallucinogens. Answers include:

1. LSD, DMT, STP/DOM, MDA, and many other synthetics
2. Peyote or mescaline, a product of a type of cactus
3. Morning glory seeds, a natural source of LSD
4. Psilocybin, a type of mushroom, also very similar to LSD in its chemistry and effects
5. Ergot, a type of spore or mold that grows on grains, especially rye
6. Belladonna alkaloids, found in plants including jimsonweed and deadly nightshade
7. Australian toad sweat—the secretions of a certain type of toad native to that continent

    The duration of the effects of hallucinogens is highly variable, depending on method of use and type and amount of drug, and may include:

Positive Effects	Negative Effects
Feeling of heightened or expanded awareness	Drowsiness*
Hallucinations*	Nausea*
No medical use	Birth defects*
	Delayed flashbacks, especially under stress
	Disorientation*
	Hallucinations*
	Distorted perception of time and space*
	Panic*
	Induced psychosis*
	With overdose, death*
	With chronic use, psychological addiction

* These effects, positive and negative, are also often seen in users of other classes of drugs.

Inhalants

Ask students to list inhalants. Answers include:

1. Anaesthetics including nitrous oxide (laughing gas) and ether—used medically, in auto racing, and as aerosol propellant
2. Commercial chemicals: gasoline, paint, paint thinner, correction fluid, glue, freon, and others
3. Vasodilators including amyl nitrate and butyl nitrate

Effects of inhalants may last from less than 1 minute to 4 hours, depending on method of use and type and amount of drug, and may include:

Positive Effects	Negative Effects
Rush-type euphoria or bliss*	Nausea*
Reduction of pain and discomfort*	Drowsiness*
Sleep-inducing*	Dizziness*
	Fainting
	Headache*
	High blood pressure*
	Bronchial spasms (choking in chest)
	Damage to skin, liver, kidneys, throat, lungs, and central nervous system
	Seizures*
	Brain damage*
	Carcinogenic*
	Tolerance with chronic use*
	Psychological addiction*
	Sudden death due to heart arrhythmia or respiratory depression (aka SSDS or Sudden Sniffing Death Syndrome)

* These effects, positive and negative, are also often seen in users of other classes of drugs.

Phencyclidine Polychloride (PCP)

Ask students to state which category PCP belongs in. *Answer:* It has characteristics of a *stimulant*, a *depressant*, and a *hallucinogen*.

PCP is used by itself or added to other drugs, especially marijuana. Its effects may last from 2 hours to 90 days, depending on dosage and combination with other drugs, and may include:

Positive Effects	Negative Effects
Reduction of physical pain/discomfort*	Hallucinations*
Giddiness, euphoria*	Distorted perception of time and space*
Increased sense of well-being*	Drowsiness or insomnia*
Sometimes, increased energy, speed, strength*	Dizziness*
	Disorientation*
	With higher doses, nausea*
	Muscle damage sometimes leading to damage in other organs and body systems including kidney failure
	Dangerously high blood pressure*
	Heart failure due to cardiac arrhythmia*
	Seizures*
	Coma*
	Psychotic episodes ranging from 6 to 90 days, panic,* rage,* self-mutilation

* These effects, positive and negative, are also often seen in users of other classes of drugs.

Anabolic Steroids

These are different from other drugs discussed so far, in that the effects usually sought are more physical than mental or emotional, and also that the user seeks long-lasting or permanent effects. These are used in pursuit of increased muscle mass, strength, and aggressiveness, often by athletes trying to improve their performance. Effects of steroids may last from hours to a lifetime, and may include:

Positive Effects	Negative Effects
Increased muscle mass and strength*	Carcinogenic*
Increased confidence and aggressiveness*	Development of unwanted secondary sexual characteristics—altered body hair patterns, voice changes, growth or shrinkage of breasts, testicles, etc.*
Physical and psychological addiction*	Damage to endocrine system and many internal organs*
	Acne*
	High blood pressure*
	Altered moods—irritability, rages, depression, paranoia*
	Withdrawal with chronic use*

* These effects, positive and negative, are also often seen in users of other classes of drugs.

CONCLUSION

Review of earlier material:

1. Psychoactive drugs are chemicals that influence the mind and mental processes in any of several ways.
2. Since prehistory, people have used several categories of psychoactive drugs. More recently, new drugs have been added in each of these categories, and the categories of inhalants, PCP, and steroids have been added.
3. People use drugs for effect, for social/popularity reasons, and as part of cultural and religious customs.
4. Drug use becomes a problem when the drug's negative effects outweigh the benefits but a person keeps using it anyway.

This presentation has presented information about four categories of drugs—hallucinogens, inhalants, PCP, and steroids. The other categories—depressants, stimulants, cannabis, and narcotics—are covered in a different presentation.

REVIEW OF LEARNING GOALS AND POSTTEST

Demonstrate knowledge of general categories of psychoactive drugs and effects

QUESTIONS/DISCUSSION BEFORE POSTTEST

ADMINISTER POSTTEST

QUESTIONS/DISCUSSION AFTER POSTTEST

Participant Handout
Psychopharmacology Part 2

1. Review — definition of a psychoactive drug: A chemical that influences _____

_____

_____

_____

2. Review — reasons people use drugs are: _____

_____

_____

_____

3. Review — drug use becomes a problem when: _____

_____

_____

_____

4. Types of drugs not used before modern times include: _____ , _____ ,

_____ , and _____ .

5. Hallucinogens: Drugs in this category include: _____

_____

_____

_____

Effects may last _____ . Positive and negative effects can include:

<u>Positive</u>   <u>Negative</u>

6. Inhalants: Drugs in this category include: _____
_____
_____
_____

Effects may last _____ . Positive and negative effects can include:

Positive   Negative

7. PCP: Drugs in this category include: _____
_____
_____
_____

Effects may last _____ . Positive and negative effects can include:

Positive   Negative

8. Anabolic steroids: Drugs in this category are: _____
_____
_____
_____

Effects may last. Positive and negative effects can include:

Positive   Negative

Name: _____ Date: ____/____/____

Pretest/Posttest
Psychopharmacology, Part 2

1. Review: A psychoactive drug is a chemical that affects the _____ or _____ .

2. Name up to three reasons people use psychoactive drugs: _____
_____
_____

3. When does use of psychoactive drugs become a problem for a person? _____
_____
_____

4. Name four categories or classes of psychoactive drugs not discussed in Psychopharmacology Part 1, and list at least two positive and two negative effects of drugs in each category or class.

Category/Class: Positive Effects: Negative Effects:

_____   _____   _____

                         _____   _____

_____   _____   _____

                         _____   _____

_____   _____   _____

                         _____   _____

_____   _____   _____

                         _____   _____

5. Matching: Match the drugs with the correct descriptions:

   a. PCP _____   1) "Poppers"
   b. Morning glory seeds _____   2) Commercial chemical associated with Sudden
                                              Sniffing Death Syndrome
   c. Amyl nitrate _____   3) Synthetic hallucinogen
   d. Anabolic steroids _____   4) Organic source of LSD
   e. LSD _____   5) Hallucinogen derived from mushrooms
   f. Belladonna alkaloids _____   6) Often linked with self-mutilation
   g. Peyote _____   7) Often abused by bodybuilders
   h. Ergot _____   8) Inhalant used as dental anaesthetic
   i. Freon _____   9) Hallucinogenic fungus
   j. Nitrous oxide _____   10) Hallucinogens found in jimsonweed

Name: _____   Date: ____/____/____

INTRODUCTION

Subject and Why It Is Important

Point out that more than half the adult population of the United States drinks alcohol. Many use other drugs as well. But most of these people do not become chemically dependent, what is commonly called being alcoholic or addicted. Ask the question: *What causes some people to become chemically dependent?* Write answers on board or flip chart and facilitate a short discussion.

Point out that this group is made up of people who have been diagnosed as chemically dependent, know someone who is chemically dependent, or are at high risk of becoming chemically dependent, so this is a personal concern for each member. Note that some members may agree with this diagnosis, others may not, but either way, because they have been given this label, they have more reason than most people to be concerned with what it means to be addicted.

Also, addiction and alcoholism run in families. Group members have reason to learn as much as they can about this to teach their children and other family members and help them as soon as possible if they start to show early signs of becoming addicted to alcohol or other drugs.

Class Policy

LEARNING GOALS

1. Upon completion of this class, participants should demonstrate understanding of the physical and psychological processes of addiction by defining, without notes or references, the terms "addiction," "alcoholism," and "chemical dependence."
2. Upon completion of this class, participants should demonstrate understanding of the physical and psychological processes of addiction by listing, without notes or references, phases of at least one model of addiction and at least two typical events or experiences in each phase.

QUESTIONS As the instructor, you may ask participants to hold questions until the end or ask them at any time during class. If participation is a high priority, we recommend allowing questions at any time; if brevity is more important, it works better to hold questions until the end.

PRETEST Pass out the pretest if you choose to use it, asking participants to fill out and turn in their answer sheets without putting names on them; tell them the posttest will be given at the end of class.

Background and Lead-In

Ask the discussion question, What is addiction or alcoholism? Ask group members to name or describe what comes to mind for them when they hear the words "addict" and "alcoholic"; write their answers on the board or flip chart, then lead a short discussion (optional, based on time). Then give these definitions:

Addiction is the same thing as *chemical dependence*: one definition will do for both. Doctors and counselors use the description in the *Diagnostic and Statistical Manual of Mental Disorders,* 4th edition (*DSM-IV*), which says that a person is addicted to a chemical if he or she has three or more of the following behavior patterns in his or her life over a period of at least a year:

1. *Tolerance*: need to drink/use more to get same effect, or diminished effect with same amount.

2. *Withdrawal*: physical/emotional withdrawal symptoms, or drinking/using more to relieve or avoid withdrawal symptoms.

3. *Loss of control*: drinking/using more, or for longer, than intended.

4. *Attempts to control*: persistent desire or efforts to cut down or control drinking/use of the substance, including making rules for self about when, where, what to drink/use, etc.

5. *Time spent on use*: spending a great deal of time getting the substance, drinking/using it, or recovering from drinking/use.

6. *Sacrifices made for use*: giving up or reducing social, work, or recreational activities that are important to the person because of conflicts with drinking/using.

7. *Use despite known suffering*: continuing to drink/use despite knowing one has a physical or psychological problem that is caused or made worse by drinking/using.

    Alcoholism is more specific and means addiction to a specific psychoactive drug, namely, alcohol.

    Point out that a person is chemically dependent, addicted, or alcoholic when he or she has at least three of these patterns in his or her life. Chemical dependence is very destructive to a person's health, family, work, social life, finances, and legal status. But many addicts and alcoholics are hard-working, intelligent, and successful (for a while); this is known as being a "functioning" alcoholic or addict. The popular image of the addict or alcoholic as homeless or otherwise down-and-out applies only to some.

    Ask for group members' thoughts on this—does this change their feelings about the words addict and alcoholic?

    Ask for opinions about how information on phases and symptoms of addiction would be useful to a functional addict or alcoholic. Then give this answer: If a person is still at the functional stage, knowing the phases and being able to see the process in action may save him or her from having to go through a lot of suffering before seeing the need to take drastic action to change these patterns.

THE PROCESS OF ADDICTION (LECTURE FORMAT)

Phases of Addiction

Jellinek's Model: Jellinek was a pioneer in getting chemical dependence recognized as a disease. Before his work, which was mainly during the 1950s, many people believed dependence was a matter of being weakwilled or being morally defective. Jellinek described chemical dependence as having four phases:

a. *Contact phase*: During this phase, one comes into contact with the drug, begins drinking or using, and becomes psychologically dependent. This means that there are no physical withdrawal symptoms if one doesn't drink or use, but one feels the need to drink or use to deal with life. The contact phase may last many years.

b. *Prodromal phase:* In the next phase, tolerance starts to increase—it takes more of the drug to get the same effect. It is often during the prodromal phase that one starts experiencing blackouts (if the drug is alcohol); begins to hide from others the amount one is drinking or using; begins drinking/using faster, or in other words, strictly for the effect; begins avoiding talking about one's drinking/use with others; and experiences loss of control and physical withdrawal.

c. *Crucial phase:* In the third phase, loss of control progresses, so that one can't be sure how much one will drink or use once begun. Alcoholics and addicts in this stage often quit for a while to prove they aren't really dependent, but return to uncontrolled drinking or using when they try to resume moderate use. They then begin trying other ways to control their drinking or using, and to escape the consequences. The instructor may quote the *Book of Alcoholics Anonymous* (the Big Book): "Here are some of the methods we have tried: Drinking beer only, limiting the number of drinks, never drinking alone, never drinking in the morning, drinking only at home, never having it in the house, never drinking during business hours, drinking only at parties, switching from scotch to brandy, drinking only natural wines, agreeing to resign if ever drunk on the job, taking a trip, not taking a trip, swearing off forever (with and without a solemn oath), taking more physical exercise, reading inspirational books, going to health farms and sanitariums, accepting voluntary commitment to asylums—we could increase the list ad infinitum" (p.31).

The addict or alcoholic in the crucial stage starts experiencing more physical and psychological damage; other people will notice that one's health and personality are going downhill. The dependent person's life is more and more disrupted and full of conflict as the crucial stage progresses. Prolonged periods of use start—benders for an alcoholic, several-day runs for a methamphetamine user, etc.

d. *Chronic phase*: This is the final stage. In the chronic stage, life falls apart, if it hasn't already. This is the stage where people may drop out of their previous family and social situations, become unemployed, become homeless, be hospitalized due to effects of long-term drinking/using, and have frequent encounters with the law. This is the stage where some people die and others hit bottom and decide to do whatever it takes to change.

Nonphysiological Model (can apply to other compulsive behaviors as well):

a. *Contact phase*: As in Jellinek's stages, this is the stage where one first experiences the drug or behavior and finds that one likes it—it either gives one pleasure or reduces unpleasant feelings.

b. *Serendipitous phase*: Serendipity means finding something good that you weren't expecting. In this phase, one discovers that using the drug or engaging in the behavior helps one deal with a situation one had difficulty with before. For example, a shy person discovers that a drink makes it easier to talk to another person; a depressed person finds that he or she feels less depressed after eating a big meal, or getting angry, or doing something dangerous.

c. *Instrumental phase*: In the instrumental phase, one begins to deliberately use the drug or behavior to cope with difficult situations. In this stage, the use of the drug or behavior becomes a routine.

d. *Dependent phase*: In the final phase, one comes to feel unable to cope with life without the drug or behavior. One experiences loss of control (with either a drug or a behavior), followed by unpleasant consequences for self and others, regrets, guilt, and promises not to "do it again." At the same time, one feels trapped because one cannot cope without the drug or behavior, and may even feel by this time that it is a part of one's basic nature and cannot be changed. For this reason, one continues engaging in the drug use or compulsive behavior in spite of more and more painful results.

Note: Non-drug-using behaviors that fit this pattern may include overeating; bingeing and purging; dieting, with or without physical exercise; physical exercise alone; gambling; spending money; religion; outbursts of rage and violence; sexual acting out; workaholism; and hobbies such as surfing the Internet.

CONCLUSION

The process of addiction is an important subject for the members of the group because of concerns they may have for themselves and for others, especially family members. We covered the *DSM-IV* definition of chemical dependence and two models of the process of addiction, one focused strictly on chemical dependence and one that includes other behaviors.

REVIEW OF LEARNING GOALS

1. Understanding of the physical and psychological processes of addiction and ability to define the terms addiction, alcoholism, and chemical dependence.
2. Knowledge of phases of at least one model of addiction and at least two typical events or experiences in each phase.

QUESTIONS/DISCUSSION BEFORE POSTTEST

ADMINISTER POSTTEST

QUESTIONS/DISCUSSION AFTER POSTTEST

Participant Handout
The Process of Addiction

1. Definitions: Chemical dependence, addiction, and alcoholism require _____ or more of these symptoms over a period of _____ or longer:

    a. Tolerance: _____

_____

_____

_____

    b. Withdrawal: _____

_____

_____

_____

    c. Loss of control: _____

_____

_____

_____

    d. Attempts to control: _____

_____

_____

_____

    e. Time spent on use: _____

_____

_____

_____

    f. Sacrifices made for use: _____

_____

_____

_____

    g. Use despite known suffering: _____

_____

_____

_____

2. Jellinek's Phases: There are _____ phases in this sequence. They are:

    a. The _____ phase: the preaddictive phase. Events during this phase include:

_____

_____

_____

    b. The _____ phase: the early phase of addiction. Events during this phase include:

_____

_____

_____

    c. The _____ phase: the middle phase of addiction. Events during this phase include:

_____

_____

_____

    d. The _____ phase: the late phase of addiction. Events during this phase include:

_____

_____

_____

3. Nonphysiological Model Phases: These describe both chemical dependency and other addictive behaviors. The four phases are:

    a. The _____ phase: the discovery phase. Events during this phase include:

_____

_____

_____

    b. The _____ phase: the beginning-use phase. Events during this phase include:

_____

_____

_____

    c. The _____ phase: the beginning-abuse phase. Events during this phase include:

_____

_____

_____

    d. The _____ phase: the compulsive phase. Events during this phase include:

_____

_____

_____

Name: _____   Date: ____/____/____

Pretest/Posttest
The Process of Addiction

1. Name at least four signs or symptoms of addiction: _____

_____

_____

2. What is the difference between addiction and alcoholism? _____

_____

_____

3. Briefly describe the mental picture you get when you think of the word "addict": _____

_____

_____

4. Now do the same for the word "alcoholic": _____

_____

_____

5. Name three types of addictive or compulsive behavior not involving alcohol or other drugs: _____

_____

_____

6. Name four phases of addiction and two symptoms or signs you might see in each phase:

Phase   Symptoms or Signs

_____   _____

_____   _____

_____   _____

_____   _____

7. What is the difference between addiction and alcoholism? _____

_____

_____

8. What does it mean to be a functioning addict or alcoholic? _____

_____

_____

Name: _____   Date: ____/____/____

INTRODUCTION

Subject and Why It Is Important

Ask participants why they think a class on the process of relapse is important, and briefly discuss their answers. Point out that this session will define relapse, map its progression, discuss types of relapse, and examine early warning signs of relapse. Inform participants that they will learn in other classes to anticipate situations and events that might trigger relapse and develop a plan to avoid or cope with them.

Class Policies

Explain to participants that they will be evaluated on their accomplishment of these learning goals:

LEARNING GOALS

1. Upon completion of this class, participants will be able to describe, without notes or references, typical events in the progression of relapse.
2. Upon completion of this class, participants will be able to identify, without notes or references, three types of relapse.
3. Upon completion of this class, participants will be able to identify, without notes or references, early warning signs of relapse in several areas of a person's life.

QUESTIONS As the instructor, you may ask participants to hold their questions until the end or ask them at any time during the presentation.

PRETEST Distribute the pretest if you decide to use it, asking group members to complete it and turn it in to the instructor. Participants are not asked to put their names on the pretest. Inform participants that a posttest will be completed at the end of class time and that they will be given an opportunity to ask questions prior to taking the posttest.

Background and Lead-In

Ask participants to define relapse and write their answers on the board. Compare with the dictionary definition of relapse: "to slip or fall back into a former condition, especially after improvement or seeming improvement; specifically (a) to fall back into illness after recovery or seeming recovery; (b) to fall back into bad habits, wrongdoing, error, etc.; to backslide." In other words, *getting sick again.* In the case of the recovering addict or alcoholic, this means returning to an addictive lifestyle as well as to using drugs, including alcohol. Note: It is helpful to compare addiction to other illnesses and diseases that result in people getting sick again if care not taken (e.g., diabetes).

Ask the question, *Is there more than one type of relapse? Answer:* Yes, and they are:

- Therapeutic relapse: A relapse that scares the person so much that he or she returns to abstinence and becomes more serious and motivated about staying in recovery.
- Pathological relapse: A relapse that leads to a lasting return to addictive behavior—the person returns to out-of-control substance use.
- Fatal relapse: A relapse that results in death by substance-induced accident, suicide, or overdose, or other results of substance abuse.

PROGRESSION OF RELAPSE AND EARLY WARNING SIGNS
Where Does Relapse Start

Discuss the idea that the drug use or drink is the completion of the relapse process, not its start. Relapse is the process of returning to an addictive lifestyle. Just as recovery involves changing not only the substance use but other habits, relationships, and patterns of thoughts and feelings, relapse is a change in all these areas back to their addictive versions. Usually, the other changes take place well before the return to substance abuse and can be identified by the recovering person or by others who know what to look for. If participants have not identified this as an important reason to attend this class, offer it to them at this time.

What Is Happening during the Early Phase (Before Actual Using or Drinking) in a Typical Relapse?

Encourage class participants to recall past relapses and to compare the following early warning signs with what occurred prior to their last use. The relapse process takes place in several areas of a person's life:

1. Thoughts and attitudes: Several changes in mental state can be part of relapse:
    (a) Growth of denial, minimization, or exaggeration of problems
    (b) Becoming rigid, obsessive, or avoidant about recovery
    (c) Unrealistic expectations of situations, self, and others
    (d) Becoming apathetic
    (e) Justifying or making excuses for using/drinking
    (f) Nostalgia about using/drinking—"good old days" effect
    (g) Thinking about drug/alcohol much of time

2. Feelings and moods: Some changes that mean a relapse is in progress:
    (a) Increased depression, guilt, self-pity, regrets
    (b) Increased anger at self or others, general hostility
    (c) Increased boredom
    (d) Increased euphoria—"pink cloud" effect
    (e) Increased loneliness
    (f) Loss of self-confidence or false air of superiority

3. Behavior changes: The most visible outward signs of a relapse in progress:
    (a) Stops participating in recovery activities
    (b) Isolates self
    (c) Returns to old using activities, places, and people
    (d) Dishonesty, secretiveness
    (e) Growing inconsistency, undependability
    (f) Increased complaining
    (g) Creating crises
    (h) Rejecting help/concern
    (i) Irregular eating and sleeping patterns
    (j) Increased impulsivity

CONCLUSION

Recapitulate the following key points:

1. Definition of relapse: *Getting sick again*
2. In the progression of relapse, the return to using or drinking is the completion of the relapse process, not its start.
3. There are early warning signs that indicate that a relapse is in process. They occur in the areas of thoughts, emotions, and behaviors.
4. There are three types of relapse: therapeutic, pathological, and fatal.
5. Your own and other people's past experiences of relapse are worth evaluating to spot warning signs and triggers and prevent future relapses.

REVIEW OF LEARNING GOALS

1. Upon completion of this class, participants will be able to describe, without notes or references, typical events in the progression of relapse.
2. Upon completion of this class, participants will be able to identify, without notes or references, three types of relapse.
3. Upon completion of this class, participants will be able to identify, without notes or references, early warning signs of relapse in several areas of a person's life.

QUESTIONS/DISCUSSION BEFORE POSTTEST

ADMINISTER POSTTEST

QUESTIONS OR ADDITIONAL COMMENTS OR DISCUSSION

1. Definition of relapse: Getting _____ _____ . In the case of the recovering addict or alcoholic, this would mean a return to _____ as well as a return to using drugs, including alcohol.

2. There are three types of relapse:

   a. _____ _____ : This is a relapse that scares the person so much that he or she returns to abstinence and becomes more serious and motivated about _____ .

   b. _____ _____ : This is a relapse that leads to a lasting return to addictive behavior — the person returns to out-of-control substance abuse.

   c. _____ _____ : This is a relapse that results in death by substance-induced accident, suicide, or overdose, or other results of substance abuse.

3. Where does relapse start? The return to drug use or drinking is the _____ of the relapse process, not its _____ .

4. What is happening during the early phase (before actual using or drinking) in a typical relapse? The relapse process takes place in several areas of a person's life:

   a. Thoughts and attitudes: Several changes in mental state can be part of relapse.

      1) Growth of _____ , _____ , or _____ of problems

      2) Becoming _____ , _____ , or _____ about recovery

      3) _____ expectations of situations, self, and others

      4) Becoming _____ , feeling little or no emotion

      5) _____ or _____ _____ for using/drinking

      6) Nostalgia about using/drinking— " _____ _____ _____ " effect

      7) Thinking about drug/alcohol _____ _____ _____ _____

   b. Feelings and moods: Some changes that may mean a relapse is in progress:

      1) Increased _____ , _____ , self-pity, regrets

      2) Increased _____ at self or others, general _____

      3) Increased _____

      4) Increased euphoria — " _____ _____ " effect

      5) Increased _____

      6) Loss of _____ - _____ or false air of

   c. Behavior changes: The most visible outward signs of a relapse in progress:

      1) Stops participating in _____ _____

      2) _____ self

      3) Returns to old using _____ , _____ , and _____

      4) _____ , secretiveness

      5) Growing _____ , undependability

6) Increased _____

7) Creating crises — the " _____ _____ " effect

8) Rejecting _____ / _____

9) Irregular _____ and _____ patterns

10) Increased _____

Relapse Warning Signs and Triggers I Might See in Myself, Based on My Own and Others' Experiences:

Thoughts and Attitudes: _____

_____

_____

_____

_____

_____

_____

_____

_____

_____

Feelings and Moods: _____

_____

_____

_____

_____

_____

_____

_____

_____

_____

_____

Behavior Changes: _____

_____

_____

_____

_____

_____

_____

_____

_____

_____

Name: _____   Date: ____/____/____

1. Define "relapse" as used in describing alcoholism or addiction: _____

_____

_____

_____

_____

2. Is there more than one type of relapse? _____ . If yes, how many types, and what are they? _____

_____

_____

_____

_____

3. The return to drug use or drinking is the _____ of the relapse process.

      a. beginning   b. completion   c. neither

4. Describe typical changes in thoughts and attitudes you might expect to see in a person who is relapsing into addiction: _____

_____

_____

_____

_____

5. Describe typical changes in feelings and moods you might expect to see in a person who is relapsing into addiction: _____

_____

_____

_____

_____

6. Describe typical changes in behavior you might expect to see in a person who is relapsing into addiction: _____

_____

_____

_____

_____

Name: _____   Date: ____/____/____

Chapter 10

Recovery Resources and Skills

Materials for Use in Psychoeducational Groups

Chapter 9 focused on the problem of addiction; with Chapter 10, we begin offering materials oriented toward teaching clients about solutions. The presentation materials in this chapter are focused on methods and information that chemically dependent people can employ to change the self-destructive patterns that have characterized their lives, both in terms of the use of alcohol and other drugs and in relation to emotional difficulties and self-care skill deficits that accompany an addictive lifestyle and can set the stage for relapse into active addiction.

The materials included in this chapter employ the same multiple-learning-modalities approach and cognitive orientation as those in Chapter 9:

The Process of Recovery

Recovery Programs and Resources

Lifestyle Changes: Alternatives to Substance Abuse or Other Compulsive Behaviors

Common Problems and Issues in Recovery

Relapse Prevention Planning, Part 1

Relapse Prevention Planning, Part 2

Physical and Emotional Self-Care

Stress Management

Coping with Anger and Resentment

Coping Skills for Depression and Anxiety

Resisting Open and Hidden Pressures to Drink or Use

INTRODUCTION

Subject and Why It Is Important

The need for a class on the process of recovery is self-evident—is there anyone who does not have questions or concerns about how recovery will work?

Group Policy

Explain to participants that they will be evaluated at the end of the class period to check the accomplishment of these goals.

LEARNING GOALS Upon completion of this presentation participants:

- Should demonstrate the ability to define the terms "abstinence," "sobriety," and "recovery."
- Will be able to discuss the difference between recovery and being recovered.
- Should demonstrate understanding of the stages, events, and experiences people typically go through in recovering from chemical dependence.

QUESTIONS As the instructor, you may ask students to hold questions until the end or ask them at any time during class.

PRETEST Distribute the pretest if you choose to use it, ask participants to fill it out and return their answer sheets to the instructor without putting their names on them; tell them the posttest will be completed at the end of the presentation.

Background and Lead-In

Ask class members for definitions of "abstinence," "sobriety," and "recovery." Write responses on the board, then compare with the following definitions from *Webster's New Universal Unabridged Dictionary:*

- *Abstinence:* "the refraining from an indulgence of appetite, or from customary gratification of one's appetites; it denotes a total forbearance, as in fasting or in giving up the drinking of alcoholic liquors."
- *Sobriety:* a two-part definition: "the state or quality of being sober; specifically, (a) temperance or moderation, especially in the use of drink; (b) seriousness, solemnity, gravity, or sedateness of manner or appearance."
- *Recovery:* four definitions. "(a) The act or power of regaining, retaking, or conquering again; (b) a getting well again, coming or bringing back to consciousness, revival of a person from weakness; (c) a regaining of balance . . . a return to soundness; (d) the time needed for recovering."

Discuss differences between the definitions for abstinence and sobriety on one hand and for recovery on the other. Discuss that abstinence and sobriety are necessary conditions for recovery, but not everyone who is abstinent is in recovery. Emphasize that recovery indicates changes to lifestyle patterns and interactions. Offer simple definitions:

1. *Abstinence:* No use of any drug of abuse; in some cases, may also mean no participation in nondrug compulsive behaviors that have been part of one's addictive pattern.

2. *Sobriety:* Usually used in treatment and 12-Step programs to mean the same as abstinence. However, because it can mean not getting high or drunk, some use it to mislead, telling themselves that even though they used or drank it wasn't enough to get them high or drunk, so they were still sober.

3. *Recovery:* Changing from a lifestyle of addiction and other self-destructive, dishonest behavior to one of abstinence and healthy, honest behavior.

Solicit and discuss input on the difference between "recovered" and "recovering"; comparison to recovery from other illnesses can be useful, for example, a chronic illness, an illness that has no cure but is treatable, and one that can be fatal if not managed (i.e., diabetes). It may be useful to discuss the similarities between diseases such as diabetes, heart disease, etc., and chemical dependency as a disease. Explain that complete recovery (to be recovered) is an ideal that no one ever achieves, just like any other ideal.

STAGES, EVENTS, AND EXPERIENCES OF RECOVERY

Remind participants that an important aspect of recovery is that it is a process, much like learning to walk, to play the piano, to type; as a process, it involves stages that occur over time and build upon skills learned in previous stages. It is also important to point out that there is no definitive time frame of recovery that occurs for everyone; for many there are "stuck points" or "backslides" when one must determine how to make progression forward. Further, some events improve simply by passage of time.

Early Recovery: Turning Things Around

This stage typically lasts for the first few months of recovery.

1. Getting physically clean: Getting through withdrawal; coping with life without chemical filters/distortion/insulation; regaining physical balance from rebound effects. This may last for days or for as long as several weeks depending on the drug(s) and the length and amount of use.

2. Growing awareness: As the "clearing of the fog" continues, newly recovering people often feel the following:

   (a) Hope and exhilaration—Sometimes called the "pink cloud effect," this is the sometimes giddy feeling that comes from having hope after having felt despair.

   (b) Enthusiasm and determination—Often, drug-dependent people spend a long time, maybe all their lives, feeling that there is something basically wrong with them, or that there is no explanation for what is going on in their lives, or that substance-abusing behavior is part of their basic nature and therefore unchangeable. Newly recovering people find explanations for their behavior that make sense, that doesn't label them defective, and that offers solutions. The natural reaction is to latch on with both hands. At the same time, most people feel:

   (c) Letdown and fear—"Quitting was supposed to make my life better, and now I have more problems than before! I don't know if I can deal with all these problems!" What is really happening: They're starting to see problems to which they were blind before (though others may have tried to point the problems out) and realizing the size of the mess they've made for themselves and now have to clean up. The tasks ahead may look overwhelming. This feeling is often intensified by:

(d) Frustration—"Nobody respects what I'm trying to do. They won't believe I've changed." Because part of the addictive lifestyle has usually been lying to and hurting themselves and others, newly recovering people may find that others are reluctant to trust them this time, thinking that this is just another lie, another promise that will be broken or attempt at sobriety that will fail. Also, because many people don't understand addiction and think it is a sign of weak will or defective character, they may think the recovering person is unable to change. Either way, it hurts to go to people to seek support, and to start making amends, and be rejected or scorned.

(e) Connection to others—"I finally fit in somewhere." After spending a lifetime feeling out of place and misunderstood, newly recovering people find themselves surrounded by others who can relate to them and have had similar experiences. They often say that they feel as if they've finally found their real families or that they're home at last. At the same time, they may feel:

(f) Loneliness—"All my old friends still use/drink!" Human beings are drawn to connect with other people, and part of recovery is usually building a new network of friends and activities. At the beginning, this new social life may not exist at all, or some people may have some drug-free friends to start with. They may also be troubled by:

(g) Feeling strange or out of place—"I don't know how to act!" Because psychoactive drug abuse usually stops emotional growth and development of social skills at the age when heavy use begins, people in their 20s, 30s, or older may be picking up where they left off as teens, and have the same confusion as a teenager trying to figure out how to stop being a child and become an adult.

3. Ongoing cravings and urges to use/drink: Habits take time to change, and drug habits are among the strongest—they have actually made physical changes in the body and brain. These cravings may hit at times of stress, or they may hit with no apparent reason at a time when things seem to be going well or nothing seems to be going on. Either way, cravings are normal and skills can be learned to cope with them without using or drinking.

4. Questions about spirituality and values: The 12-Step programs emphasize a relationship with a higher power, and recovery involves a shift in values and ethics in daily life. At the same time, many newly recovering people feel they have been hurt or deeply disappointed by the God they may have been taught about as children, and they may have reason to doubt or reject the proclaimed religion, values, and ethics others have urged on them so far in their lives. This phase may see newly recovering people seeking answers to these questions in a variety of places, including 12-Step programs, other self-help programs, churches, books, and the guidance of others they trust.

5. Step work during early recovery: During this stage, newly recovering people are laying the foundation for a new life and beginning to build on that foundation. In the 12-Step programs, this process is given structure by steps 1 through 7. In these steps, people come to a realistic view of themselves and their situations; break through their isolation to establish healthy relationships with other people and with a higher power; and begin the process of changing the patterns in their lives that have been destructive.

Middle Recovery: Solidifying Change and Putting One Foot in Front of the Other

New patterns and stability: During this time, the new patterns established in early recovery are being strengthened and becoming habits themselves. The old life had a structure built on drug and alcohol use and impulsive and compulsive behavior; the new life also needs a structure, and one built on new routines and new ways of coping with life is becoming stronger and more comfortable. Experiences and feelings during this stage include:

a. Settling in—As new practices become habits, they become automatic, and recovering people find themselves noticing that they are doing different things and responding differently to people, places, and things in different ways, without having to stop and think about it as often. Others also notice and comment. New acquaintances who find out about the past may express surprise and say that sounds unlike the people they see.

b. Growing strength and confidence—Recovering people at this stage find themselves less fearful and anxious and start noticing the distance they have come, especially when they see newcomers who remind them of their earlier selves. They find they have much to offer others. They may need to be on guard at this stage against:

c. Overconfidence—It can be tempting to think that they have changed and gained control over their lives to such a degree that they can now handle either some drug use or other behaviors that they were unable to control before. They may think to themselves, "Maybe I'm not really an addict or alcoholic after all—maybe it just got away from me before." It is a good idea at this stage to talk with a trusted friend who knows them well and understands how their addiction works. At the same time, however, there may be:

d. New awareness of addictive behavior in other areas—As people continue to grow in emotional and mental health and experience of recovery, they may realize additional ways they are still acting like addicts and alcoholics, usually in family, work, and social situations.

Continued improvement in quality of life: These are seen in several areas:

a. Physical health and feeling of well-being

b. Improvement of moods—relief of chronic depression, anxiety, anger

c. Rebuilding or improving relationships with others—family, work, social

d. Financial situation

e. Relationship with spiritual side of life or higher power

f. Plans, goals, and prospects for future

Step work during middle recovery: During this stage, recovering people are continuing the process of change begun in early recovery and extending it into more areas of their lives. In the 12-Step programs, this continuation is supported by steps 8 through 10. In these steps, people continue to clean up the wreckage of their past and work daily to avoid losing ground gained in the areas of honesty and creating new patterns during early recovery.

Late Recovery: Maintenance and Continued Growth

Maintenance activities: During this stage, the emphasis for most people is on relapse prevention, avoiding falling back into old patterns.

a. Continued attendance at meetings

b. Feedback from others

c. Continued study and emphasis on recovery (Step study groups, etc.)

Greater focus on helping others: Helping others, with addiction-related issues and in general, comes to feel more and more natural and necessary.

a. Others seek out advice

b. Sponsorship, speaking at meetings, starting new groups, service tasks

Tackling new problems and issues: As people integrate new values and attitudes into their basic outlook on life, they find themselves acting on the new awareness they found in middle recovery in areas where they need to make changes. They often seek to apply the same methods that have helped them overcome addiction.

a. Using known tools (12-Step program, other resources) on new issues

b. Starting participation in other programs (may have started earlier)

12-Step work during late recovery: During this stage, the focus is on maintenance, as noted above, and on gradual continued growth. In the 12-Step programs, this is supported by steps 10 (which also fits into middle recovery) through 12. In these steps, people work to strengthen and deepen the habits and values that have changed their personalities and to bring their lives into closer harmony with these principles.

CONCLUSION

Recovery is a process in which people coping with substance abuse and chemical dependency learn to live life without chemicals and other self-defeating behaviors. People learn that there is hope as well as challenge to managing life in more productive ways. Recovery encompasses the substance-abusing behavior, and also provides hope that other life areas will improve.

REVIEW OF LEARNING GOALS

Ask questions to probe class members' learning:

1. Ability to define the terms abstinence, sobriety, and recovery.
2. Knowledge of the stages, events, and experiences people typically go through in recovering from chemical dependence.

QUESTIONS/DISCUSSION BEFORE POSTTEST ADMINISTRATION

ADMINISTER POSTTEST

QUESTIONS/DISCUSSION AFTER POSTTEST

1. Definitions from Webster's New Universal Unabridged Dictionary:

    1. **Abstinence:** "the refraining from an indulgence of appetite, or from customary gratification of one's appetites; it denotes a total forbearance, as in fasting or in giving up the drinking of alcoholic liquors."

    2. **Sobriety:** a two-part definition: "the state or quality of being sober; specifically, (a) temperance or moderation, especially in the use of drink; (b) seriousness, solemnity, gravity, or sedateness of manner or appearance."

    3. **Recovery:** four definitions. "(a) The act or power of regaining, retaking, or conquering again; (b) a getting well again, coming or bringing back to consciousness, revival of a person from weakness; (c) a regaining of balance . . . a return to soundness; (d) the time needed for recovering."

Simple Definitions:

    1. **Abstinence:** No use of any _____; in some cases, may also mean no participation in nondrug compulsive behaviors that have been part of one's addictive pattern.

    2. **Sobriety:** Usually used in treatment and 12-Step programs to mean _____ . However, because it can mean _____ . some use it to mislead, telling themselves that even though they used or drank it wasn't enough to get them high or drunk, so they were still sober.

    3. **Recovery:** Changing from a lifestyle of _____ and other _____ to one of _____ and _____ .

Stages, Events, and Experiences of Recovery

    a. Early Recovery: Turning Things Around

        1) Getting physically clean:

            (a) Getting through

            (b) Coping with life without

            (c) Regaining from rebound effects

This may last for days, or for as long as several weeks depending on the _____ and the _____ .

        2) Growing awareness: As the "clearing of the fog" continues, newly recovering people often feel the following:

            (a)_____

            (b)_____

            (c)_____

            (d)_____

            (e)_____

            (f) _____

            (g)_____

        3) Ongoing _____

        4) Questions about _____

        5) Step work during early recovery: Steps _____ through _____

b. Middle Recovery: Solidifying Change and Putting One Foot in Front of the Other

   1) New patterns and stability: During this time, the new patterns established in early recovery are being strengthened and becoming habits themselves.   The old life had a structure built on drug and alcohol use and compulsive behavior; — the new life also needs a structure, and one built on new routines and new ways of coping with life is becoming stronger and more comfortable. Experiences and feelings during this stage include:

   (a)_____

   (b)_____

   (c)_____

   (d)New awareness of _____

   2) Continued improvement in quality of life:

   (a)_____ and feeling of well-being

   (b)Improvement of _____ — relief of _____

   (c)Rebuilding or improving relationships with others — family, work, social

   (d)_____

   (e)Relationship with _____

   (f) _____

   3) Step work during middle recovery: Steps _____ through _____

c. Late Recovery: Maintenance and Continued Growth

   1) Maintenance activities: During this stage, the emphasis for most people is on relapse prevention, avoiding falling back into old patterns.

   (a)Continued _____.

   (b) _____ from others.

   (c)Continued study and emphasis on recovery (_____ groups, etc)

   2) Greater focus on:

   (a)_____

   (b)_____, _____ , starting _____ _____,

   3) Tackling _____ :

   (a)Using _____

   (b)Starting _____ (may have started earlier)

   4) 12-Step work during late recovery: Steps _____ through _____

Notes/Comments/Questions: _____

_____

_____

_____

_____

_____

_____

_____

Name: _____   Date: ____/____/____

Pretest/Posttest
The Process of Recovery

1. Simple definitions of terms. Match the term with the definition.

Abstinence   Means no use of any drug of abuse, often used to mislead if use occurred but not to the point of intoxication.

Sobriety   Lifestyle of healthy, honest behavior, in addition to no use of any drug of abuse

Recovery   No use of any drug of abuse

2. Discuss the difference between being in recovery and being recovered. _____
_____
_____

3. We discussed three stages in the process of recovery: early, middle, and late. For each stage, list three common events or experiences people typically go through.

     a. Early recovery:

         (1)_____
_____

         (2)_____
_____

         (3)_____
_____

     b. Middle recovery:

         (1)_____
_____

         (2)_____
_____

         (3)_____
_____

     c. Late recovery:

         (1)_____
_____

         (2)_____
_____

         (3)_____
_____

Name: _____   Date: ____/____/____

INTRODUCTION

Subject and Why It Is Important

Solicit input from class members about why they think it is important to know about, and use, recovery programs and resources; write their answers on the board and discuss them. If it has not come up in discussion, point out that most addicts and alcoholics know they have problems and have done their best to solve them alone. If they succeed, they succeed—if not, they end up in treatment programs, or elsewhere.

Quote an anonymous member of a 12-step program: "My best thinking and hardest efforts got me where I was when I started this program."

Discuss that most people cannot recover alone through their own insight or willpower, but most addicts and alcoholics who work together with others are able to recover if they make a wholehearted, unreserved effort. Most need tools and support, and this class is about where to find them and how to use them. It has been helpful to point out that frequently, when using has caused problems and people have attempted to discontinue using behavior and felt they had to or could do so alone, efforts were unsuccessful. Also point out that people frequently consult with professionals for legal problems, when buying a home, and so forth, rather than making a major life decision without help from an authority.

Ask class participants to discuss what support services exist in their community; make a list. Point out that this presentation will discuss the services on the list as well as others they may not have been aware of and what each serves to address.

Group Policy

Explain to participants that they will be evaluated on their accomplishment of the following learning goals.

LEARNING GOALS Upon completion of this presentation, participants will demonstrate:

- Knowledge of recovery programs available to help people overcome both chemical dependence and other problems.
- Knowledge of resources, techniques, and practices for making most effective use of recovery programs.

QUESTIONS Instructor can either ask students to hold questions until the end or ask them at any time during class.

PRETEST Distribute the pretest if you decide to use it, asking group members to fill out and return their completed forms to the instructor without putting their names on them; tell them the posttest will be done at the end of the presentation. Explain that the purpose of the pre- and posttest is for participants to assess their own level of understanding.

Background and Lead-In

Ask class members to name programs for chemical dependence available in their community; list them on the board.

Ask class members to name other problems that people have that are not necessarily associated with chemical dependency (i.e., depression), and list programs for those problems available in the community.

RECOVERY GROUPS AND PROGRAMS FOR CHEMICAL DEPENDENCE

12-Step programs: These programs are all based on the same twelve steps of recommended action that give members a structure or framework to guide them in changing their behaviors to become free of substance abuse. 12-Step programs make a point of welcoming all who want to join and giving suggestions but not requirements for participation. They include Alcoholics Anonymous, Narcotics Anonymous, and Cocaine Anonymous. These programs have existed longer than any others, have more members, and claim the highest success rates. There are Alcoholics Anonymous meetings, Narcotics Anonymous meetings, Cocaine Anonymous meetings available within the community or agency (inform clients of availability of each program).

Key parts of working a 12-Step program:

1) Working the steps

2) Establishing a relationship with a higher power

3) Attending meetings frequently

4) Working with a sponsor, a mentor with experience in the program

5) Studying program literature such as the *Big Book, 12 Steps and 12 Traditions,* etc.

6) Having at least one home group

7) Applying the steps to all areas of life as well as to chemical use

Functions a 12-Step group provides that are unavailable to those working alone:

1) Definitive, structured guidance about how to proceed from others who are successful

2) Frequent feedback to correct distorted thinking and perceptions

3) Knowledgeable peer group or "family" (both support and peer pressure for efforts to maintain recovery)

4) Frequent activities to help restructure daily routine

5) Popular answers to many questions and issues that trouble most chemically dependent people

6) Worldwide availability at no cost

Other recovery programs

Rational Recovery: For people who can't accept the 12-Step programs' views on a higher power, based on rational-emotive therapy (RET), the idea that all dysfunctional actions are based on mistaken beliefs and that correcting those beliefs will correct the actions. It may be useful to provide a simplified lesson of RET here or create another lesson to teach in more detail. Include the following components:

A = Activating Event (situation, event, feeling)

B = Belief (irrational or rational)

C = Consequence (thoughts, feelings, results)

Many people believe that A causes C; in RET, it is taught that it is our belief (B) about A that causes C. Provide a general example and then relate it to substance-abusing behavior. It is also helpful to provide a sample of irrational beliefs people may hold that support substance-abusing behavior. Point out that this is a useful way to address substance-abusing behavior separate from a specific support group.

This program is centered primarily on alcohol abuse, but its principles can be applied to other chemical dependence as well. Report if any of these meetings are available in the area.

Synanon: This is a California-based program that split from Narcotics Anonymous over disagreements with the nondirective format of the 12-Step approach—in a Synanon group, members are expected to submit to strict discipline and may be physically punished or kicked out for failure to follow program rules. This program has never been widely successful and has had legal difficulties over allegations of violence against critics and people who left the program, and is sometimes referred to as a cult.

Formal treatment programs

Four basic types of treatment exist and often seek to involve people in 12-Step programs as a part of treatment. Point out which program the members are involved in.

1. Inpatient or residential treatment: This is the most intensive type of treatment program. In this program, people are hospitalized, are not free to come and go, and may receive medical and psychiatric treatment for other problems in addition to being treated for addictions. This is usually for people who either have medical problems that would endanger them if they were not closely monitored, or are so likely to relapse that they must be denied any chance to use or drink. For obvious reasons, it is the most expensive type of treatment and may last anywhere from several days to several months. Components included are medically supervised detox, psychiatric or psychological therapy, and medical monitoring.

2. Intensive outpatient treatment: This is less intensive than inpatient treatment but is still much more thorough than the other two types to follow. In an intensive outpatient program, the staff seeks to "saturate" people and provide a lot of therapeutic impact and education in a short time. This type of program is aimed at people who do not need inpatient treatment but appear to need more intensive treatment than the other types below. This type of treatment may last as long as inpatient treatment but is less expensive because it does not provide housing, food, and medical supervision, and the movements of people are generally not restricted.

3. Other outpatient group treatment: The typical format for a less intensive outpatient treatment program is for people to attend a group session once or twice a week for several weeks, and sometimes to have homework assignments between sessions. This is designed for people who need some treatment and education but appear to have good prospects for success with fairly limited supervision and support. This is the least expensive form of treatment in most cases.

4. Individual treatment: Individual therapy may be used in some cases where a person is not required and not willing to participate in a group or is not expected to succeed in a treatment group for any of a number of reasons such as mental disorders that would cause them to be disruptive in a group. This is not the preferred method but may be the only approach available in some cases.

Other Types of Programs and Resources

A variety of books, workbooks, audiotapes, videotapes, and so on offer recommended ways to overcome addiction, usually based on research or existing treatment programs. Many of these are available at large bookstores, typically located in the self-help or psychology sections, and there are bookstores that specialize in recovery-type resources. It is also useful to ask others support group meetings about other resources that are recommended.

RECOVERY GROUPS AND PROGRAMS FOR OTHER PROBLEMS

12-Step programs: The 12-Step approach is successfully applied to several other problems with compulsive behavior that do not necessarily involve drugs. Some of these are:

1. Overeaters Anonymous: This program is for people who eat compulsively, using food as a drug in ways that harm them. It applies the 12 steps to overcoming this form of addiction. Discuss if meetings of this type are available within the community.

2. Gamblers Anonymous: This is a program to help compulsive gamblers overcome their addiction to the excitement of gambling, and is similar to AA and NA. Discuss if meetings of this type are available within the community.

3. Debtors Anonymous: This program is for people who spend money compulsively and seem unable to control themselves in this area; it applies the 12 steps to overcoming this addictive behavior. Discuss if there are DA meetings in the community.

4. Sex and Love Addicts Anonymous: This is a program for people who are compulsive about sexual behavior to the extent that they endanger their lives, health, and relationships and are unable to stop on their own. It also uses the 12 steps. Discuss if there are any meetings addressing this topic within the community.

5. Emotions Anonymous: EA is for people who are unable to control their emotional reactions without help, and blends the 12 steps with rational-emotive therapy to help them regain control of their feelings and actions. Discuss if any EA meetings exist in the community or within your agency.

6. Parents Anonymous: This program is for parents who either have lost control with their children and behaved abusively, or fear they will do so without help. Discuss if PA meetings exist within the community.

7. Al-Anon, Nar-Anon, Gam-Anon: These programs help adult partners, family members, and close friends of alcoholics, addicts, gamblers, and so on cope with the stresses they experience due to the addictive behavior and to avoid being compulsive, abusive, or over controlling themselves as a result. Do these meetings exist in your community?

8. Ala-Teen: This is similar to Al-Anon, except that it is for adolescent children of alcoholic parents. Discuss if these meetings exist within your community. Often, meetings are held at the same time and often in the same place as AA, NA, and CA meetings, which allows teens and their parents to attend their respective meetings.

9. Adult Children of Alcoholic and Dysfunctional Families: This group aims at helping members identify connections between present-day problems and patterns they learned as children, and to correct those problems by changing their behavior patterns. Discuss where clients may find information about these meetings.

10. CoDependents Anonymous: This group is for people trying to control the lives of others, or feeling responsible for the happiness of others (often the others are addicts or alcoholics), and feeling that their own lives are out of control as a result. Direct participants where they may find information about CoDA meetings in their area.

Additional Information about 12-Step Meetings

Types of meetings and groups:

1. Open—meetings open to the public
2. Closed—for alcoholics and addicts only
3. Speaker—one speaker or several share their "story"
4. Discussion—invites group participation; people are either called on by the chairperson or volunteer to share
5. Stags—men-only or women-only meetings; members are more comfortable talking about some issues in a single-gender group; a very important support for men and women
6. Book or step study—members read from and discuss literature

The concept of anonymity: For protection of individual members; allows the meetings to be a safe place to share; means what is said at a meeting stays at a meeting

The concept of sponsorship: Working closely with other recovering people who are willing to share with you how to work the program; men sponsor men and women sponsor women; typical to seek sponsor with greater length of time in the program who has done step work. There is no perfect sponsor; newly recovering individuals should choose someone who has what they want and someone they can be honest with.

The concept of fellowship: When one's sponsor is unavailable, there are others who are available; based on founder Bill W.'s realization that helping other alcoholics was necessary for him to stay sober.

Other Recovery and Support Programs

1. Compulsive overeating: Weight Watchers, Taking Off Pounds Sensibly (TOPS), and others are not 12-Step programs but do assist with learning healthy ways to eat and exercise.

2. Emotional/behavior control: Recovery Incorporated is a support group for people with mental and emotional disorders and their family and friends, there are usually meetings in the community. Direct members where they may find information about the existence of such meetings.

3. Coping with trauma: Discuss support groups or therapy available for survivors of molestation/incest, rape, deaths of children, and suicide by family members or friends and where they might access more information.

Treatment Programs

Treatment facilities offer programs for the following:

1. Stress and anger management
2. Depression
3. Coping skills
4. Molestation and incest
5. Family relationship issues
6. Helping children cope with divorce
7. Others

RESOURCES, TECHNIQUES, AND PRACTICES FOR MAKING MOST EFFECTIVE USE OF RECOVERY PROGRAMS

Some of these are already covered in the information about the 12-Step programs. However, for both those and other programs, the following may be helpful and may make the programs more effective:

- Keeping journals or diaries
- Learning additional information about the subject
- Participating in a church or worship group if this is consistent with beliefs
- Asking trusted friends and relatives for support and feedback
- Setting aside time daily to think, meditate, reflect, pray
- Using affirmations (positive self-talk)
- Planning ahead, in writing, to either cope with or avoid stressful situations
- Rewarding oneself for successes in healthy ways
- Combining support group participation work with personal therapy
- Spending time on helping others with similar issues

CONCLUSION

A variety of support groups and therapies exist for individuals coping with chemical dependency and other issues. Many of these programs are available in the community. Most support groups are free of charge, but individuals may want to research this before they attend. We have also discussed ways to make the most effective use of other resources. It is sometimes helpful to point out to class participants that if they are willing to put as much time and effort into recovery as they put into substance-abusing behavior, they will likely do very well.

REVIEW OF LEARNING GOALS

Upon completion of this presentation, participants should demonstrate:

- Knowledge of recovery programs available to help people overcome both chemical dependence and other problems.
- Knowledge of resources, techniques, and practices for making most effective use of recovery programs—specifically, those that are available in their community.

QUESTIONS/DISCUSSION BEFORE POSTTEST

ADMINISTER POSTTEST

QUESTIONS/DISCUSSION AFTER POSTTEST

Participant Handout
Recovery Programs and Resources

1. Personal reflection question: Do you feel you will have a better chance at recovery if you are using a recovery program? Why or why not? _____
_____
_____

2. Recovery Groups for Chemical Dependence
    a. 12-Step programs: Points of interest about these programs:
       1) Names of programs for chemical dependence: _____ , _____ , _____ .
       2) Key parts of working a 12-step program:
          (a)_____.
          (b)Establishing a relationship with _____ .
          (c) _____ frequently.
          (d)Working with a _____ .
          (e) Studying _____ .
          (f) Having at least one _____ .
          (g)Applying the steps to _____ .
       3) Functions a 12-step group provides that are unavailable to those working alone:
          (a) _____ about how to proceed.
          (b) _____ to correct distorted thinking and perceptions.
          (c) A _____ .
          (d)Frequent activities to help _____ .
          (e) _____ that trouble most chemically dependent people.
          (f) _____ at _____ .
    b. Other chemical dependence recovery programs:
       1) _____
       2) _____
    c. Formal treatment programs:
       1) _____ treatment: this is the _____ type of treatment program.
       2) _____ treatment: this is less intensive than _____ treatment but is still much more thorough than the two types that follow.
       3) Other outpatient _____ treatment.
       4) Individual treatment: may be used in some cases where a person is unwilling or unable to participate in a group.
    d. Other types of chemical dependence programs/resources: Books, workbooks, audiotapes, videotapes, etc.

3. Recovery Groups and Programs for Other Problems
    a. 12-step programs: The 12-step approach is successfully applied to several other problems with compulsive behavior that do not necessarily involve drugs. Some of these are:
       1) _____ Anonymous: This program is for people who _____ .
       2) _____ Anonymous: This is a program to help compulsive _____ overcome their addiction to the excitement of _____ .

3) _____ Anonymous: This program is for people who _____ _____ compulsively.

4) _____ Anonymous: This is a program for people who find they are compulsive about _____ behavior, to the extent that they endanger their lives, health, and relationships and are unable to stop on their own.

5) _____ Anonymous: This program is for people who are unable to control their _____ reactions without help.

6) _____ Anonymous: This program is for who _____ either find they have lost control with their _____ and behaved abusively, or fear they will.

7) _____ These are for adult partners, family members, and close friends of _____ .

8) _____ . This is similar to _____, except that it is for adolescent children of _____ .

9) Adult Children _____ . This group aims at helping members identify connections between present-day problems and patterns they learned as children, and to correct those problems by changing their behavior patterns.

10) _____ Anonymous. This group is for people trying to control the lives of others.

b. Other recovery/support programs:
1) Compulsive overeating
2) Emotional/behavior control
3) Coping with trauma: Groups available in the area include groups for survivors of

c. Treatment programs: Treatment programs are available for a variety of other issues, including:

1) _____   4) _____
2) _____   5) _____
3) _____   6) _____

4. Resources, Techniques, and Practices for Most Effective Use of Recovery Programs
    a. Keeping _____
    b. Learning _____ about the subject
    c. Participating in a _____
    d. Asking _____ for support and feedback
    e. Setting aside time daily to _____
    f. Using _____ (positive self-talk)
    g. Planning ahead, in writing, to either _____ or _____ stressful situations
    h. Rewarding oneself for successes _____
    i. Combining support group participation work with personal therapy
    j. Spending time helping others with similar issues

5. Personal reflection question: What programs would you benefit from being involved with? What programs will you use in your recovery program? _____
_____
_____
_____

Name: _____   Date: ____/____/____

Pretest/Posttest
Recovery Programs and Resources

1. List two recovery groups/programs available in your community to help with chemical dependency.

_____

_____

_____

_____

2. List at least three recovery groups/programs available in your community to help with other problems.

_____

_____

_____

_____

_____

_____

_____

_____

3. List three ways to make the most effective use of recovery programs.

_____

_____

_____

_____

_____

_____

Name: _____   Date: ____/____/____

Facilitator's Guide
Lifestyle Changes: Alternatives to Substance Abuse or Other Compulsive Behaviors

INTRODUCTION

Subject and Why It Is Important

Ask how many class members think there are good reasons to use drugs, including alcohol. Then offer the suggestion that people may use drugs for good reasons, that a drug meets some need in every case, but the problem is that the price is too high. The key to recovery is not denying one's needs, but finding other ways to meet them without paying such a high cost in health, freedom, relationships, money, and self-respect.

Group Policy

Explain to participants that they will be evaluated on their accomplishment of these goals. Inform them that the learning goals will also provide them useful information on what they have learned.

LEARNING GOALS Upon completion of this presentation, group members will demonstrate:

- awareness and acceptance of personal needs that were met in the past by using drugs, including alcohol.
- knowledge of alternative ways to meet the same personal needs.

QUESTIONS Instructor can either ask students to hold questions until the end or ask them at any time during class.

PRETEST Distribute the pretest if you choose to use it, ask participants to complete it to the best of their ability and return it to the instructor without putting their name on it; tell them that the posttest will be administered at the end of the presentation.

Background and Lead-In

IDENTIFYING NEEDS Ask class members to name some needs drugs meet for people; write their answers on the board; discuss how drugs meet the needs identified.

PERSONAL NEEDS LEADING PEOPLE TO USE DRUGS

The reasons can be divided into two main categories: seeking pleasure and avoiding pain. These are basic survival instincts possessed by all creatures, without which we would die. Drugs may meet these needs, at least in the short run, in ways including the following (compare with class members' responses on board):

Seeking Pleasure/Reward

1. Emotional pleasure—euphoria, bliss, rush, feeling of well-being, excitement
2. Physical pleasure—intensified sensory awareness, hallucinations (for some)
3. Social pleasure—shared activity with others, status, acceptance

Avoiding Pain

1. Reducing emotional pain—relief for depression, anxiety, fear, anger
2. Reducing physical pain—aspirin to morphine
3. Reducing social pain—overcome loneliness, inhibitions; fit in

In-Class Exercise: Cost-Benefit Analysis

On the board, set up four columns: benefits of drug use, costs of drug use, benefits of abstinence, and costs of abstinence. For each, ask group members to give input; write their answers on the board, then guide discussion of the "balance sheet" and the decisions it suggests.

ALTERNATIVES TO SUBSTANCE ABUSE

Without erasing previous material, ask class members to list ways they have found, or are considering, to achieve the benefits listed under "benefits of drug use." Guide them in a discussion of the costs of these alternatives, and compare to the costs listed for drug use. Alternatives include:

Talk to nonusing friends, loved ones	Martial arts	Going to a meeting
Music (playing or listening)	Swimming	Talking to a sponsor
Movies	Biking	Playing with one's children
Camping, hiking	Rock climbing	Playing with a pet
Church	Join a club	Taking flying lessons
Prayer, meditation	Reading	Taking scuba lessons
Cooking, eating a favorite meal	Writing	Painting or drawing
Taking a nap	Dancing	Taking a vacation
Running	Fishing	Existing hobbies—collections, etc.
Lifting weights	Going for a drive	Finding a new hobby

Ask each class members to identify which three alternative activities are most interesting to him or her, and to say what he or she has done or can do to pursue those alternatives.

CONCLUSION

Ask class members to discuss what they learned about their own needs met by substances and the possibility of alternative activities to incorporate from this point on.

REVIEW OF LEARNING GOALS

Upon completion of this presentation, participants should demonstrate:

• an awareness & acceptance of personal needs that were met in the past by using.
• knowledge of alternative ways to meet the same personal needs.

QUESTIONS/COMMENTS

ADMINISTER POSTTEST

QUESTIONS/DISCUSSION AFTER POSTTEST

1. Personal Needs Leading People to Use Drug

   a. Seeking pleasure/reward:

      1) _____ pleasure

      2) _____ pleasure

      3) _____ pleasure

   b. Avoiding pain:

      1) Reducing _____ pain

      2) Reducing _____ pain

      3) Reducing _____ pain

In-Class Exercise: Cost-Benefit Analysis

Drug Use		Abstinence	
Benefits	Costs	Benefits	Costs
_____	_____	_____	_____
_____	_____	_____	_____
_____	_____	_____	_____
_____	_____	_____	_____
_____	_____	_____	_____
_____	_____	_____	_____
_____	_____	_____	_____
_____	_____	_____	_____
_____	_____	_____	_____
_____	_____	_____	_____
_____	_____	_____	_____
_____	_____	_____	_____
_____	_____	_____	_____
_____	_____	_____	_____
_____	_____	_____	_____
_____	_____	_____	_____
_____	_____	_____	_____
_____	_____	_____	_____
_____	_____	_____	_____
_____	_____	_____	_____
_____	_____	_____	_____

Alternative Activities to Get Same Benefits:

_____   _____
_____   _____
_____   _____
_____   _____
_____   _____
_____   _____
_____   _____
_____   _____
_____   _____
_____   _____
_____   _____
_____   _____
_____   _____
_____   _____
_____   _____
_____   _____

Alternatives Most Interesting to Me Personally:

_____   _____
_____   _____
_____   _____
_____   _____
_____   _____
_____   _____
_____   _____
_____   _____
_____   _____
_____   _____
_____   _____
_____   _____
_____   _____
_____   _____
_____   _____
_____   _____
_____   _____
_____   _____
_____   _____

Name: _____   Date: ____/____/____

Pretest/Posttest
Lifestyle Changes: Alternatives to Substance
Abuse or Other Compulsive Behaviors

1. What two needs do people seek to meet with chemical use? _____

_____

_____

_____

_____

2. What are at least five alternative methods for meeting these needs that do not involve chemical use?

_____

_____

_____

_____

_____

_____

_____

_____

_____

_____

_____

_____

Name: _____ Date: ____/____/____

INTRODUCTION

Subject and Why It Is Important

Ask each participant to identify the biggest problem he or she is experiencing in connection with recovery, other than just staying chemical-free. Write their answers in a vertical column on the board, flip chart, or transparency sheet, using check marks to show duplicate answers. Tell the group that this presentation's topic will be problems and issues of this type.

Group Policy

Explain to participants that they will be evaluated on their accomplishment of these goals.

LEARNING GOALS Upon completion of this presentation, participants should demonstrate understanding of common problems and issues in recovery by listing, without notes or references, at least four common problems encountered by many newly recovering alcoholics and addicts.

Upon completion of this presentation, participants should demonstrate understanding of common problems and issues in recovery by listing, without notes or references, at least one coping skill and/or resource to use in handling each problem/issue they list in their answers to the first learning goal.

QUESTIONS As the presenter, you may ask participants to hold their questions until the end or to ask them at any time during the presentation. If participation is a high priority, we recommend allowing questions at any time; if brevity is more important, it works better to hold questions until the end.

PRETEST Pass out the pretest if you choose to use it, asking participants to fill out and return their answer sheets without putting names on them; tell them the posttest will be done at the end of the presentation.

Background and Lead-In

Ask the group how each problem could affect a newly recovering person's abstinence from substance use or other addictive or compulsive behaviors. Ask if any of the problems identified can be solved by abstinence from substance use without other changes in lifestyle. State that the information in this presentation is based on the experiences of many others who have been in the position participants are in now, and is given to increase group members' chances of success and help them achieve the best quality of life they can.

COMMON PROBLEMS AND ISSUES IN EARLY RECOVERY

Dislike of Meetings

This may be a common complaint if your program requires participants to attend AA, NA, or other community recovery program meetings. Many people find they initially dislike 12-Step meetings and attend only because they are required to do so; later, they find that they come to value the meetings and want to continue. This process often takes weeks or months. The following are methods used by many to make meetings more enjoyable:

1. Shop around: Go to as many different groups as possible, and find the ones you like best. Try other programs as well as groups in your main program. Every group has its own personality; some will fit you, others won't. Find people you have a lot in common with and ask which meetings they like best.

2. Go with friends: Attending a meeting with friends or family members, then discussing it afterward, makes it a more interesting and enjoyable experience. This is sometimes described as "the meeting after the meeting," which takes place in the car or van on the way home (or back to a treatment center). Going with friends can also help when people are nervous about going to meetings they have not attended before.

3. Participate—read, help out, and speak up at meetings: Even if they only bring someone a cup of coffee, or give their names and a brief comment—for example, mentioning that they could relate to something someone said—most people leave a meeting feeling better than if they do and say nothing to interact with others.

4. Find the type of meeting you prefer: Some people prefer step study or book study meetings, some like speaker meetings, some like open-topic or sharing meetings; pick the format you like best and seek out meetings with that format. You may also find that you are most comfortable in a meeting that is small or large, smoking or nonsmoking, open or closed, stag (single-gender) or mixed, oriented toward a certain age range, gay/lesbian, in a language other than English, and so on.

5. Go a little early/stay a little late: Most meetings include some socializing before and after, and people are usually friendly but not nosy. This is a good chance to meet people one-on-one and ask questions you might not want to ask of the whole room.

6. Pick a home group: A home group is like a second family, where you are known, accepted, expected, and missed if you aren't there. That's a good feeling for most of us.

7. Help start a new meeting: If you are one of a small group that gets in at the beginning of a group's formation, that group's personality will be partly based on your personality and preferences. If you are looking for a particular type of meeting or one at a certain time, chances are other people are too. It is a good idea to have at least a couple of people with a few years of recovery to help launch a new meeting, but you can do a lot to help and put your own stamp on it.

8. Give the meetings time: For most people, meetings feel strange at first. Give yourself a chance to get used to the experience, and you may come to look forward to them.

Higher Power Issues

Most people have trouble with the idea of surrendering to a higher power: It doesn't fit with our beliefs and values, it doesn't seem to make sense, and it doesn't fit with the pattern many addicts have of trying to control and manipulate everything and everyone around them. Here are some tactics that have worked for people:

1. Read the words "as we understood him" and think about their meaning: the 12 Steps don't ask anyone to believe in a particular version of God, Allah, Buddha, the Great Spirit, the Force, or whatever. If you can believe that there could be a power greater than you, that's all you need to start with. People have chosen as their higher power any of the following, or many more:
   a. Their principles of right and wrong
   b. Their groups
   c. Their conscience or "inner voice"
   d. The God they were raised to believe in
   e. A mystery they hope to understand later on
   f. Nature
   g. Time

2. Find someone you can relate to at a meeting, and ask his or her views about the higher power: Many people struggle with this issue. If you feel you have a lot in common with someone the chances are he or she had the same doubts you have, and if that person found a solution that works for him or her it might work for you too.

3. Read about it: Good material about this issue exists in the AA Big Book's *Chapter to the Agnostic,* in other books in sections of bookstores devoted to both religion and addiction and recovery, in workbooks, and in pamphlets available at some meetings.

4. Design your own God: Think about what you were taught about God, then ask yourself what kind of God would make sense to you and how people might be able to see that God at work in the world: in other words, what would the evidence be? Then wait and see.

5. Bring the subject up at a meeting: If one person raises the topic and says he or she is having trouble with the concept of a higher power, others will respond to say "Me, too!" or to share their experience in resolving this dilemma. There's nothing wrong with having doubts and questions; in a healthy group, they will be respected and accepted, though others may disagree and share their own views, hoping you can find something in them with which you agree.

6. Talk about it with your sponsor: If you have chosen a sponsor with whom you feel comfortable and with whom you have much in common, he or she may have gone through the same struggle and have found a solution you can use.

Resistance to Change

Deep down, many of us find that there are many parts of ourselves and our addictive lifestyles we really don't want to let go of. Here are some ways others have successfully tackled this problem:

1. "I want to want to": If we can't honestly say we want to change something, at least we can say we wished we wanted to change it. That's a good start—give yourself credit for effort and keep working on it.

2. Accept the feelings, but control the actions: Sometimes we can't leave a character trait behind as long as we're trying to get rid of it. We can control the action, and that may be all for a while. And that's okay—because once we accept our feelings with the hope that they will leave us one day, often they do start changing.

3. Find replacement activities: Often, it isn't the chemical itself we crave, but something else that happened when we consumed it. Find new ways to get that something else (think about the class on Lifestyle Changes: Alternatives to Substance Abuse). Figure out what the payoff was, and find another way to get it without paying such a high price.

4. Set small goals and reward yourself: This is a good way to build new habits. It takes about three weeks of practice for most people to get a new habit formed; give yourself little rewards several times during that period for sticking to it. Give yourself time!

5. Hang around with people who are the way you want to be: You'll learn things from them, and some of their attitudes and habits may rub off on you.

Anger, Fear, and Hopelessness or Depression

One of the reasons we use and drink is to block negative emotions, and when we quit it can seem as if they're spinning out of control. To get through this phase, try some of these approaches:

1. Talk about the feeling: If you talk about it with a trusted friend or at a good meeting, you'll understand it better and feel more peaceful, and chances are someone else will say "Me, too!" and add some insights that may help you even further.

2. Take care of yourself: If you eat a healthy diet, get enough sleep, and get regular exercise in a way you enjoy, negative emotions will diminish and be more manageable.

3. Give yourself at least one good laugh a day: Hearty laughter changes your brain chemistry the same way hard exercise or some prescription drugs do—it releases natural antidepressants and painkillers, with no side effects. Think about collecting comedy videos or books, and turn to them when you're having a bad day.

4. Look out for distorted thinking: Think out loud and get feedback from a friend, or listen to yourself, and figure out what beliefs are behind your negative feelings. Often, we are trying to live up to some ridiculous rules and expectations we haven't really thought about. When we get them into consciousness and take a close look at them, a lot of negative feelings may go away.

5. Get some counseling: See a therapist. He or she may be able to help you get past the negative feelings.

6. Give yourself some time: Remember that this is a normal, but temporary, part of recovery, and it won't last as long as it seems. You've been emotionally numb, and now things are coming back to life. Think about what happens when your leg "goes to sleep," then gets its circulation back -- it feels crazy, but only for a short time.

Relationships with People (Significant Others, Family, Friends, Supervisors, and Coworkers)

Some of these people may be very angry, hurt, and suspicious because of our past actions, or they may like us better sick and undermine our recovery, or they may just not understand and cause us problems for that reason. Often, they are trying to decide whether to stay in a relationship with us, and when they see us start changing it's both hopeful and frightening for them. They may also have their own drug and alcohol problems, which make our recovery seem threatening to them. These are some time-tested solutions to these relationship problems:

1. Listen to others and let them vent: Give them a chance to tell you how they feel about whatever may have happened between you. Don't argue, explain, or defend yourself: Just listen closely, then tell them what you believe you heard them say. They will either agree, disagree and correct you, or stay mad and keep blasting you. Keep listening and reflecting back what you hear, and they will run out of steam, usually sooner than you expect, and start noticing the changes in you. Then you can explain yourself if you feel the urge.

2. Help others understand: Explain to them what you are doing, if you feel safe trusting them with that information—but if they knew about your addiction, you might as well tell them about your recovery. Give them the chance to read some literature about what you are doing. Invite them to attend open meetings with you.

3. If they seem interested, encourage them—gently, in a nonpushy way—to get involved in their own recovery programs such as Al-Anon, AlaTeen, CoDependents Anonymous, or others.

4. Make your amends, and give them time: As you change, most people will eventually come around to seeing, accepting, and trusting the new you. Some may not, but that's beyond your control.

5. Take care of yourself: Don't put yourself in situations where you are being used or abused or where your recovery is being undermined. Take action to avoid, change, or leave those situations.

Work, Money, and Time-Management Problems

These can seem overwhelming, especially when they require you to make major changes in your habits. It can be very difficult to adjust, especially when your body is still getting used to being without the drug, your schedule may be busier than it's ever been, and you're trying to juggle meetings with work and other activities. Here are some ways to make this easier:

1. Make your routine consistent: Give yourself a regular schedule—structure lowers your stress level by reducing the number of little decisions you have to make. If you always get up at the same time, you don't have to decide when to get up; if you always go to the same meeting, you don't have to decide what to do at that time. In a short time, the new routine will become as strong a set of habits as the old one was.

2. Get help from others: It helps to have other people both encouraging us and depending on us—get a workout partner, join a car pool, seek the advice of someone wise you trust, get others (sponsor and program friends) to help you by pointing out to you if they see you straying from your plan and when they see you doing well at it.

3. Reward yourself for success: Give yourself little rewards often as you score small victories. Mention them at meetings, take yourself for a walk, treat yourself to a movie and dinner if you can—and don't wait until you accomplish something great, but reward yourself after some of the "baby steps" you take. And as always, give yourself time to adjust.

4. Get organized: Get and use a notebook-type organizer, a calendar, a filing system, schedule regular times for things like paying the bills, balancing the checkbook, and so on. Make yourself checklists for things you have to do. Set aside time at the beginning or end of the day to go over what you need to do or what you've done that day.

Legal Problems

It is best to tackle legal problems head on and get them over with (we often have no choice, because they tackle us). As long as these are hanging over our heads, we have a hard time relaxing and being comfortable with ourselves, and our stress level stays higher than if they were dealt with. If you have legal problems, talk with your lawyer and do what you have to do to get them resolved if you can. Sometimes your willingness to deal with your problems will make a strong favorable impression on people and show them you're changing, too.

Health problems

Hopefully, once your system is drug-free, these will clear up quickly. If not, don't be stubborn about it—see a doctor and take care of yourself. If your physical health is not good, it will make the rest of your recovery more difficult. As recommended above, it's important to eat a healthy diet and get enough rest and exercise, and it's a good idea to have at least one good hard laugh every day if you can.

Further, as your body repairs itself from months or years of abusive use of alcohol and/or chemicals, you may experience aches, pains, symptoms of fatigue, or other illnesses. This is a normal part of the healing process and will lessen with time. It is also a good idea to get a physical from a physician to assess your general medical health.

CONCLUSION

Recovering people often experience several common types of problems beyond abstinence from substances. By understanding these problems and learning about solutions, group members can improve their chances of success and reduce the stress of recovery.

REVIEW OF LEARNING GOALS

Upon completion of this presentation, participants should demonstrate:

1. Understanding of common problems and issues in recovery by listing, without notes or references, at least four common problems encountered by many newly recovering alcoholics and addicts.
2. Understanding of common problems and issues in recovery by listing, without notes or references, at least one coping skill and/or resource to use in handling each problem/issue they list in their answers to the first learning goal.

QUESTIONS/DISCUSSION BEFORE POSTTEST

ADMINISTER POSTTEST

QUESTIONS/DISCUSSION AFTER POSTTEST

1. Dislike of meetings: Many people find they initially dislike 12-step meetings and attend only because they are required to do so, but later find that they come to value the meetings and want to continue. This process often takes weeks or months. Some suggested ways to make meetings more enjoyable:

    a. _____

    b. Go with _____

    c. _____ at meetings

    d. Find a _____ you like

    e. _____ / _____

    f. Pick a _____

    g. Help _____

    h. Give the meetings _____ _____

2. Higher power issues: Most people have trouble with the idea of surrendering to a higher power: It doesn't fit with our beliefs and values, it doesn't seem to make sense, and it doesn't fit with the pattern many addicts have of trying to control and manipulate everything and everyone around them. Here are some tactics that have worked for many people:

    a. Read the words "as we understood him" and think about their meaning: The 12 Steps don't ask anyone to believe in a particular version of God, Allah, Buddha, the Great Spirit, the Force, or whatever. If you can believe that there could be a power greater than you, that's all you need to start with. People have chosen as their higher power any of the following, or many more:

        1) Their _____

        2) Their _____

        3) Their or _____

        4) The God they were raised to believe in

        5) A _____

        6) Nature _____

        7) Time _____

    b. Find someone at a meeting you can _____ , and _____

    c. _____ about it

    d. _____

    e. Bring the subject up _____

    f. Talk about it with _____

3. Resistance to change: Deep down, many of us find that there are parts of ourselves and our addictive lifestyles we really don't want to let go of. Here are some ways others have successfully tackled this problem:

    a. "I _____ want to"

    b. Accept the _____ , but control the _____

    c. Find _____

    d. Set _____ and _____ yourself

    e. Hang around with people who _____

4. Anger, fear, and hopelessness or depression: One of the reasons we use and drink is to block negative emotions, and when we quit it can seem as if they're spinning out of control. To get through this phase, try some of these approaches:

    a. _____ the feelings

    b. _____ yourself

    c. Give yourself at least _____ a day

    d. Look out for _____ thinking

    e. Get some _____

    f. Give yourself some _____

5. Relationships with people (significant others, family, friends, supervisors, and coworkers): Some of these people may be very angry, hurt, and suspicious because of our past actions, or they may like us better sick and undermine our recovery, or they may just not understand and cause us problems for that reason. Often, they are trying to decide whether to stay in a relationship with us, and when they see us start changing it's both hopeful and frightening for them. They may also have their own drug and alcohol problems, which make our recovery seem threatening to them. These are some time-tested solutions to these relationship problems:

    a. Listen to them and _____

    b. Then help them _____

    c. If they seem interested, encourage them — gently, in a nonpushy way — to _____

    d. Make your _____, and give them _____

    e. _____ yourself

6. Work, money, and time-management problems: These can seem overwhelming, especially when they are requiring you to make major changes in your habits. It can be very difficult to adjust, especially when your body is still getting used to being without the drug, your schedule may be busier than it's ever been, and you're trying to juggle meetings with work and other activities. Here are some ways to make this easier:

    a. Make your _____ consistent

    b. _____

    c. _____ yourself for _____

    d. Get _____

7. Legal problems: Tackle legal problems head on and _____

8. Health problems: Hopefully, once your system is drug-free, these will clear up quickly. If not, don't be stubborn about it — and take care of yourself. If your physical health is not good, it will make the rest of your recovery more difficult. As recommended above, it's important to _____ and get enough _____ and, _____ and it's a good idea to have at least one good _____ every day if you can.

Name: _____   Date: ____/____/____

Pretest/Posttest
Common Problems and Issues in Recovery

1. List four common problems or issues beyond just remaining free of alcohol and other drugs which you have encountered, or seen or heard of others encountering, in early recovery from chemical dependence: _____

_____

_____

_____

_____

_____

_____

_____

_____

_____

2. List at least one coping skill and/or resource to use in handling each problem/issue listed for question #1 above: _____

_____

_____

_____

_____

_____

Name: _____   Date: ____/____/____

INTRODUCTION

Subject and Why It Is Important

Review the information covered in the process of relapse presentation. Ask participants to identify why it is important to design a relapse prevention plan. Write answers on the board, flip chart, transparency. It has been useful to point out components of all prevention plans (e.g., fire prevention)—warning signs, dangers, methods to employ to prevent situation from occurring, backup plan if one method does not work. Ask group members to discuss areas to address in designing a relapse prevention plan. Inform group members that this presentation is about learning what places them at risk to relapse, in another lesson (if you choose to use them separately), they will learn effective strategies for trigger situations that can and those that cannot be anticipated.

Group Policy

Explain to participants that they will be evaluated on their understanding of the following learning goals.

LEARNING GOALS Upon completion of this presentation, group participants will demonstrate understanding of the components of an effective relapse prevention plan.

Upon completion of this presentation, group participants will be able to identify their own warning signs and relapse triggers.

QUESTIONS As the presenter, you may ask participants to hold their questions until the end or to ask them at any time during the presentation.

PRETEST Distribute the pretest if you choose to use it, asking participants to complete it to the best of their ability and return it to the instructor. Inform them that the posttest will be completed at the end of the presentation to assess learning on the topic of relapse prevention planning.

Background and Lead In

Explain to group participants that relapse is a symptom of the disease of chemical dependency and that every dependent person runs the risk of relapse. Note that a percentage of individuals attempting recovery are successful at avoiding relapse, a percentage of individuals relapse and then become successful in recovery, and another percentage relapse and die. Empower clients to determine what course of action is in their best interest and how they might go about living this course of action. Reiterate that relapse does not begin with the first drink or use: The time to prevent relapse is before they return to using behavior. As one progresses in the recovery process, one moves further away from a possible relapse. Also point out that recovery is a process that requires lifestyle changes; therefore, indicators of relapse occur in many areas of one's life, including physical, social, and psychological. Relapse, like recovery and addiction, is a process that can be changed or interrupted at any time—the earlier the better.

WARNING SIGNS OF IMPENDING RELAPSE

Refer clients to presentation on the process of relapse and ways in which people's thoughts, feelings, and behaviors change even prior to using a chemical. Further, many steps are taken before use occurs, and if you regularly note the warning signs that point to impending relapse, the chances of avoiding relapse are much stronger. Warning signs of relapse are different for each individual, and usually several signs are present rather than just one. Once a pattern begins and if denial keeps an individual from identifying what is happening, other old behaviors may be reactivated. These occur in addition to the ones listed below:

General Signs of Impending Relapse

1. Dishonesty
2. Exhaustion
3. Denial returns
4. Argumentativeness
5. Depression
6. Frustration
7. Stuck in self-pity
8. Overconfidence
9. Complacency and procrastination
10. Expecting too much from others
11. Avoiding daily structure
12. Use of mood-altering drugs/chemicals
13. Wanting too much too quick
14. Not going to aftercare
15. "It can't happen to me" syndrome
16. Eating and sleeping irregularly

Knowing Your Own Warning Signs

For those group members who have relapsed, have them take some time to check the above factors that were happening prior to their last use. For those group members who have not had experience with relapse, have them think about times that they felt pressure of wanting to use. You can get this information from the following sources:

1. What happened in your own past experiences of relapses
2. The experiences of others, especially those people with whom you can identify
3 Literature, classes, and other external sources

Core Issues That May Lead to Relapse

Below is a list of issues that may precede a relapse. Awareness of them and ways to cope with them are strong indicators that relapse can be prevented. They include:

Cravings, urges	Loneliness	Anger and resentment
Relationships	Sexual issues	Guilt and shame
Fear of abandonment	Illnesses, chronic pain	Thinking problems
Financial stressors	Low self-worth	Family issues
Discovering/accepting emotions		

Identifying Likely Triggers/Pressures in Advance

Discuss that being prepared assists with higher rates of success in avoiding relapse. Many people believe that preparation is not necessary and that they will handle things "as they come up." Others believe that their desire to remain free of chemicals is the only preparation they need. It may be helpful to ask the question "Has anyone ever wanted to stay sober and free of substances and then found that they returned to the use of substances?"

Discuss the fact that there are both internal and external triggers and pressures that precede relapse. These include:

1. External pressures:
   a. Social situations
   b. Relationships
   c. Environment
   d. Stagnation in recovery
2. Internal pressures:
   a. Feelings, thoughts, attitudes, memories, resentments
   b. Testing control—purposely putting oneself in drinking or using situations to see if use can be avoided; having one drink to see if can stop; keeping paraphernalia or a "stash" around the house to see if use can be avoided.
   c. Senses—familiar sights, sounds, smells, tastes
   d. Physical health—sleep problems, chronic pain, etc.

Knowing Your Own Relapse Triggers in Advance by Reviewing the Following Areas

1. Times and situations when you often used/drank in the past
2. Situations likely to place you in conflict with family or friends
3. Life events or losses you feel you couldn't handle clean and sober
4. Situations that make you angry
5. Situations that make you lonely
6. Situations that scare you
7. Situations that depress you
8. Situations that make you overconfident

Have group members make a list of their own triggers or pressures that place them at high risk for relapse. It is important for class participants to complete this prior to discussing the second part of this presentation so they may use specific situations to design actions and strategies for dealing with each. If this is prepared prior to Part 2 of the Relapse Prevention Planning presentation, they are able to receive feedback from other group members.

CONCLUSION

This presentation covered general and specific warning signs and high-risk situations that precede relapse. Point out that relapse is preventable and the material covered in this presentation is designed to assist them in preparing themselves to cope with relapse, which occurs in response to chemical dependency.

REVIEW OF LEARNING GOALS

Upon completion of this presentation, clients will demonstrate:

1. Knowledge of components of an effective relapse prevention plan.
2. Understanding of their own warning signs and relapse triggers.

QUESTIONS/DISCUSSION BEFORE POSTTEST

ADMINISTER POSTTEST

QUESTIONS/DISCUSSION AFTER POSTTEST

Participant Handout
Relapse Prevention Planning, Part 1

1. Relapse is a _____ of chemical dependency and everyone runs a risk of having one.

2. Warning signs of impending relapse:

    a. General signs:

    1) _____   9) _____

    2) _____   10) _____

    3) _____   11) _____

    4) _____   12) _____

    5) _____   13) _____

    6) _____   14) _____

    7) _____   15) _____

    8) _____   16) _____

Place a (*) next to those that occurred prior to the last time you contemplated returning to use.

    b. Knowing your own warning signs. This information can be obtained from:

    1) _____

    2) _____

    3) _____

    c. Other core issues that may precede relapse:

    1) _____   2) _____   3) _____

    4) _____   5) _____   6) _____

    7) _____   8) _____   9) _____

    10) _____   11) _____   12) _____

    13) _____

    d. Identifying likely triggers and pressures in advance:

    1) External pressures:

        (a)_____

        (b)_____

        (c)_____

        (d)_____

2) Internal pressures:

(a)_____ , _____ , _____ , _____ , _____

(b)_____ — purposely putting myself in drinking/using situations to see if use can be avoided; having one drink to see if I can stop; keeping "stash" to see if use can be avoided.

(c)_____ — familiar sights, sounds, smells

(d)_____ health — sleep problems, chronic pain, etc.

e. Knowing own relapse triggers in advance by review following areas:

1) _____ and _____ when often drank in the past.

2) Situations likely to place you in _____ .

3) _____ .

4) Situations that make you _____ .

5) Situations that make you _____ .

6) Situations that make you _____ .

7) Situations that make you _____ .

8) Situations that make you _____ .

3. Personal notes: _____
_____
_____
_____
_____
_____
_____
_____
_____
_____
_____
_____

Name: _____   Date: _____/_____/_____

Pretest/Posttest
Relapse Prevention Planning, Part 1

1. List three components of an effective relapse prevention plan. _____
   _____
   _____
   _____

2. List five warning signs that indicate a relapse may be in progress. _____
   _____
   _____
   _____
   _____
   _____

3. List three relapse triggers (events, situations, or feelings). _____
   _____
   _____
   _____

Name: _____   Date: ____/____/____

INTRODUCTION

Subject and Why It Is Important

Ask "Why should you do relapse prevention planning?" Write participants' responses on the board, flip chart, or transparency sheet. Ask "Who wants to maintain sobriety from all mind-altering substances?" State that the purpose of this presentation is to define the most appropriate actions for yourself and those around you to minimize the destructive potential of relapse and to provide newly recovering individuals with a sense of what they should be doing to maintain sobriety, as most have little experience with sobriety and don't yet trust their internal feelings of what is healthy and what is unhealthy for their continued recovery.

Group Policy

Explain to participants that they will be evaluated on what they have learned.

LEARNING GOALS Upon completion of this presentation, participants will demonstrate understanding of effective strategies to employ in high-risk situations, both those they can anticipate and those they are unable to anticipate, by themselves and with the assistance of supportive people.

Upon completion of this presentation, participants will develop a plan of action for coping with high-relapse-risk situations.

Upon completion of this presentation, participants will demonstrate knowledge of effective ways to avoid high-risk situations, both alone and with the help of others.

QUESTIONS As the presenter, you may ask participants to hold their questions until the end or to ask them at any time during the presentation.

PRETEST Distribute the pretest if you choose to use it, asking participants to fill out and turn in their completed form; tell them the posttest will be administered at the end of the presentation.

Background and Lead-In

Review the process of relapse and indicators that a relapse may be in process. When members have prepared the information from Relapse Prevention Planning, Part 1, this presentation will address individual participants' information specifically and will allow other group members to provide feedback regarding effective versus ineffective strategies and possible alternatives. State that this presentation's aim is to teach members strategies for avoiding high-risk situations and developing a plan of action for times when they are faced with high-risk situations. Point out that a relapse prevention plan is a work in progress and that it needs continual maintenance; as their recovery progresses, items and strategies will be added and changed as individuals themselves change. Further, information will be presented on methods to use alone and with other people.

Inform group members that most relapses are unnecessary. Discuss the two major causes of relapse: lack of understanding of how to prevent relapse and lack of understanding of signs and symptoms of relapse.

RELAPSE PREVENTION PLANNING

Actions/Strategies to Prevent Relapse

Draw a box on the board and divide it in half vertically. In the left column, write "with others" and in the right column write "alone." Choose a trigger of relapse and have participants brainstorm options to deal with that specific trigger, both how they will cope with it alone and how they will cope with it with the help of others. Generate as many responses as possible for each box so that group members may visualize a variety of options available to them to avoid using/drinking. Encourage clients to do this with each of the triggers, pressures, and high-risk situations they have identified for themselves. It is sometimes useful to divide the group into several smaller groups and have members work with each other to complete their strategy boxes. Reassemble as one large group and have members share what they came up with.

Suggestions of Other Actions or Strategies to Use When Confronted with High-Risk Using Situations, Pressures, and Triggers

(Group members may have already generated some of these options; share those that no one thought of and have members add them to their boxes accordingly.) Point out that individuals should list items and actions that are realistic and that they are able to do at this time. Choosing options that are not realistic sets one up for failure. Below is a list of methods and techniques that can be utilized:

1. Talk to others: Have group members list who they have available to talk with if needed. Plan how they will ask others for help. Preplanning this reduces stress.

2. Be active: Have group members list three activities they could do to take their mind off using or drinking.

3. Positive affirmations: Suggest positive thoughts to replace negative thoughts, for example, replacing "I can't stand this anymore" with "I can do this today." Have group members list three positive thoughts.

4. Substitute rewards: List ways that people can reward themselves: watching a movie, taking a walk, talking on the phone, eating a favorite food, taking a bath, buying or listening to a favorite CD, taking a nap, cooking a meal, exercising, watching TV, reading a comic book. Have group members list three rewards for themselves.

5. Attend a support group meeting: Have group members specify how many meetings they will attend, where, days, and times. Planning this out ahead of time gives the individual something to look forward to and reduces the stress of having to decide on a daily basis.

6. Preplan how to deal with loneliness, conflict, fear, losses, stress, anger, etc.: Have group members list how they will deal with difficult feelings and situations before they happen or to plan how they will identify these feelings early and stop them from progressing to out-of-control proportions.

7. Make healthy choices in the areas of relationships, finances, health, time-management, etc.: Ask participants to assess areas of difficulty in life functioning and develop a plan to deal with them, complete with start and target dates. Point out that they do not have to resolve all of them in the next week, but having a plan to address them assists with stress reduction.

8. Find and contact a sponsor.

9. Read program or spiritual literature; recite the Serenity prayer.

10. Plan how to start and end each day.

11. Make a gratitude list.

12. Make and review a list regarding the positive aspects of being sober.

13. Get into the company of others who are recovering.

14. Get task-focused: Ask, "How will I deal with this situation right now?" "How will I avoid worrying about tomorrow, next week, etc.?"

15. Read through a list of program slogans and decide how they apply.

16. Leave a situation that is making you uncomfortable or stressed. Plan how to do this.

17. Refer to this prevention plan: Keep it located in a place that you have access to and refer to it often.

Assign group members to discuss their strategy and action list it with their sponsor or someone else who is in recovery for additional suggestions, to screen for being realistic, and to increase commitment to follow through.

It is useful to emphasize that the more comprehensive and detailed the relapse prevention plan, the more useful it will be when one is confronted with the desire, urge, or thought to use.

Evaluating Your Relapse Prevention Plan

On a periodic basis, you must take a look at your overall recovery program and relapse prevention plan to assess how it is working for you. What things are particularly useful? What things seem to work only some of the time? Is it helping you identify early warning signs? Is it helping you feel more comfortable and sure of yourself? What obstacles do you continually encounter and how have you managed them? Encourage participants to take a daily inventory to assess their progress in living a healthier lifestyle and taking responsibility for putting learning into practice. Whatever is working for them may be of benefit to someone else who is having a difficult time managing urges and cravings to use—ask members to share what you have learned. Remind group participants that an effective relapse prevention plan is one that is useful, works to prevent one from going back to old behaviors, helps one avoid high-risk situations and manage those that cannot be avoided, and allows one to feel more confident. Remind group participants that as they practice these skills, the skills will become more automatic and natural.

CONCLUSION

Relapse is a process, not an event; it is preventable when we can identify red flags that indicate that it is beginning or in process. By identifying the warning signs and the high-risk situations, it is possible to develop a plan to avoid returning to use. This presentation covered strategies for dealing with high-risk using situations, triggers, and pressures, both alone and with the help of others.

REVIEW OF LEARNING GOALS

Upon completion of this presentation, group members should be able to demonstrate:

1. Understanding of effective strategies to employ in high-risk situations, those they can anticipate and those they are unable to anticipate, by themselves and with the assistance of supportive people.

2. The knowledge to develop a personal plan of action for coping with high-risk situations.

3. Knowledge of effective ways to avoid high-risk situations, both alone and with the help of others.

QUESTIONS/DISCUSSION BEFORE POSTTEST

ADMINISTER POSTTEST

QUESTIONS/DISCUSSION AFTER POSTTEST

Participant Handout
Relapse Prevention Planning, Part 2

1. Relapse Prevention Planning

    a. Suggested actions and strategies to prevent relapse:

    1) _____ .

    List of people to call: How will I ask each of them whether I can call on them?

    2) Be _____ .

    Three activities I can do:

        (a)_____

        (b)_____

        (c)_____

    3) Positive.

    Three positive thoughts I will use:

        (a)_____

        (b)_____

        (c)_____

    4) Substitute.

    Three rewards I will utilize:

        (a)_____

        (b)_____

        (c)_____

    5) Attend.

        (a) How many groups will I attend per week? _____

        (b) List dates, times, locations: _____

    6) Plan to deal with.

        (a) Feelings I have difficulty with: _____

        (b) My plan to deal with each includes: _____

    7) Healthy.

        (a) Areas of difficulty for me are: _____

        (b) I will deal with each by doing: _____

    8) Find and contact a _____ .

9) Read _____ .

10) Plan _____ .

11) Make a _____ list.

12) Make and review a list of _____ .

13) Get into the company of _____ .

14) Get _____ .

15) Read through a list of and apply them to me _____ .

    Those that are particularly helpful include: _____

16) Leaving a situation: How will I do this?

17) Refer to my relapse prevention plan

    I will keep this _____ .

    I will review and revise if necessary _____ .

2. Personal Notes and Reflections:

_____

_____

_____

_____

_____

_____

_____

_____

_____

_____

_____

_____

_____

_____

_____

_____

_____

_____

Name: _____   Date: ____/____/____

Pretest/Posttest
Relapse Prevention Planning, Part 2

1. List five effective strategies for avoiding or dealing with high-risk situations that can be done alone.

_____
_____
_____
_____
_____
_____
_____
_____
_____
_____
_____
_____
_____

2. List five effective methods for avoiding or dealing with high-risk situations with the assistance of other people. _____

_____
_____
_____
_____
_____
_____
_____
_____
_____
_____
_____
_____
_____

3. Choose one high-risk situation for yourself: _____
What will you do to avoid relapse if presented with this high-risk trigger or stressor utilizing the help of others, and what will you do alone? _____

_____
_____
_____
_____
_____

Name: _____   Date: ____/____/____

INTRODUCTION

Subject and Why It Is Important

Ask how many participants feel they have the knowledge they need to take good care of themselves physically and emotionally; ask what impact this might have on their ability to stay clean and sober. State that this presentation will cover the basics of physical and emotional self-care because there is a strong link between how well recovering people take care of themselves and how successful they are at staying clean and sober.

Group Policy

Explain to participants that they will be evaluated on their accomplishment of these goals.

LEARNING GOALS Upon completion of this presentation, participants should demonstrate understanding of the basics of physical self-care by listing, without notes or references, at least four considerations in physical self-care.

Upon completion of this presentation, participants should demonstrate understanding of the basics of emotional self-care by listing, without notes or references, at least four considerations in emotional self-care.

QUESTIONS As the presenter, you may ask participants to hold their questions until the end or to ask them at any time during the presentation. If participation is a high priority, we recommend allowing questions at any time; if brevity is more important, it works better to ask them to hold questions until the end.

PRETEST Pass out the pretest if you choose to use it, asking participants to fill out and return their answer sheets without putting names on them; tell them the posttest will be done at the end of the presentation.

Background and Lead-In

Ask the discussion question "What is self-care?" List participants' answers on the board, flip chart, or transparency sheet, and facilitate a brief discussion. Then provide the following working definition: *Self-care is composed of two elements: One is positive, providing for one's own needs, and one is negative, preventing harm to oneself.*

PHYSICAL SELF-CARE

Providing for Needs

Ask participants to list physical needs; write these on the board, then add any of the following they omit, and discuss:

1. Nutrition: Point out that studies of people completing treatment and monitored for one year afterward showed lower relapse rates for those eating healthy diets and higher relapse rates for those eating more junk food.
   a. Balanced diet—low-fat, moderate lean protein, moderate carbohydrates
   b. Nutrients—take vitamins; eat fruits and vegetables, low-fat dairy products
   c. Fluids—lots of water, juices, milk; describe the dehydrating effects of alcohol and some other drugs, including caffeine.
2. Environment: Shelter, clothing—protection from the elements
3. Hygiene: Vital for protection from disease and parasites
4. Sleep: Sleep deprivation weakens the body's immune system. Give participants the following tips:
   a. Keep as regular a schedule as practical.
   b. Avoid caffeine for several hours before sleep.
   c. Avoid vigorous aerobic exercise for 2 to 3 hours before sleep.
   d. Avoid long mid-day sleep periods (catnaps don't usually interfere).
   e. Eat only mild foods before bedtime.
   f. Arrange for a quiet period to collect thoughts—write in journal, read, meditate.
   g. Keep paper and pen near bed to write down troubling thoughts.
   h. Screen out distractions—use ear plugs and sleep mask if necessary.
5. Exercise: Regular exercise keeps the body working at its best, helps optimize weight, improves appearance and endurance, improves moods, raises one's energy level, and increases resistance to illness.
   a. Set up a regular routine, getting the advice of someone qualified if you are not familiar with the type of exercise program you are starting.
   b. Find an exercise partner—two can keep each other motivated, and some forms of exercise are unsafe alone.
   c. Do 20 to 30 minutes of some aerobic exercise 3 to 5 times each week—walk, run, swim, bike, play basketball, play a racket sport, etc. Pick something you enjoy and something that fits your schedule and lifestyle.
   d. Frequency is more important than length or intensity.
   e. Avoid over-strenuous exercises (too long, too hard, overstressing specific parts of your body).
   f. Use the right equipment; get training as needed.
   g. Stretch, warm up, and cool down.
   h. Back off at signs of impending injury or strain.
   i. Include adequate time for muscles to rest and loosen up before more exercise.
   j. Be extra careful regarding sun, heat, cold, dehydration.

Protecting against Harm

Types of physical harm we may be able to prevent:

1. Injury
   a. Avoid too risky behaviors and situations—this includes being in abusive relationships!
   b. Use protective equipment where appropriate (seat belts, sports equipment, etc.) Use sunscreen and avoid dehydration, overheating, getting too cold.
   c. Warm up and stretch before strenuous activities.
   d. Don't do risky activities alone.
   e. Stop if pain indicates possible injury.

f. When hurt, get medical attention as appropriate.

g. Be careful regarding meds and risk of masking pain and increasing injuries.

h. People with medical problems should seek doctor's advice before exercising.

2. Illness

a. Keep resistance up—diet, exercise, rest, stress management.

b. Avoid needless exposures and disease-promoting actions (e.g., smoking).

c. Take protective measures—safe sex; hand washing; inoculations; proper protective clothing and equipment when needed.

d. Get regular physical exams—catch low-profile problems earlier (for example, high blood pressure detectable without medical attention).

e. Get medical attention when needed, and follow doctor's instructions.

Interaction between Substance Abuse and Medical Problems

1. Substance abuse causing medical problems

a. Accidents, fights, etc. while under the influence

b. HIV, herpes, other STDs resulting from unsafe sex while under the influence and judgment impaired

c. Illness because of substance abuse damaging the immune system and reducing the body's resistance to getting sick

d. Direct tissue damage from substance abuse, such as cirrhosis of the liver from chronic excessive drinking

2. Medical problems contributing to substance abuse

a. Pain leading to self-medication with alcohol or other nonprescribed drugs

b. Abuse of prescribed medications for either pain management or pleasure-seeking

c. Becoming addicted to prescribed meds after long use

EMOTIONAL SELF-CARE

Providing for Needs

Ask participants to list what they consider their emotional needs; write these below previous answers; lead a brief discussion. Add the following:

1. Feeling of being loved, accepted, and valued—We get this from supportive relationships.

2. Feeling of having some ability to control events around us—We can gain this by planning, having a routine, and avoiding no-win situations when possible.

3. Feeling of competence and that one's activities are worthwhile—This is often based on a person's job but can stem from volunteer activities, hobbies or clubs, and family activities; again, avoid no-win situations when possible.

4. Feeling of safety—We must plan, and avoid needless risky situations.

Protecting against Harm

What are the types of emotional harm we may be able to prevent?

1. Emotional abuse or neglect by others or self—Don't do it, don't tolerate it. If you have questions about what's abusive or negligent, discuss it with someone you consider wise and trustworthy.
2. Isolation—Avoid this by staying connected to important others.
3. Depression, anxiety, etc.—These can have physical causes also; it is important to get help as needed.
4. Burnout—This leads to relapse. It is vital to keep balance in one's life.
5. Distorted thinking—check with healthy people for feedback.
6. If any of the above problems or other problems become a significant source of distress, get help when needed.

Overall Tools and Resources

The following are useful in both positive and negative self-care:

1. One's own attitudes and knowledge
2. Personal relationships that provide support and information
3. Recovery support groups and other community activities or facilities
4. Therapy
5. Other sources of information and support—books, hotlines, etc.

CONCLUSION

Physical and emotional self-care directly affects one's chances of success in staying clean and sober. This presentation has discussed elements of both types of self-care, the interactions between substance abuse and self-care, and tools and resources that are available to help recovering people take care of themselves.

REVIEW OF LEARNING GOALS

Upon completion of this presentation, participants should demonstrate

1. Understanding of the basics of physical self-care by listing, without notes or references, at least four considerations in physical self-care.
2. Understanding of the basics of emotional self-care by listing, without notes or references, at least four considerations in emotional self-care.

QUESTIONS/DISCUSSION BEFORE POSTTEST

ADMINISTER POSTTEST

QUESTIONS/DISCUSSION AFTER POSTTEST

```
┌─────────────────────────────────────────────┐
│              Participant Handout              │
│       Physical and Emotional Self-Care        │
└─────────────────────────────────────────────┘
```

1. We are talking about this subject because there is a strong link between _____ and _____ .

2. Taking care of ourselves has two parts, one positive and one negative:

    a. _____ .

    b. _____ .

3. Physical needs:

    a. _____ : direct impact on relapse rates after treatment.

       1) Balanced _____ — low _____, moderate lean _____ , moderate _____

       2) Key _____ — vitamins; fruits and vegetables; low-fat dairy products

       3) _____ — lots of _____ , _____ , _____ ;
dehydration increased by alcohol, some other drugs, caffeine

    b. Environment: _____ , _____ , _____ ,

    c. _____: avoid deprivation — hurts immune system — tips:

       1) Keep a regular _____

       2) Avoid _____ for several hours before _____

       3) Avoid _____ for 2–3 hours before _____

       4) Avoid long mid-day _____

       5) _____ before bedtime

       6) _____ — write in journal, read, meditate

       7) Keep _____ near _____

       8) Screen out _____

    d. Exercise: Keep the body working at its best, optimize weight, etc. — beyond making one
stronger and enhancing endurance, this increases resistance to illness.

       1) Set up a _____

       2) Find an exercise _____

       3) Engage in _____ minutes of some aerobic exercise _____ times each week: walk,
run, swim, bike, basketball, racket sports, etc. — something you _____ and something that
_____ your _____ .

       4) _____ is more important than length or intensity.

       5) Avoid overstrenuous exercises (length, intensity, specific stresses).

       6) Use the right _____ , and get training as needed.

       7) _____ , _____ , and _____ .

       8) Back off at signs of _____ , _____ .

       9) Include adequate time for tissues to rest before more exercise.

       10) Be extra careful regarding _____ , _____ , _____ , _____ .

4. Physical harm: Types of physical harm we may be able to prevent:

    a. Injury:

       1) Avoid _____ and _____ — including relationships!

       2) Use _____ seat belts, sports equipment, sunscreen,
gear to avoid dehydration, overheating, getting too cold.

3) _____ and _____ before strenuous activities.

4) Don't do risky activities _____ .

5) Stop if pain indicates possible injury.

6) When hurt, get medical attention as appropriate.

7) Be careful regarding meds and risk of _____ and increasing injuries.

8) People with medical problems should seek doctor's advice before excercising.

b. Illness:

1) Keep _____ up — diet, exercise, rest, stress management.

2) Avoid needless _____ and disease-promoting _____ .

3) _____ — safe _____ ; _____ ; inoculations; proper protective clothing and equipment when needed.

4) Regular _____ — catch low-profile problems earlier.

5) Get medical attention when needed and follow doctor's instructions.

5. Overall Physical Self-Care Tools and Resources:

    a. Own attitudes and knowledge

    b. Relationships (information, shared activities)

    c. Services and community resources

    d. All sources of information

6. Emotional needs: What are our emotional needs?

    a. Feeling of being _____ , _____ , _____ — supportive relationships

    b. Feeling of having ability to _____ — plan, have routine; avoid no-win situations when possible

    c. Feeling of _____ and worthwhile activities — job, volunteer, hobbies and clubs; again avoid no-win situations when possible

    d. Feeling of _____ — plan and avoid needless risky situations

7. Emotional harm: What types of emotional harm may we be able to prevent?

    a. Emotional _____ , _____ by others or self — Don't do it, don't tolerate it. If you have questions about what's abusive or negligent, investigate.

    b. _____— stay connected to important others.

    c. Depression, anxiety, etc. — Get help as needed.

    d. _____ — leads to relapse — Keep balance in life.

    e. _____ thinking — check with healthy people for feedback.

    f. Get help when needed.

8. Overall Emotional Self-Care Tools and Resources:

    a. Own attitudes and knowledge

    b. Personal relationships

    c. Recovery support groups

    d. Therapy

    e. Other sources of information & support — books, hotlines, etc.

Name: _____   Date: ____/____/____

Pretest/Posttest
Physical and Emotional Self-Care

1. List four aspects of physical self-care for people recovering from chemical dependence or abuse:

_____

_____

_____

_____

_____

_____

_____

_____

_____

2. List four aspects of emotional self-care for people recovering from chemical dependence or abuse:

_____

_____

_____

_____

_____

_____

_____

_____

Name: _____   Date: ____/____/____

Facilitator's Guide
Stress Management

INTRODUCTION

Subject and Why It Is Important

Ask class members if they have noticed any connection between stress and their own using or drinking; list responses. All people experience stress in their daily life. Additional stress comes with recovering from chemical dependency and substance abuse as multiple changes are occurring. Often, people began using to relieve feelings of stress. What people discovered early is that alcohol and other drugs were temporary fixes or solutions that were short term. Eventually, the use of chemicals or alcohol created more stress. Managing stress in early recovery is an important part of avoiding a return to use and maintaining a program of recovery.

Group Policy

LEARNING GOALS Upon completion of this presentation, participants will be able to identify the relationship between chemical dependency and stress and sources of stress in early recovery.

Upon completion of this presentation, participants will be able to identify the symptoms of stress.

Upon completion of this presentation, participants will be able to identify common ways people cope with stress.

QUESTIONS As the instructor, you can ask group members to hold their questions until the end of the presentation or to ask them at any time during the presentation.

PRETEST Distribute the pretest if you choose to use it, asking group members to complete it and return it to the instructor. Remind group members that they will be asked to complete a posttest at the end of the presentation to assess what they have learned from the presentation.

Background and Lead-In

What is stress? Tell group members that the definition of stress includes strain, pressure, urgency, tension. A useful visual of stress is to tell group members to imagine that they are holding an uncooked spaghetti noodle between their two index fingers. Have them visualize what would happen to the noodle if the lightly pressed their fingers together (the noodle would bend). Ask them what would happen if they released the stress (it would return to its original shape). Now ask them to visualize what would happen to the noodle if they applied more stress (eventually the noodle will break). This is useful to compare to what happens when people are exposed to stress: They change shape when a little pressure is applied and they can have their shape altered if pressure is not released.

To understand stress more completely, we must look at stressful situations and their effect on the body, mind, and spirit. Have group members generate a list of stressful situations. Tell students that stress can be both positive and negative. Negative stress is when you feel overwhelmed; positive stress gets people's attention and motivates people to make changes. Some examples of stressful situations include:

1. Meeting new people
2. Change in employment status (new job, fired, layoff, promotion, demotion)
3. Breaking up of significant relationship
4. Getting married
5. Losing your house key or car keys
6. Graduating
7. Entering or leaving treatment
8. Going to your first support group meeting
9. Finding and talking with a sponsor
10. Taking a test
11. Talking in a group

SYMPTOMS OF STRESS (PHYSIOLOGICAL, PSYCHOLOGICAL, BEHAVIORAL RESPONSES)

Physiological Symptoms of Stress

1. Tension
2. Aches and pains
3. Rapid heart rate
4. Indigestion

Psychological/Emotional Symptoms of Stress

1. Anger, irritability
2. Lack of motivation
3. Confusion
4. Fatigue
5. Anxiety and worry
6. Tearfulness
7. Increased emotionality, hypersensitivity

Behavioral Symptoms of Stress

1. Argumentativeness
2. Withdrawal, isolating from peers or activities
3. Insomnia or excessive sleep
4. Accident-prone
5. Inattention, short attention span, difficulty concentrating
6. Return to old self-defeating behaviors
7. Overeating, loss of appetite, smoking

RESPONDING AND MANAGING STRESS

Stressful Situations Common in Early Recovery

1. Giving up old acquaintances and developing healthy sober friendships
2. Addressing old situations for the first time without a chemical filter
3. Coping with new situations without mood-altering substances
4. Communicating with your family on issues you previously avoided
5. Experiencing some feelings, multiple feelings for the first time

Responding to Stress in Unhealthy Ways

1. Avoiding the situation by leaving or not becoming emotionally involved
2. Creating win-lose situations (fighting) and using control to win
3. Tackling the situation indirectly or "sideways"; this is often referred to as a passive–aggressive way of managing stress

Managing Stress in Healthy Ways (Ways That Support Recovery)

1. Get physical exercise: Work it off—this can be done by taking a walk—rigorous and strenuous exercise is not necessary.
2. Talk with others: Share your concerns with others you trust—this may be a way to get feedback and also to see that you may not be alone in what you feel.
3. Let go and accept the situations and events that are out of your control: personal limitations, resentments, legal problems, financial situation, relationship difficulties, family's attitude toward recovery attempt, and so on. People spend a lot of time, energy, worry, and stress on the things in their life that they have no control. Recite the Serenity Prayer.
4. Get adequate sleep, rest, and nutrition: Our bodies require this to work efficiently; without rest or sleep, people are unable to deal with stress effectively; normal sleep patterns may take several months to return; avoid the intake of stimulants—what you put in your body will influence how you handle stress (for more on how diet, rest, and exercise effect recovery, see presentation on self-care).
5. Help someone else: This aids in getting the focus of attention off yourself; provides a diversion to think about something else.
6. Be honest: Often during the time you were drinking or using you spent a lot of time hiding, making excuses, covering your tracks; learning to live honestly reduces the worry and stress associated with dishonesty.
7. Focus on the present: Avoid dwelling on guilt over past situations or worrying about the future.
8. Learn effective relaxation techniques: Give yourself a break.
9. Practice patience and flexibility: Learn to admit mistakes, accept others opinions or stances, give up the need to be right, allow things to happen as they happen. Many people recovering from addictions feel that they need to be further along than they are. It is important to point out that long-term positive changes come with learning new skills, practicing consistently over a period of time. Many recovering people want to perform perfectly and when they do not, they experience stress and frustration.
10. Learn to laugh at yourself and life's problems.
11. Avoid competitiveness: comparing yourself, what you have, what you've done, with everybody else; always wanting to win or come out on top.
12. Act; avoid procrastination.

13. Confront your fears: Not confronting fears can lead to excessive worry as fears grow bigger than the fear of the original situation.

14. Ask for help: Often, solutions to the difficulties you are experiencing are outside yourself. Typically, people use/drink in isolation; break this old pattern and use the resources around you.

15. Practice time management: Establish and maintain a daily schedule and routine that is realistic; often, people need to learn how to prioritize tasks and to learn that not everything is a crisis or that it is sometimes not possible to get everything done in a particular time frame.

CONCLUSION

This presentation covered the symptoms of stress on the body, how stress is related to addiction and recovery, and ineffective and effective ways to manage stress. Reiterate that the goal is not to eliminate stress from our lives, as this is impossible and positive stress exists. The goal is to learn to create low-stress living and find effective ways to manage stress before it reaches crisis proportions. Point out to group members that the more they practice these skills, the better they will become at integrating them into their life.

REVIEW OF LEARNING GOALS

Upon completion of this presentation, participants should be able to identify:

1. The relationship between chemical dependency and stress and sources of stress in early recovery.
2. The symptoms of stress.
3. Common ways people cope with stress.

QUESTIONS/DISCUSSION BEFORE POSTTEST

ADMINISTER POSTTEST

QUESTIONS/DISCUSSION AFTER POSTTEST

Participant Handout
Stress Management

1. Symptoms of Stress (physiological, psychological, behavioral responses)
   a. Physiological symptoms of stress:
      1) _____
      2) _____
      3) _____
      4) Indigestion
   b. Psychological/emotional symptoms of stress:
      1) Anger, _____
      2) Lack of _____
      3) _____
      4) _____
      5) Anxiety and worry
      6) Tearfulness
      7) Increased _____ , hypersensitivity
   c. Behavioral symptoms of stress:
      1) _____
      2) _____ , isolating from peers or activities
      3) Insomnia or excessive sleep
      4) Accident-prone
      5) _____ , _____ , _____
      6) Return to old _____ behaviors
      7) Overeating, loss of appetite, smoking

2. Responding and Managing Stress
   a. Stressful situations common in early recovery:
      1) Giving up _____ and developing _____
      2) Addressing _____ for the first time without a chemical filter
      3) Coping with _____ without mood-altering substances
      4) _____ with your family on issues you previously avoided
      5) Experiencing some feelings, multiple feelings for the first time
   b. Responding to stress in unhealthy ways:
      1) Avoiding the situation by leaving or _____
      2) Creating _____ (fighting) and using control to win
      3) Tackling the situation _____ or _____

c. Managing stress in healthy ways (ways that support recovery):

    1) _____ : Work it off; this can be done by taking a walk.

    2) _____ : Share your concerns with others you trust; this may be a way to get feedback and also to see that you may not be alone in what you feel.

    3) _____ the situations and events that are out of your control: Recite the Serenity Prayer.

    4) Get _____

    5) Help someone else: This aids in getting the focus off attention of yourself.

    6) Be _____ .

    7) Focus on the _____ : Avoid dwelling on guilt over past situations or worrying about the future.

    8) Learn effective _____.

    9) Practice _____: Learn to admit mistakes, accept others' opinions or stances, give up the need to be right, allow things to happen as they happen.

    10) Learn to laugh at yourself and life's problems.

    11) Avoid _____: comparing yourself, what you have, what you've done,. with everybody else; always wanting to win or come out on top.

    12) Act; avoid _____ .

    13) Confront your _____: Not confronting fears can lead to excessive worry as they grow bigger than the fear of the original situation.

    14) Ask for help.

    15) _____ management: Establish and maintain a daily schedule and routine.

3. Personal Reflections: Make a list of stressful situations you are dealing with at this time. After each item, write down what you will do today to address it.

_____

_____

_____

_____

_____

_____

_____

_____

_____

_____

_____

_____

_____

_____

_____

_____

Name: _____   Date: ____/____/____

Pretest/Posttest
Stress Management

1. List three symptoms of stress:

_____

_____

_____

_____

_____

_____

2. List one common situation in recovery that causes stress:

_____

_____

_____

3. What is the relationship between stress and relapse?

_____

_____

_____

4. List three ways to manage stress effectively:

_____

_____

_____

_____

_____

Name: _____   Date: ____/____/____

INTRODUCTION

Subject and Why It Is Important

Ask group participants to name any connections they have noticed between anger and their own using or drinking (e.g., anger results in using/drinking; using/drinking results in feelings of anger; using/drinking is a method used to cope or avoid anger reactions, etc.). Ask members to discuss any ways anger has undermined their intentions in recovery or other areas of their lives; list responses. Explain that anger is a feeling everyone has, that it is normal, healthy, and constructive; it tells us that we are alive. State that what becomes abnormal, unhealthy, or destructive is the way we handle or deal with our feelings of anger. It is possible to learn different ways to deal with anger. Inform participants that when anger is mismangaged or not managed at all it sets people up to return to old patterns of behavior of using/drinking.

Group Policy

Explain to group participants that they will be evaluated on the information presented to see what they have learned. This will be done by a pretest at the beginning of group and a posttest following the presentation.

LEARNING GOALS Upon completion of this presentation, participants will be able to identify what anger and resentment are and demonstrate an ability to recognize symptoms of anger and resentment before a crisis.

Upon completion of this presentation, participants will demonstrate knowledge of coping methods to handle anger without causing harm to themselves or others.

QUESTIONS As the presenter, you may ask participants to hold their questions until the end of the presentation or to ask them at any time during the presentation.

PRETEST Distribute the pretest if you choose to use it, asking participants to fill it out and return the completed form to the instructor.

Background and Lead-In: Feelings vs. Behaviors

1. Feelings: State as a fact that anger is a feeling and is part of us. Affirm that all feelings are okay. Inform participants that feelings don't always make sense, as we can have two or three different feelings at the same time; that we can feel anger without knowing the specific reason; that feelings don't always make sense (e.g., we can love someone we are mad at or who hurts us).
2. Behaviors: State that not all behaviors are okay. Define behavior as the way we choose to react to our feelings. We can control our behaviors—we always have a choice of which behavior we will use. We can change our behaviors—even old behaviors. Sometimes, feelings are used as excuses or justifications for our behaviors. For example, "I had to hit him, because he made me angry."

WHAT IS ANGER? WHAT IS RESENTMENT?

Definitions

Ask group participants for definitions of anger and resentment, then provide the following definitions from *Webster's Unabridged:*

1. Anger: "a strong feeling excited by real or supposed injury;" it's root means regret, anguish, fear.
2. Resentment: "holding an attitude from something that is in the past; resentment is old anger."

Flight, Fight, or Freeze Reactions

Anger includes physical reactions. For most of human experience, our common stressors have been physical dangers, and coping methods were to fight back, run away, or freeze and go unnoticed. Our bodies are still conditioned that way and release chemicals to help: epinephrine (i.e., adrenaline) for fight/flight and norepinephrine for freeze reactions. Too bad we can't use physical combat, escape, or hiding to deal with overdue bills, the boss, relationships, and so on. Chemicals in the bloodstream help us to react physically with more speed and strength but put stress on the body if we don't react with physical action.

IDENTIFYING OUR ANGER EARLY (NOTE RESEMBLANCE OF SYMPTOMS TO EFFECTS OF STIMULANT DRUGS)

Physical symptoms

1. Muscle tension—clenched jaw, tightened shoulders and neck, fists, drumming fingers, vibrating feet and legs
2. Breathing and heart rate speed up
3. Sharpened senses
4. Increased energy and reactivity—jumpy, shaky, restless
5. Clammy skin—blood moving into deep muscles, internal organs
6. Digestion stops—possible nausea, "butterflies"

Mental/Emotional Symptoms

1. More alert
2. Strong feelings—urge to attack or run; sometimes exhilaration
3. Racing thoughts and sense of urgency (or brain freeze)—either way, it makes clear thinking more difficult
4. Recall of past stressful situations
5. Feeling of oncoming loss of control
6. Thinking shifts to black-and-white; able to see fewer options
7. Feeling of power and certainty in some people

COPING WITH ANGER WITHOUT HARM TO SELF OR OTHERS

Acknowledge and Accept the Feelings

1. Tell self what the feeling is and that it's okay to feel that way right now.
2. Remind self that feelings and actions are separate; feeling angry does not mean acting it out.

Reverse the Physical/Emotional/Mental Preparation for Fight/Flight/Freeze

1. Sit down.
2. Begin breathing slowly and deeply.
3. Relax muscles in one part of the body at a time; it may help to tense extra hard for several seconds and release.
4. Visualize a relaxing scene or memory.

Start a Coping System

1. Find out where anger came from; identify the trigger (where's the threat?).
   a. The past? Does it remind me of another situation? Let go!
   b. The present? What need am I afraid won't be met? Express it!
   c. Fear of what will happen in the future? Act *now!*
   d. What is actually likely to happen? How likely is it? Is the threat real or perceived? How bad would it be? Could I stand it?
2. Consider the consequences of acting from anger: What would happen afterward?
3. What are my other options (time out, talk it out directly or at a meeting, walk away)?
4. Visualize a good outcome: Picture yourself handling the situation successfully.
5. Carry out a nonharmful situation: Do this in a timely fashion so it does not turn into resentment.
6. If successful, think about what happened.
7. Relax.
8. Get some physical exercise to burn off the fight or flight chemicals in the system.
9. Talk it over with someone you trust.
10. Give yourself credit for what you did well in this situation—tell someone; this is hard at first but gets easier with practice.
11. Plan for the future: How can I avoid this happening again or be ready for it when it does happen?

FACTORS THAT AFFECT OUR ABILITY TO HANDLE ANGER

General Physical State

1. Sleep deprivation
2. Hunger
3. Influence of chemicals—judgment is impaired, inhibitions are lowered; body is already in a fight or flight state
4. Lack of exercise—accumulation of fight or flight chemicals in the bloodstream

Mental/Emotional Factors

1. Resemblance to past stressful situations may set off reaction out of proportion to the here-and-now; buttons getting pushed
2. Preexisting stress: "I have one nerve left and you're getting on it"
3. Relation of negative parts of self-image: getting buttons pushed
4. Loneliness: lack of emotional support
5. Unrealistic expectations—rules, musts, shoulds. We can only be disappointed if we have expectations that aren't met; if we have expectations that can't be met, we will be disappointed. (Refer to the list of unrealistic thinking that is included in the presentation on depression and anxiety.)

PROTECTION AGAINST FUTURE PROBLEMS WITH ANGER

Self-Care

Keep your resistance to stress as high as possible.
1. Adequate rest
2. Healthy diet
3. Regular exercise
4. Supportive relationships through program meetings and sponsorship

Self-Monitoring: HALT

If feeling Hungry, Angry, Lonely, Tired, act to correct the problem. Get in the habit of regular self-checks throughout the day.

Correct Distorted Thinking Patterns

Address Past Resentments

Resentments put recovering people at high risk to relapse.

Practice Coping Skills

1. Practice steps from this class.
2. With the input and feedback from people you trust, mentally rehearse or brainstorm situations you have trouble handling.

CONCLUSION

This presentation defined what anger and resentment are and how they put people at high risk to relapse. It presented practical ways to learn to cope with a normal feeling of anger in a way that is constructive and does not harm you or others. Remind class participants that old behaviors can be changed by increasing personal awareness of anger problems and utilizing new tools. Coping effectively with anger is difficult at first but gets easier with practice.

REVIEW OF LEARNING GOALS

Upon completion of this presentation, participants should demonstrate:
1. An ability to identify what anger and resentment are and demonstrate an ability to recognize symptoms of anger and resentment before a crisis.
2. Knowledge of coping methods to handle anger without causing harm to themselves or others.

QUESTIONS/DISCUSSION BEFORE POSTTEST

ADMINISTER POSTTEST

QUESTIONS/DISCUSSION AFTER POSTTEST

Participant Handout
Coping with Anger and Resentment

1. Definitions:
    a. Anger: _____
    b. Resentment: _____

2. Identifying anger early:
    a. Physical symptoms:
        1) _____ tension
        2) _____ increase
        3) Sharpened _____
        4) Increased _____
        5) Clammy skin
        6) Digestion stops
    b. Mental/emotional symptoms:
        1) More _____
        2) Strong feelings — urge to _____
        3) Racing thoughts
        4) Recall of _____
        5) Feeling of _____
        6) Thinking shifts to _____
        7) Feeling of power and certainty

3. Coping With Anger Without Harm to Self or Others
    a. Acknowledge and _____
        1) Tell self what the feeling is and that it's okay to feel that way right now.
        2) Remind self that feelings and actions are separate; feeling angry does not mean acting it out.
    b. Reverse the physical/emotional/mental preparation for fight/flight/freeze:
        1) Sit down.
        2) Begin _____.
        3) _____.
        4) Visualize _____.
    c. Start a _____.
        1) Find out where it came from; identify the trigger (_____).
            (a) The past? Does it remind me of another situation? _____ .
            (b) The present? What need am I afraid won't be met? _____
            (c) Fear of what will happen in the future? _____ .
            (d) What is actually likely to happen? How likely is it? Is the threat real or just perceived? How bad would it be? Could I stand it?
        2) Consider the consequences of acting from anger: _____.
        3) What are my other options (time out, talk it out directly or at a meeting, walk away)?
        4) Visualize a good outcome: _____.
        5) Carry out a nonharmful solution. Do this in a timely fashion so it does not turn into resentment.
        6) If successful, think about what happened.

7) _____ .

8) Get some physical exercise to _____ .

9) Talk it over with someone you trust.

10) Give yourself credit for what you did well in this situation — tell someone; this is hard at first but gets easier with practice.

11) _____ How can I avoid this happening again or be ready for it when it does happen?

4. Factors That Affect Our Ability to Handle Anger

    a. General physical state:

        1) _____ deprivation

        2) _____

        3) Influence of chemicals — judgment is impaired, inhibitions are lowered; body is already in a fight or flight state.

        4) Lack of _____

    b. Mental/emotional factors:

        1) Resemblance to past stressful situations may set off reaction out of proportion to the here-and-now; _____

        2) Preexisting stress: "I have one nerve left and you're getting on it"

        3) Relation of negative parts of self-image: getting buttons pushed

        4) _____ : lack of emotional support

        5) _____ — rules, musts, shoulds. We can only be disappointed if we have expectations that aren't met; if we have expectations that can't be met, we will be disappointed.

5. Main Topic: Protection Against Future Problems With Anger

    a. Self-care: Keep your resistance to stress as high as possible.

        1) Adequate _____

        2) Healthy _____

        3) Regular _____

        4) Supportive relationships through program meetings and sponsorship

    b. Self-monitoring: : If feeling Hungry, Angry, Lonely, Tired, act to correct the problem. Get in the habit of regular self-checks throughout the day.

    c. Correct distorted thinking patterns.

    d. Address past resentments: Resentments put recovering people at high risk to relapse.

    e. Practice _____ .

        1) Practice steps from this class.

        2) With the input and feedback from people you trust, _____ situations you have trouble handling.

6. Personal Reflections: This is one thing I learned in this class that I will start practicing in my daily life:

Name: _____ Date: ____/____/____

Pretest/Posttest
Coping with Anger and Resentment

1. Anger is: _____

_____

_____

_____

_____

2. Resentment is: _____

_____

_____

_____

_____

3. List three signs of anger: _____

_____

_____

_____

4. What are the steps in managing anger effectively without harming oneself or others? _____

_____

_____

_____

_____

_____

_____

Name: _____   Date: ____/____/____

Facilitator's Guide
Coping Skills for Depression and Anxiety

INTRODUCTION

Subject and Why It Is Important

Ask group members how many have felt depressed or anxious often in the past year. Ask them to suggest what relationship this has to substance abuse for them and for people in general. Ask them what they would like to see happen in connection with their feelings of depression and anxiety the next year. Negative moods and depression are common feelings during recovery. Depression and anxiety are problems in their own right. However, they are particular problems for someone attempting to maintain sobriety because they can cause relapse. Often, people return to using/drinking as a method to cope with depression and anxiety. The catch is that using is an ineffective way to manage negative moods and serves only to make the individual more depressed or anxious in the long run.

Group Policy

Explain to group members that they will be evaluated on the following learning goals through the use of a pretest/posttest:

LEARNING GOALS Upon completion of this presentation, participants will demonstrate understanding of how depression and anxiety affect thoughts, perceptions, and behaviors.

Upon completion of this presentation, participants will demonstrate knowledge of skills and resources to cope with depression and anxiety.

QUESTIONS As the instructor, you can ask students to hold their questions until the end or to ask them at any time during class.

PRETEST Distribute the pretest if you decide to use it, asking group members to fill out and return their completed forms to the instructor without putting their names on them; tell them the posttest will be done at the end of the presentation. Explain that the purpose of the pre- and posttests is for participants to assess their own level of understanding.

Background and Lead-In

1. Definitions of depression:

   a. *Webster's Unabridged* defines depression as "low spirits, gloominess, sadness . . . a decrease in force, activity . . . a feeling of inadequacy . . ."
   b. Clinicians, psychiatrists, doctors, and others define depression using the *DSM-IV* and describe a major depressive episode as five of nine of the following symptoms for two weeks or more:
      i. Depressed mood most of the time
      ii. Loss of pleasure in most/all activities
      iii. Significant weight loss/gain or a change to appetite
      iv. Unable to sleep or sleeping too much
      v. Physically dragging or agitation
      vi. Fatigue or loss of energy nearly every day
      vii. Difficulty thinking/concentrating, indecisiveness
      viii. Feeling worthless or excessively guilty
      ix. Recurrent thoughts of death, suicidal thoughts/plan/attempt

2. Definition of anxiety: *Webster's* dictionary defines anxiety as "concern . . . regarding some event, future or uncertain, which disturbs the mind."

     It is important to note that symptoms of anxiety and depression can range from mild to moderate to severe.

TRIGGERS OF DEPRESSION AND ANXIETY

Physical Triggers

1. Chemical imbalances: Correctable using medications; may be temporary in response to some traumatic event, or permanent due to permanent imbalance

2. Results of substance abuse: Either during use, as a withdrawal effect, or more long term due to excessive abuse of certain substances

   a. Some drugs are depressants (like alcohol), which means they depress functioning in many areas

   b. Other drugs are stimulants, which means they stimulate functioning to higher than normal levels; the body tries to restore normal levels, resulting in a rebound effect when the drug is removed from the system. Examples include coming down from methamphetamine use especially after prolonged use over days, or the "crash" associated with cocaine use.

3. Other physical causes:

   a. Sleep deprivation

   b. Hunger

   c. Physical illness

   d. Chronic pain

Emotional/Environmental Triggers

1. Crisis, where a person feels overwhelmed or out of control of a situation

   a. Relationships (death, breakup, divorce, children leaving, etc.)

   b. Job (loss of employment, retirement, change, etc.)

   c. Financial

   d. Legal

   e. Loss of structure (move, change of job)

   f. Health

   g. High stress of other kinds

2. Emotional isolation especially common for:

   a. Adolescents

   b. Elderly individuals

   c. Chemically dependent individuals

3. Distorted thinking patterns: Explain that many approaches to the treatment of depression specifically address identifying thinking patterns that support depression and anxiety. Further, treatment of depression addresses changing negative thoughts, which in turn changes behavior. Basic distortions of reality occur on three levels: unrealistic negative view of self, negative interpretations of events, and unrealistically negative expectations for the future.

   a. Seven common patterns of distorted thought/perception:

    i. Leaping to negative conclusions with little evidence

    ii. Focusing on the bad, ignoring the rest of the picture

    iii. Overgeneralizing from one or a few negative incidents to expect every situation to turn out badly

    iv. Magnifying or minimizing the importance of events—typically, magnifying the negative and minimizing the positive events

    v. Taking everything negative personally or seeing the worst possible outcome of events

    vi. Thinking in extremes, no gray area: perfect/worthless, success/failure, winner/loser, etc.

    vii. Jumping to negative conclusions

b. Unrealistic expectations or rules for self, others, and situations:

    i. It is not okay for me to feel angry in this situation.

    ii. If I feel angry, I can't control my actions.

    iii. It's not acceptable for me to make a mistake—if I do, I'm a failure.

    iv. It's not okay for me not to know something—if I don't, I'm stupid.

    v. I'm weak if I need or ask for help.

    vi. If he/she gets mad at me, he/she does not care about me.

    vii. Other people make me unhappy, and I have no control over this.

    viii. My past experiences and events determine my present behavior, and their influence is too strong for me to overcome.

    ix. There is a right, perfect solution to every problem, and I have to find it or the results will be disastrous.

    x. Other people must treat me fairly; if they don't it is terrible and I can't bear it.

COPING SKILLS FOR DEALING WITH DEPRESSION AND ANXIETY

Correct Physical Causes

1. Get drugs out of the system: Allow your body to regain its homeostasis; understand that there are ways to cope with depression and anxiety and that these states are temporary.
2. Observe basic self-care: Getting appropriate diet, rest, and exercise builds up one's resistance; when people's bodies are not working at optimum functioning, feelings are elevated, especially negative moods.
3. Treat illness or injury by seeking medical consultation.
4. Medications prescribed by a psychiatrist after thorough evaluation and detox period may be necessary.

Correct Emotional/Environmental Causes

1. Address crisis situations if possible: This sometimes means professional help; emotional support and time are also important.
2. Emotional isolation: increase interaction/involvement with others—friendships, organizations, volunteer work, recovery programs, reconnect with supportive family members.
3. Distorted thinking patterns: Learn corrective thinking skills and practice them.

       It is helpful at this point to review RET, discussing that in this view behaviors and feelings are results of irrational or distorted beliefs or interpretations of events. To correct faulty, self-destructive behavior, one must learn to identify and challenge one's faulty beliefs and replace them with healthy, productive, rational beliefs. A suggested exercise to help participants become familiar with this is to review the list of unrealistic rules that are discussed earlier in the presentation and replace each with a more realistic rule.

4. Act on positive, healthy thoughts and beliefs: Identifying your negative thoughts is not enough; sometimes by acting differently, you can change old thinking habits and reinforce new ones. These activities have been effective for people attempting to change their behavior and becoming successful at overcoming depression and anxiety:

    a. Solve problems—Many times, problems have accumulated and new ones arise as a result of drinking/using; worrying about them does not change them, it only serves to increase depression and anxiety, which increases the level of hopelessness. Be active in solving problems in healthy ways (see presentation on effective problem solving for more details).

    b. Change your activity level—Activity improves mood; more activity begets more energy; more activity increases motivation. When you do more, you cannot blame yourself for doing nothing.

    c. Increase pleasurable activities—Often, depressed and anxious individuals isolate and avoid doing anything. Plan activities that you can do alone and those that you can do with others—and *do* them.

    d. Reward yourself for accomplishing tasks, no matter how small, then assess those areas where you may be able to make improvements. Put a plan in motion.

    e. Design and follow a daily schedule that is flexible and realistic.

    f. Involve other people in your life.

CONCLUSION

This presentation covered the negative feelings of depression and anxiety and suggested methods to assist in coping with depression and anxiety without the use of substances. Reiterate that this is common in recovery and may precede relapse, but it is correctable with knowledge and practice of skills. Challenge group participants to design as part of their relapse prevention plan methods they will employ to cope with depression and anxiety if they arise in the course of their recovery.

REVIEW OF LEARNING GOALS

Upon completion of this presentation, participants should demonstrate:

1. Understanding of how depression and anxiety affect thoughts, perceptions, and behaviors.
2. Knowledge of skills and resources to cope with depression and anxiety.

QUESTIONS/DISCUSSION BEFORE POSTTEST

ADMINISTER POSTTEST

Provide same instructions that you provided when you administered the pretest.

QUESTIONS/DISCUSSION AFTER POSTTEST

1. Definitions of Depression:

    a. Webster's Unabridged: "low spirits; gloominess; dejection; sadness . . . a decrease in force, activity . . . a feeling of inadequacy . . ."

    b. DSM-IV (Major Depressive Episode): 5 of 9 symptoms in 2-week period:

        1) _____

        2) _____

        3) _____

        4) _____

        5) _____

        6) _____

        7) _____

        8) _____

        9) _____

2. Definition of Anxiety: Webster's Unabridged: "concern . . . regarding some event, future or uncertain, which disturbs the mind."

3. Triggers of Depression and Anxiety:

    a. Physical causes:

        1) _____ imbalances

        2) Results of _____ .

        3) Other physical causes: _____, _____ , _____ , _____ .

    b. Emotional/environmental causes:

        1) _____

        2) _____

        3) Distorted thoughts and perceptions

    a) Common patterns of distorted thought/perception:

        i) _____

        ii) _____

        iii) _____

        iv) _____

        v) _____

        vi) _____

        vii) _____

    b) Unrealistic expectations — Five examples that apply to me are:

        i) _____

        ii) _____

iii) _____

iv) _____

v) _____

4. Coping Skills for Dealing with Depression and Anxiety

    a) Correct physical causes in four ways:

        1) _____

        2) _____

        3) _____

        4) _____

    b) Correct emotional/environmental causes:

    1) Solve crisis if possible

    2) Increase involvement with others

    3) Correct distorted thinking

    4) Six techniques for acting on healthy, positive thoughts and beliefs:

        i) _____

        ii) _____

        iii) _____

        iv) _____

        v) _____

        vi) _____

5. Personal Reflection: Something I learned today that I will practice for the next seven days is:

_____

_____

_____

_____

_____

_____

_____

_____

_____

_____

_____

_____

_____

_____

_____

_____

_____

_____

Name: _____   Date: ____/____/____

Pretest/Posttest
Coping Skills for Depression and Anxiety

1. List four causes of depression and anxiety:

_____

_____

_____

_____

_____

_____

_____

_____

_____

2. Describe a common pattern of distorted thinking and discuss how this may result in someone experiencing depression or anxiety: _____

_____

_____

_____

_____

_____

_____

3. List three ways to cope with depression or anxiety or decrease feelings of depression or anxiety:

_____

_____

_____

_____

_____

_____

Name: _____   Date: ____/____/____

Facilitator's Guide
Resisting Open and Hidden Pressures to Drink or Use

INTRODUCTION

Subject and Why It Is Important

Ask for a show of hands of group members who don't think they will be confronted with any pressures to return to drinking or drug use, either during or after treatment. If any raise hands, discuss briefly, letting other group members challenge the hand-raisers. Then ask, of members expecting to encounter such pressures, how many think all of those pressures will be open and easy to identify.

Point out (to whatever degree applies, depending on treatment setting) that clients may be completely or partially sheltered from pressures to engage in the addictions that brought them to treatment—but they will soon be back in their normal environment, facing pressures they were unable to resist before.

Ask clients to think about any examples of posttreatment success or failure in maintaining abstinence among people they know, then reflect on what pressures to relapse those people encountered, and how they dealt with the pressures.

Point out that many people with intelligence, willpower, and motivation to stay clean and sober have left treatment planning to stay abstinent, only to relapse in the face of pressures to return to active addiction; at the same time, others facing the same or tougher pressures have succeeded in resisting. Suggest that the key factors are not strength, intelligence, or luck, but information and action—knowing how to identify pressures and what to do and what to avoid doing. Emphasize that this presentation will give them information about both open and hidden pressures that may influence them toward relapse, along with positive actions that have been helpful for many people and negative actions that have contributed to problems for others before them.

Group Policy

Explain to participants that they will be evaluated on their accomplishment of these goals.

LEARNING GOALS Upon completion of this presentation, participants should demonstrate with an accuracy rate of at least 80%, knowledge of open and hidden pressures to drink or use by labeling, without notes or references, various situations as open or hidden pressures to relapse.

Upon completion of this presentation, participants should demonstrate understanding of techniques of resisting open and hidden pressures to drink or use by listing, without notes or references, at least three sources of support and three strategies to resist either open or hidden pressures to return to addictive behaviors.

QUESTIONS As the presenter, you may ask participants to hold their questions until the end or to ask them at any time during the presentation. If participation is a high priority, we recommend allowing questions at any time; if brevity is more important, it works better to hold questions until the end.

PRETEST Distribute the pretest if you choose to use it, asking participants to fill out and turn in their answer sheets without putting names on them; tell them the posttest will be done at end of the presentation.

Background and Lead-In

Ask whether anyone present has had experience with reentry into their normal existence after a previous treatment experience, and if so, what difficulties they experienced. Ask the discussion question: *What people and situations may pressure me to relapse, and how might they do so?* Write answers on a board, flip chart, or transparency sheet and facilitate a short discussion.

TECHNIQUES OF RESISTING OPEN AND HIDDEN PRESSURES TO DRINK OR USE

Identifying Pressures to Drink or Use

1. Open pressures: Because they are open, these are easy to identify, though they may be either easy or hard to resist. Refer to previous feedback from group members and cover the following types of open pressure to relapse:

   a. Peer pressure—Individual friends (and family members) with whom a person formerly used alcohol or other drugs may urge the client returning from treatment to return to the addictive behavior for several reasons:

      i. They may be uneasy about their own substance abuse and react defensively when someone they know rejects that behavior; this often takes the form of feeling insulted when someone refuses to drink or use with them.

      ii. They may rely on selling drugs for income and see abstinence as a direct economic threat.

      iii. They may sincerely believe substance use to be harmless and even beneficial; they may see it as "the thing to do."

   b. Situational pressure—A social or even a work-related situation may include substance abuse as an important element, creating pressure to drink or use:

      i. Group recreational activities may always include alcohol or other drugs.

      ii. Religious or social rituals may involve consuming alcohol or other drugs, such as sacramental services involving wine and drinking of toasts at weddings.

      iii. Work group parties (office Christmas parties, etc.) may involve alcohol or other drugs, and the client may be required or pressured to attend and participate.

      iv. Clients may not have any social groups or activities that don't involve drinking or using, and it may seem that to be abstinent means to always be alone.

2. Hidden pressures

   a. A powerful source of pressure to return to drinking or using may be one's own self-image and the meaning one has learned to associate with substance use or abuse. Ask group members how many feel they were taught that drinking or other drug use (including smoking tobacco) was a sign of sophistication, being a success in life, being attractive to the opposite sex, and so on. Ask how many sometimes feel like failures because they can't be controlled drinkers/users. Ask how many had key role models who drank or used heavily. Note that part of recovery is rethinking these points and creating a new self-image that includes positive views about abstinence and finding new role models that don't drink or use.

   b. Often, newly recovering people either relapse or come close to doing so by sheer unconscious reflex, because it is such an ingrained habit or because some situation is such a strong cue for substance use. Ask for examples; provide some if group members don't (the person who always drinks beer at baseball games, the gambler who automatically buys a lottery ticket at the convenience store, etc.). Note that studying one's past patterns of addictive behavior is important because it helps make us aware of these unconscious habits and cues.

c. The newly clean and sober person may encounter painful rejection from others either because they dislike the change or because they refuse to believe that the change is sincere and will last. Often, these others will not openly say that they dislike the person's new sobriety or that they don't trust him or her, but they will withdraw and/or become hostile without saying why or even while denying they are doing it. If the rejection seems stronger when the newly recovering person talks about his or her sobriety or is acting very different than while drinking, using, or engaging in other addictive behaviors, the rejection is more likely to be in response to the change. Because they have grown up believing that they have to please others, many people find this rejection particularly difficult.

d. A final factor that often makes maintaining abstinence hard is the simple lack of knowledge of, and practice with, effective alternatives. All alcoholics, addicts, and people engaged in other compulsive patterns of behavior originally did so for similar reasons: They liked the way it made them feel—it made them feel good, relieved an unpleasant feeling, or it helped them cope with a situation, or both. Part of recovery is finding new ways to feel good, to get relief for unpleasant feelings, and to cope with situations one used to handle with addictive behaviors. But at first, these new patterns may seem uncomfortable, awkward, or difficult, and they will probably not be the first alternative that comes to mind.

Resisting Open Pressures to Drink or Use

1. Awareness/anticipation: This is the easy part of open pressures. Because they are open, the newly recovering person *knows* he or she is being pressured. By anticipation, we mean looking ahead and knowing when this is likely to happen, for example, the first time one meets an old using friend after returning from treatment.

2. Avoidance when possible: As this implies, the easiest and best way to handle open pressure to use or drink is to avoid it if one can: Don't see the person, don't go to the place. Unfortunately, this is often impossible, so it cannot be effective as a primary strategy.

3. Coping when avoidance isn't practical: In the majority of situations where the person returning from treatment must face at least some sources of pressure to drink, use, or return to other compulsions, these coping strategies are useful:

   a. Preparation is vital: Think about how you will feel and what you will say or do. Very few people do their best thinking or decision making in a hurry or under high stress, so the time to think and decide is in advance, when the pressure is not on yet and there is plenty of time.

   b. Support is vital: If possible, ensure support from someone who is actually present when the pressure takes place, and if not, support from someone important in your life who is not hard to get in contact with. The best way to obtain this kind of support is often to give a straightforward explanation of what you are trying to do together with a sincere request for the other person's help. Most people love to feel needed and helpful and will respond positively if approached in this way. Support can come from individuals—friends, family members, a sponsor, a coworker (even a therapist or counselor!)—or from groups such as a family, an AA or other 12-Step group, or a therapy group.

   c. Planning specific strategies is also wise. These may include:

   Planning to have one's own transportation

   Planning a reason to leave a situation early

   Planning what one will say and do if confronted or ridiculed

   Planning to consume only nonalcoholic beverages, etc.

Resisting Hidden Pressures to Drink or Use

1. Awareness/anticipation: This is more tricky but also more important with hidden pressures. The best ways to be aware of and anticipate such pressures are to analyze one's own past patterns and to discuss this with others and get their ideas, especially before occasions when hidden pressures may arise.
2. Avoidance when possible: Again, if possible, the simplest and easiest way to handle hidden pressures to drink or use is to avoid them completely. But this is harder to do and will often be impossible, especially for the hidden pressures that come from within.
3. Coping when avoidance isn't practical:
   a. Preparation is even more important with hidden pressures than with open ones. Again, think about how you will feel and what you will say or do. Because under stress one may lose awareness of hidden pressures, plan to give yourself reminders.
   b. Support is vital with hidden pressures even more than with open ones. Hidden pressures often consist largely of what we think others expect of us, and their power comes from our desire to be liked and accepted; thus, someone showing us that we may be more liked and accepted if we are sober is offering us a powerful reason to be abstinent.
   c. Strategies in coping with hidden pressures are more subtle, like the pressures themselves, and often don't involve direct confrontation. The most effective strategies often involve ways to maintain one's awareness of the danger together with proactive planning for use of alternative ways to feel better or handle difficult situations.

CONCLUSION

Few people leaving treatment intend to relapse, but many do. Open and hidden pressures to relapse have a lot to do with this. The keys to resisting such pressures are information and action. This presentation provided important information and suggested actions that can help group members stay clean, sober, and abstinent when they face pressures to return to their old lifestyles. The presentation covered types of open and hidden pressures and ways to resist both.

REVIEW OF LEARNING GOALS

Upon completion of this presentation, participants should demonstrate:

1. With an accuracy rate of at least 80%, knowledge of open and hidden pressures to drink or use by labeling, without notes or references, various situations as open or hidden pressures to relapse.
2. Understanding of techniques of resisting open and hidden pressures to drink or use by listing, without notes or references, at least three sources of support and three strategies to resist either open or hidden pressures to return to addictive behaviors.

QUESTIONS/DISCUSSION BEFORE POSTTEST

ADMINISTER POSTTEST

QUESTIONS/DISCUSSION AFTER POSTTEST

1. Techniques of Resisting Open and Hidden Pressures to Drink or Use
   a. Identifying pressures to drink or use:
      1) Open pressures: Because they are open, these are _____ to identify, though they may be either easy or hard _____ .
         (a)_____ pressure: Friends or family may pressure someone returning from treatment to relapse for several reasons:
            i. They may be _____ about their own substance abuse and react _____ when someone they know rejects that behavior.
            ii. They may rely on _____ drugs for _____.
            iii. They may sincerely believe substance use to be harmless.
         (b)_____ pressure: A _____ or _____ -related situation may include substance abuse as an important element, creating pressure to drink or use. This may include:
            i. _____ activities that always include alcohol/other drugs
            ii. _____ or social rituals
            iii. _____ parties
            iv. Sometimes people don't have any social groups or activities that don't involve drinking or using, and it may seem as if being sober means to always be alone.
      2) Hidden pressures:
            i. One's own _____ - _____ and the meaning a person has learned during their life to associate with substance use or abuse: Seeing drinking or other drug use (including _____ _____) as a sign of sophistication, being a success in life, being attractive to the opposite sex, etc. This may come from having key _____ _____ who drank or used heavily.
            ii. Sheer _____ reflex, because it is such an ingrained habit or because some situation is such a strong cue for substance use. Studying one's past patterns of addictive behavior is important because _____ .
            iii. Painful _____ from others either because they _____ the _____ or because they refuse to _____ the change is _____ and will last.
            iv. Lack of knowledge of, and practice with, _____ _____ . Part of recovery is finding new ways to _____ _____ , and to get _____ for _____ feelings, and to cope with situations one used to handle with _____ _____ . At first, these new patterns may seem awkward, uncomfortable, or difficult, and they will probably not be the first alternative that comes to mind.
   b. Resisting open pressures to drink or use:
      1) _____ /anticipation: This is the _____ part with open pressures. Because they are open, the newly recovering person *knows* he or she is being pressured. By anticipation, we mean looking ahead and knowing _____ _____ _____ _____ _____ , for example, the first time one meets an old using friend after returning from treatment.

2) _____ when possible: This is often _____ , so it cannot be effective as a primary strategy.

       3) Coping when _____ isn't practical:

          i. _____ : Think about how I will feel and what I will say or do.

          ii. _____ : If possible, support from someone who is _____ when the pressure takes place, and if not, support from someone _____ in my life who is not hard to _____ _____ _____ _____ . Support can come from individuals — _____ _____ , members, a _____ , a _____ , (even a _____ or _____ !) Support can also come from groups such as a _____ _____ , an _____ or other _____ - _____ group, or a _____ group.

          iii. Planning specific strategies is also wise. These may include:

            Planning to have one's own _____

            Planning a reason to _____ a situation _____

            Planning what to say and do if _____ or _____

            Planning to have _____ - _____ _____

   c. Resisting hidden pressures to drink or use:

       1) Awareness/anticipation: The best ways to be aware of and anticipate such pressures are to analyze one's own _____ and to _____ this with _____ and get their ideas, especially before occasions when hidden pressures may arise.

       2) Avoidance when possible: Again, if possible, the simplest and easiest way to handle hidden pressures to drink or use is to avoid them completely. But this is harder to do and will often be impossible, especially the hidden pressures that _____ _____ _____ .

       3) Coping when avoidance isn't practical:

          i. Preparation: Again, think about how you will feel and what you will say or do. Here, because _____ _____ people may lose awareness of hidden pressures, plan to give yourself _____ .

          ii. _____ : The hidden pressures may be based on what we think _____ _____ or _____ of us, and the power of the pressures comes from our desire to be _____ and _____ .

          iii. The most effective strategies often involve ways to maintain awareness of the danger together with _____ _____ for use of alternative ways to feel better or handle difficult situations.

Notes/Questions:

_____

_____

_____

_____

_____

_____

Name: _____ Date: ____/____/____

Pretest/Posttest
Resisting Open and Hidden Pressures to Drink or Use

1. For each of the following, indicate whether it is a source of open pressure to relapse, hidden pressure to relapse, or neither:

Open   Hidden   Neither

_____   _____   _____ An old friend urging you to have "just one beer for old times' sake."

_____   _____   _____ The memory of your father, whom you admired, drinking every weekend.

_____   _____   _____ Thinking about the consequences of your last DWI.

_____   _____   _____ Talking with an AA or other 12-Step program sponsor.

_____   _____   _____ Feeling shy at a party and remembering that smoking a joint always helped.

_____   _____   _____ Your brother accusing you of being "holier than thou" and thinking you're too good to have a beer with him since you went through treatment.

_____   _____   _____ A family member insisting that you drink a toast at a wedding reception.

_____   _____   _____ Feeling bored and restless with nothing to do on Friday night, when you always used to go to a casino with friends from work.

_____   _____   _____ Experiencing intense grief at the death of a parent and not knowing whom to talk to about it or how to cope with the sadness you feel.

_____   _____   _____ Noticing that you feel calmer and less stressed after you go for a long walk.

2. List three or more individuals or groups you could use as sources of support to help you resist either open or hidden pressures to use, drink, or engage in other addictive behaviors:

_____

_____

_____

_____

3. List three or more strategies you could use to resist either open or hidden pressures to use, drink, or engage in other addictive behaviors:

_____

_____

_____

_____

Name: _____ Date: ____/____/____

Chapter 11

Other Mental Health Issues

Materials for Use in Psychoeducational Groups

With this chapter, we shift our focus to a series of problems that are separate from, but often linked with, substance abuse problems. These other mental health issues are situational problems that may be contributing causes, effects, or both of addiction and abuse. They are dangerous enough in their own right to both the client and others that they demand treatment at the same time as chemical dependence problems, and, aside from the dangers they pose in themselves, they can thoroughly undermine sobriety and recovery if left unaddressed during drug and alcohol treatment. Because these conditions and problems are so entangled with substance abuse issues, you will encounter some or all of them in many if not most of your clients.

As in Chapters 9 and 10, these presentation materials are primarily cognitive in format and combine the learning modalities of seeing the information, hearing it discussed, and experiencing it kinesthetically through the process of writing key information while filling in the blanks in the handouts.

The materials in this chapter include:

Family Dynamics

Domestic Violence

Suicide Awareness and Prevention, Part 1: Factors and Warning Signs

Suicide Awareness and Prevention, Part 2: Prevention and Response

Communication Skills

Dual Diagnosis

Codependency

Healthy Relationship Skills

Grief and Loss

INTRODUCTION

Subject and Why It Is Important

Ask class how many feel their childhoods were affected by their parents' substance abuse, and how many feel that drug and alcohol abuse was only part of the problem; finally, ask how many would like to avoid passing those experiences on to their own children.

Group Policy

LEARNING GOALS Upon completion of this presentation, participants will demonstrate an understanding of the typical roles and interaction patterns people act out in addictive/alcoholic and other dysfunctional families.

Upon completion of this presentation, participants will demonstrate an awareness of healthy alternative interaction patterns and resources available to help people change their learned role behaviors.

QUESTIONS The instructor can ask students to hold questions until the end or to ask them at any time during class.

PRETEST Distribute the pretest if you choose to use it, asking participants to complete and return them to the instructor. Inform group members that they will be given a posttest at the end of the presentation to assess their learning on this topic.

Background and Lead-In

Return to the discussion begun in the introduction. Ask how many participants have seen families in which the parents' problems caused their children to experience any of the following:

1, Being abused or neglected, emotionally or physically

2. Having to grow up too soon and take on adult responsibilities

3. Living in fear of their parents and wanting to get away from them as soon as possible

4. Being ashamed of their parents, their families, and their homes

5. Going without necessities like food, reliable shelter, and safety

Ask the question "Which of you wants your children to have that kind of a childhood?" Now ask them whether any of the parents in those situations wanted it to be that way or were happy about it. Ask the question "They wanted the same things you do and weren't able to achieve them. How will you succeed where they failed?" State that along with the willingness to work for change, the key to their success is knowledge of how to do things differently, and that's what this presentation is about.

DYSFUNCTIONAL FAMILY ROLES IN ACTION

Identifying Roles

1. Description of six common roles in chemically dependent families:

   a. *Dependent person*—This is the alcoholic or addict (or someone with another compulsive behavior).

   b. *Chief enabler*—Often the spouse or partner of the dependent person, this person's role in the family is taking care of the dependent person, cleaning up after him or her, covering up for him or her, and so on, thereby sheltering the dependent person from the consequences of his or her actions. This person is often controlling, full of self-pity and resentment, and burned out.

c. *Family hero*—Often the oldest child, this person makes the family proud, is a superachiever; his or her role is to be the one nobody has to worry about and the one who helps the family look good and healthy to the outside world. This person also tends to take care of the rest and may share common traits with the chief enabler. However, this child often feels inadequate and angry and strives for perfection to feel adequate.

d. *Scapegoat*—Often a middle child, this is the person who is always in trouble and may be blamed for the dependent person's using or drinking ("Having a kid like you would make anyone drink!"). This child's role is to be the lightning rod, the one who lets everyone else off the hook of responsibility for the family's problems, and to distract attention from the dependent person's actions.

e. *Lost child*—Often another middle or younger child, this person has developed the survival tactic of avoiding trouble by being invisible, either not being around or fading into the background when trouble erupts. His or her role is to be the one who never asks anyone for anything.

f. *Mascot*—Often the youngest child, this is the person who is always clowning around and distracting people from their problems. He or she seems never to be serious about anything, and this person's role in the family is to prevent big scenes and keep people from getting too upset by making them laugh whenever the atmosphere starts to get too tense.

Identifying Interaction Patterns

Ask the class to name unhealthy ways the members of a chemically dependent or dysfunctional family relate to one another. Write their answers on the board, then compare with this list of unhealthy behaviors:

1. Dishonesty/denial—refusing to admit how bad the problem is, covering up, avoiding confronting problems until too angry to keep silent; blaming others for problems in the family that are clearly the result of substance-abusing behavior
2. Breaking promises—not following through on commitments to children or spouse
3. Isolating—keeping secrets from "outsiders," not allowing visitors or friends to visit so there is no speculation that something is wrong in the family; instilling the "no talk rule"; sometimes withdrawing from other family members who may serve as support for the children but are merely nuisances for the adults as they may comment on the substance-abusing behavior
4. Emotional and physical abuse and neglect—parents hitting children and each other, yelling, calling names, bullying, belittling, leaving kids alone and unfed, ignoring school problems, ignoring medical needs of children
5. Parentifying children—forcing older children, while not old enough to perform responsibilities, to function as parents and caretakers to younger siblings and possibly to parents when hungover, high, drunk, or absent
6. Influencing children to be self-destructive—pressuring children to drink or use other substances with the parents, role-modeling drunk driving, avoiding addressing problems with children (e.g., shoplifting, truancy), allowing siblings to abuse one another

Family Rules and Chemical Dependency

Discuss that rules are created in family systems to keep the family in balance. Roles are adapted to cope with ongoing dysfunction in the family, rules are developed to protect and isolate family members from one another—to prevent family members from sharing their thoughts and feelings with one another and to keep distance. Discuss the following list of rules that often exist in families where substance abuse occurs:

1. It's not okay to talk about problems.

2. It's not okay to talk or express any feelings openly.

3. Always be strong, good, perfect.

4. Do as I say, not as I do.

5. It's not okay to be a child; to play.

6. Don't make waves.

7. You can't trust anyone.

8. Don't communicate in relationships directly.

9. Others' needs are more important than my own.

Predicting Outcomes

1. Adult characteristics: Ask class members to predict what a child in each of the roles will be like as an adult if he or she stayed in those roles. What strengths and problems might he or she have? Again, write their answers on the board. It is important to discuss the strengths as well as the problems that adult children tend to have as a result of growing up in an alcoholic or drug-dependent home.

2. Behavior as parents: Ask class members how they would expect each of these children to behave with their own children when they are adults; write answers on the board.

Recall the question about how many class members want to spare their children from experiences like their own and how well they could keep that promise.

Personalizing

1. Identify own role: Ask class members which role(s) they feel best fits their own behavior in childhood, explaining that people often take on different roles at different times.

2. Consider consequences: Refer to the last of family rules and explore thoughts and feelings about the possibility that clients might be that way with their own children. Ask how it would feel to look in the mirror and see their father or mother.

CHANGING ROLE BEHAVIORS

Frequently, group members comment that they do not believe their substance abuse has had any impact on their children because the children are too young or the parents never use substances around them. Other group members will express guilt regarding the evident or likely result of their substance-abusing behavior on their children. Often, parents in treatment have had their children removed from their homes due to legal and/or substance-abusing behavior. They express both guilt and anger regarding this situation and feel that it is impossible to have their children returned to them.

Goals—Knowing What We're Trying to Accomplish

It does not matter why these rules and roles were developed, the point is that they do not have to be maintained. It is important that group participants understand that they have choices and can break the unhealthy norms of the family.

1. Addressing denial regarding the impact of their own substance abuse: Discuss with class members that to prevent their children from sharing the same experience that they did, it is important (and painful) to accept responsibility for substance-abusing behavior. Point out to participants that despite the excuses that their use did not impact their children, children are aware that parents are different when high or drunk; that their needs, no matter how small, did not get met; that home does not feel safe, and so on. To assist their children, parents must recognize addiction or substance abuse as a family illness that needs family treatment.

2. Behavior changes: Ask group members to list healthy behaviors they would like to substitute in their own lives for the unhealthy behaviors listed and to describe any experiences they've had when they've acted out these healthy behaviors. To get members started, offer these examples: replace the "no talk rule" with open communication where children are encouraged to express their feelings and thoughts; avoid physical or verbal threats; avoid name calling; and make home a safe place.

3. Tools and support: Poll class members for knowledge of community and personal resources to help stay clean and sober and also to start making these changes.

   a. *Individual friends and relatives* (if they respect your health and intentions)

   b. *Support groups*—Al-Anon, AlaTeen, Codependents Anonymous, Adult Children of Alcoholic and Dysfunctional Families; less formal organizations

   c. *Other sources*—there are a lot of books on family dynamics and related issues; most large bookstores have a good selection. Two particularly useful workbooks are *Repeat After Me* by Claudia Black and *The 12-Steps: A Way Out for Adult Children.*

   d. *Therapy*—especially for some severe problems related to intense abuse from parents or residual effects that impact relationships, coping abilities, self-worth

Planning and Acting

1. How can a person systematically plan and carry through changes in these types of behaviors? Ask for input, then refer class members to steps 4 through 8 of 12-Step Programs.
2. What have class members done already to make these kinds of changes, and what do they plan to do? When will they start?

CONCLUSION

This presentation addressed roles, rules, and interaction patterns common in substance-dependent families. It also discussed common issues parents bring into treatment when addressing their own family of origin and determining what to pass on to their children.

REVIEW OF LEARNING GOALS

Upon completion of this presentation, group members should demonstrate:

1. An understanding of the typical roles, interaction patterns, and family rules people act out in addictive/alcoholic and other dysfunctional families.
2. An awareness of healthy alternative interaction patterns and resources available to help people change their learned role behaviors.

QUESTIONS/DISCUSSION BEFORE POSTTEST

ADMINISTER POSTTEST

QUESTIONS/DISCUSSION AFTER POSTTEST

1. Six common roles in chemically dependent families:

    a) _____ — the _____ or _____ (or someone with another compulsive behavior)

    b) _____ — often the spouse or partner, sheltering the dependent person from the consequences of his or her actions; often _____ , full of _____ and _____ , and _____

    c) _____ — the one who helps the family look good and healthy to the outside world

    d) _____ — the person who is always in trouble and may be blamed for the dependent person's using or drinking; the lightning rod who lets everyone else off the hook of responsibility for family problems and distracts from the dependent

    e) _____ — has developed the survival tactic of avoiding trouble by being invisible, not being around or fading when trouble erupts; the one who never asks anyone for anything

    f) _____ — always clowning around and distracting people, never seems serious about anything; role in the family is to prevent scenes by making people laugh when the atmosphere starts to get tense

2. Identifying interaction patterns:

    a) _____ / _____ — refusing to admit how bad the problem is, covering up, avoiding confronting problems until too angry to keep silent

    b) Breaking _____ — not following through on commitments to children or spouse

    c) _____ — keeping secrets from "outsiders"

    d) _____ and _____ abuse and neglect — parents hitting children and each other, yelling, calling names, bullying, belittling, leaving kids alone and unfed, ignoring school problems

    e) _____ children — forcing older children to act as _____ to younger siblings (and parents when drunk/high/hungover!)

    f) Influencing children to _____ — encouraging children to drink or use with adult, role-modeling drunk driving

3. Predicting outcomes:

    a) characteristics: What will the children in these roles be like as adults?

_____

_____

    b) Behavior as _____ :

_____

_____

4. Personalizing:

    a) Identify _____ :

    b) Consider _____ :

5. Changing Role Behaviors

    a) _____ — Knowing what we're trying to accomplish:

        1) Addressing _____

        2) _____ changes: _____

        3) _____ and _____ : _____

            (a) Individual _____

            (b)_____ groups — Al-Anon, AlaTeen, Codependents Anonymous, Adult Children of Alcoholic and Dysfunctional Families; less formal organizations

            (c) Other sources — books, workbooks, *Repeat After Me* by Claudia Black and *The 12 Steps: A Way Out for Adult Children*; can use with therapy

            (d)_____ , especially for some severe problems related to intense abuse from our parents.

    b. Planning and acting:

        1) How can a person systematically plan and carry through changes in these types of behaviors?

        Step 4: Made a _____ of ourselves.

        Step 5: Admitted to God, to ourselves, and to another human being the _____ .

        Step 6: Became willing to have God _____ .

        Step 7: Humbly asked him to _____ .

        Step 8: Made a list of all persons and became willing to _____ .

        Step 9: To such people wherever possible, except when to do so would _____ .

        2) What have you done already to make these kinds of changes, and what do you plan to do? When will you start?

_____

_____

_____

Comments / Questions / Discussion:

Name: _____ Date: ____/____/____

Pretest/Posttest
Family Dynamics

1. Match the following family roles with the behavior that best describes the role:

   Chief enabler   Immature, clowns around, assists in releasing family tension

   Dependent person   Seems to always be in trouble and blamed for the drinking/using behavior; takes focus off the addict

   Family hero   Invisible, never asks anyone for anything

   Scapegoat   Alcoholic, addict

   Lost child   Takes care of the dependent person, makes excuses for using behavior, shelters addict from consequence of using behavior

   Mascot   Superachiever; makes family look good to others outside the family

2. List three family rules that tend to exist in substance-abusing families.

   _____

   _____

   _____

3. List three interaction patterns present in chemically dependent/dysfunctional families.

   _____

   _____

   _____

4. Describe one healthy pattern of interaction that assists in breaking the pattern of dysfunction learned in family of origin where alcoholism or drug addiction was present. _____

   _____

   _____

   _____

5. Name one resource available to individuals attempting to learn how to change their learned role behaviors. _____

   _____

   _____

   _____

Name: _____   Date: ____/____/____

INTRODUCTION

Subject and Why It Is Important

Domestic violence has touched the lives of most of the program participants. There is a strong link between domestic violence and substance abuse, especially the abuse of alcohol and methamphetamine. There are no winners when people use violence to settle family conflicts, and no one feels good about the way things turn out. This is another area where you may look back and say, "I will never be like that"—but unless you learn how domestic violence works and how to do something different, your chances of slipping into familiar behaviors are great. Every year, thousands of adults and children are killed and injured in domestic violence incidents. Once violence starts in a relationship, it normally continues and keeps getting worse until it is stopped by the relationship breaking up, the death or incarceration of one partner, or an intervention involving the couple or family being sent to intensive therapy.

Group Policy

Explain to group participants that they will be evaluated on their accomplishment of the following goals.

LEARNING GOALS Upon completion of this presentation, participants will be able to identify behaviors that constitute domestic violence.

Upon completion of this presentation, participants will demonstrate understanding of the two main theories of domestic violence.

Upon completion of this presentation, participants will demonstrate understanding of healthy, nonabusive relationship interactions.

QUESTIONS Instructor can ask students to hold questions until the end or to ask them at any time during class.

PRETEST Distribute the pretest if you choose to use it, asking participants to fill it out and turn in their answer sheets to the instructor without putting their names on it; tell them the posttest will be completed at the end of the presentation.

Background and Lead-In

What is domestic violence, and what causes it? Ask class members for their definitions and views on causation. Write their answers on the board, flip chart, or transparency and discuss briefly. Compare answers with the following:

1. Definition: Domestic violence is any use of force or the threat of force in a conflict between members of a family. This includes the following:
   a. Battering or direct assault—hitting, kicking, shoving, biting, scratching, yanking hair, pinching, choking, burning, spitting, use of a weapon
   b. Grabbing or holding a person against his or her will
   c. Forced or coerced sexual intercourse
   d. Restricting a person's freedom of movement
   e. Using control of money to limit a person's freedom
   f. Preventing a person from working

g. Forcing a person to commit a crime

h. Destroying a person's property

i. Intimidation by abusing pets in a person's presence

j. Verbal or gestured threats to do any of the above

k. Using the threat of suicide or self-harm to control another person

2. Two theoretical models: Ways people conceptualize domestic violence

a. Cycle of abuse model: This describes abuse as a cycle similar to addictive behavior with a drug.

b. Power and control model: As articulated in the Duluth model (Pence & Paymar, 1993), this describes abuse as a deliberate way for one person (usually but not always a man) to control another.

THE CYCLE OF ABUSE MODEL

Domestic violence is a compulsive behavior, much like a binge-type pattern of substance abuse.

Three Stages of the Cycle of Abuse

1. Building tension: The abuser is irritable, critical, and increasingly hard to please; the victim becomes increasingly tense and nervous, trying not to upset the abuser and sometimes going to much trouble to try to please him or her.

2. Explosion of violence: The abuser "snaps" over some event, usually minor, becomes uncontrollably violent, and batters the partner, usually for a fairly short period of time—but long enough to kill or badly injure.

3. "Honeymoon" period: After the explosion, the abuser feels guilt, shame, and remorse. The abuser tries to compensate for the battering by crying, apologizing and promising it will never happen again, pampering the victim, giving gifts, tolerating verbal abuse from the victim, and so on. The honeymoon period fades as the abuser again starts to become irritable and harder to please, beginning another cycle with the "building tension" stage.

Other Information about the Cycle of Abuse

1. Over time, the cycle gets faster and more dangerous. The explosions keep getting more violent, and the honeymoon period gets shorter and eventually disappears, leaving the couple with constant tension relieved for brief periods by increasingly violent explosions.

2. This model fits the patterns of some violent couples but not others. Research and case histories show that violence between many couples does fit the cyclical pattern described here, but in other couples this is not the case. The second model, the Duluth power and control model, does a better job of explaining what appears to happen in many of those situations.

Ending the Cycle of Abuse

According to the cycle of abuse model, the way to end the abuse is to teach the violent partner communication skills, conflict resolution, and stress and anger management so that he or she is able to stop the buildup of tension and avoid future loss of control.

THE POWER AND CONTROL MODEL

In this model, presented by Pence and Paymar in the manual Education Groups for Men Who Batter (1993), domestic violence is not the result of uncontrollable outbursts of emotion; rather, it is a deliberate method used by one person to try to control another. It is a constant process rather than a cycle.

Underlying Beliefs

The Duluth power and control model is based on one partner, most often the man but in some cases the woman, believing the following things:

1. They have the right to dominate and control the other person and to be in charge of the relationship. With men, this is often based on the belief that women are inferior.
2. They have the right to choose the other partner's friends and activities.
3. They have the right to use force to exert this control.
4. The other partner really likes being dominated.
5. The other partner is manipulative.
6. The other partner is using them, sees them as a paycheck, etc.
7. The other partner's role is to serve them.
8. They have the right to punish the other partner if he or she displeases them.
9. If they are angry, they can't help getting violent—it's the other partner's fault for making them so angry.
10. Smashing property is venting, not abuse, so it's okay to do.

Power and Control Wheel

The power and control model describes eight separate facets or areas of power and control other than direct physical and sexual violence, which are used to control a partner. This is depicted (Pence & Paymar, 1993) as a wheel with eight sections:

1. Using coercion and threat—making or carrying out threats (e.g., threatening to leave, commit suicide, to make a report to Child Protective Services)
2. Using intimidation—creating fear by looks, gestures, breaking things, displaying weapons
3. Using emotional abuse—put-downs, derogatory comments, name calling, humiliation, mind games
4. Using isolation—controlling the other's actions, contacts, activities; using jealousy to control actions
5. Using minimizing, denying, and blaming—making light of the abuse, denying the abuse is happening, shifting responsibility, claiming it is the other's fault
6. Using the children—threatening to take the children, using the children to deliver messages, making other feel guilty about the children
7. Using male privilege (obviously, for male batterers)—defining men's and women's roles, treating woman as inferior or as a servant, and so on
8. Economic abuse—preventing employment, restricting money

Ending the Abuse—Shifting to the Equality Wheel

According to this model, the key to ending the abuse is to restructure the batterer's basic beliefs and attitudes, replacing the beliefs listed above with values respecting the other partner's rights as a person, giving up the idea of having the right to control the other person, and accepting responsibility for controlling his or her actions regardless of feelings. The result is summed up by an "equality wheel," which replaces the power and control wheel and also depicts eight sections:

1. Nonthreatening behavior—talking and acting in ways that allow partner to feel safe and comfortable doing things and expressing self
2. Respect—listening without judgment, valuing opinions
3. Trust and support—support goals; respect right to own feelings, social activities, opinions

4. Honesty and accountability—self-responsibility, acknowledging past violence, communicating openly and honestly
5. Responsible parenting—sharing parenting responsibilities, positive role modeling
6. Shared responsibility—making family decisions together, mutual agreement on ways household work is done
7. Economic partnership—making money decisions together, accessibility of both partners to money
8. Negotiation and fairness—effective conflict resolution, accepting change, compromising

WHAT LEADS TO CHANGE

For either model, one question is "What motivates the abusive partner to change?" In cases where change does happen, the motivating factors usually include the following:

Legal Pressure

Short of leaving and never coming back, research shows that the single most effective thing a victim of domestic violence can do to prevent recurrence is to call the police, have the batterer arrested, and press charges. Going to jail is a deterrent, and the court system will often order a couple to therapy.

Partner's Ultimatum

Sometimes it is also effective for the victim to tell the violent partner that if the abuse ever happens again, he or she will end the relationship—*and to be ready to follow through;* most people can detect a bluff. The longer the violence has been going on, the less effective and the more dangerous this tactic is.

Offender's Becoming Clean and Sober

This often makes the difference between a person being violent and nonviolent. Impulse control is increased; also, if the violent person is in a 12-Step program, the process of working the steps requires a person to evaluate his or her own actions, make amends, practice the principles of the steps in all affairs, and make every effort to avoid future abusive behavior.

Tools and Resources

These consist of therapy programs and support groups.

CONCLUSION

This presentation provided participants with information about what constitutes domestic violence, models for its explanation, and ways it can be eliminated from relationships.

REVIEW OF LEARNING GOALS

Upon completion of this presentation, participants should demonstrate:

1. Understanding of the two main theories of domestic violence.
2. Understanding of healthy, nonabusive relationship interactions.

QUESTIONS/COMMENTS BEFORE POSTTEST

ADMINISTER POSTTEST

QUESTIONS/DISCUSSION AFTER POSTTEST

1. Definition: Domestic violence is any _____ or the _____ in a conflict between members of a family — this includes the following:

    a. Battering or direct assault — _____ , _____ , shoving, _____ , _____ , _____ , _____ , _____ , burning, _____ , use of a _____

    b. _____ or _____ a person against his or her will

    c. Forced or coerced _____

    d. Restricting a person's _____

    e. Using control of _____ to limit a person's freedom

    f. Preventing a person from _____

    g. Forcing a person to _____

    h. Destroying a person's _____

    i. Intimidation by _____ in a person's presence

    j. Verbal or gestured threats to do any of the above

    k. Using the threat of _____ or _____ to control another person

2. Two theoretical models:

    a. _____ of abuse model: This describes abuse as a cycle similar to addictive behavior with a drug.

    b. _____ and _____ model: Also called the Duluth model, this describes abuse as a deliberate way for one person (usually but not always a man) to control another.

3. The _____ of Abuse Model: This explanation says that domestic violence is a _____ behavior, much like a binge-type pattern of substance abuse.

    a. Three stages:

        1) _____ : The abuser is irritable, critical, and increasingly hard to please; the victim becomes increasingly tense and nervous, trying not to upset the abuser and sometimes going to much trouble to try to please him or her.

        2) _____ of _____ : The abuser "snaps" over some event, usually minor, becomes uncontrollably violent, and batters the partner, usually for a fairly short period of time — but long enough to kill or badly injure.

        3) "_____" period: After the explosion, the abuser feels guilt, shame, and remorse. The abuser tries to _____ by crying, apologizing and promising it will never happen again, pampering the victim, giving gifts, tolerating verbal abuse from the victim, an so on. The _____ fades as the abuser again starts to become irritable and harder to please, beginning another cycle with the "building tension" stage.

    b. Other information:

        1) Over time, the cycle gets _____ and more _____ .

        2) This model fits the pattern of some violent couples but not others.

    c. Ending the cycle of abuse: According to this model, the way to end the abuse is to _____ the violent partner _____ , _____ , and _____ .

4. The Power and Control Model: This model says that domestic violence is not the result of uncontrollable outbursts of emotion. It is a _____ used by one person to try to _____, and it is a constant process rather than a cycle.

     a. Underlying beliefs: The power and control model is based on one partner, more often the man but in many cases the woman, believing the following things:

       1) They have the right to _____ and to be in charge of the relationship. With men, this is often based on the belief that women are inferior.

       2) They have the right to choose the other partner's _____.

       3) They have the right to _____ to exert this control.

       4) The other partner really _____.

       5) The other partner is _____ .

       6) The other partner is _____ them, sees them as a paycheck, etc.

       7) The other partner's role is to _____ serve them.

       8) They have the right to _____ the other partner.

       9) If they are angry, they _____ — it's the other partner's own fault for making them so angry.

       10) _____ is venting, not abuse, so it's okay.

     b. _____ and _____ wheel:

       1) _____ and threats

       2) _____

       3) _____abuse

       4) _____

       5) _____ , _____ , and _____

       6) Using _____

       7) Using _____ (obviously for male batterers)

       8) _____abuse

     c. Ending the abuse — shifting to the _____ wheel:

       1) _____ behavior

       2) _____

       3) _____ and _____

       4) _____ and _____

       5) Responsible _____

       6) Shared _____

       7) _____ partnership

       8) _____ and _____

5. What Leads to Change

     a. _____ pressure

     b. Partner's ultimatum

     c. Offender's becoming _____

     d. Tools and resources: _____ and _____

Name: _____   Date: ____/____/____

Pretest/Posttest
Domestic Violence

1. Domestic violence is defined as any use of force or the threat of force in a conflict between members of a family. Name at least three behaviors that would be considered acts of domestic violence.

_____

_____

_____

_____

_____

_____

2. The two main theoretical models of abuse are: _____

_____

_____

_____

_____

3. One way of understanding domestic violence is to see it as a pattern of seeking power and control, demonstrated by eight tactics used by batterers to exert power and control over their partners. Name three of the eight tactics: _____

_____

_____

_____

_____

4. There are eight healthy patterns that are positive counterparts to the eight tactics of batterers based on the power and control model. Name three of the eight healthy patterns:

_____

_____

_____

_____

_____

_____

Name: _____   Date: ____/____/____

INTRODUCTION

Subject and Why It Is Important

Ask for a show of hands of group members who have been affected by a suicide, suicide attempt, or suicidal threat or gesture by someone close to them, then ask in how many of those situations drinking or other drug use was a factor. Point out that suicide and substance abuse are often connected. Then ask that, without answering or raising hands, group members think about whether they have ever attempted or seriously considered suicide, and if they have, what role alcohol or other drugs played in their lives at the time.

Group Policy

Explain to participants that they will be evaluated on their accomplishment of these goals.

LEARNING GOALS Upon completion of this presentation, participants should demonstrate understanding of suicide factors and warning signs by listing, without notes or references, at least four factors in a person's life situation that would increase the risk of suicide.

Upon completion of this presentation, participants should demonstrate understanding of suicide factors and warning signs by listing, without notes or references, at least four factors in a person's lifestyle that would increase the risk of suicide.

Upon completion of this presentation, participants should demonstrate understanding of suicide factors and warning signs by listing, without notes or references, at least four warning signs that might indicate that a person was in increased danger of suicide.

QUESTIONS As the presenter, you may ask participants to hold their questions until the end or to ask them at any time during the presentation. If participation is a high priority, we recommend allowing questions at any time; if brevity is more important, it works better to hold questions until the end.

PRETEST Pass out the pretest if you choose to use it, asking participants to fill out and turn in their answer sheets without putting names on them; tell them the posttest will be done at the end of the presentation.

Background and Lead-In

Ask the discussion question, "How many feel you know enough about suicide to be able to tell when someone close to you is in danger of becoming suicidal?" Ask how many have children; how many have elderly relatives; how many have family members or close friends who have drug or alcohol problems. State that all three of these categories of people are high-risk groups for depression and suicide.

Explain that this presentation will give participants information about the state of mind that leads to suicide and about situations and lifestyle factors that increase the risk of suicide, and will teach them about the warning signs in others' behavior that may indicate greater risk of suicide. Note that after this presentation and the second presentation on suicide, which will cover what to do, the group members will probably have more knowledge on this subject than anyone else in their families or circles of friends, and that their knowledge may save a life.

SUICIDE FACTORS AND WARNING SIGNS

The Suicidal State of Mind

Ask for group members' ideas about what a person might be thinking when he or she commits suicide; write feedback on a board, flip chart, or transparency sheet. Then explain that research and interviews with people who have tried to kill themselves show that the following four factors are almost always present in suicide:

1. Intense emotional pain
2. A belief that one cannot tolerate or endure this emotional pain
3. A feeling that there is no way to escape the emotional pain except by dying
4. A feeling of being isolated, that no one understands or cares very much

Note that if any of these four factors is reduced or eliminated, the risk of suicide drops dramatically. This can happen in four ways:

1. The emotional pain is relieved
2. The person comes to believe that he or she can handle the painful situation
3. The person comes to believe there is a way to reduce or end the emotional pain without dying
4. The person comes to feel a strong emotional connection to, and to feel valued by, another person or people

Life Situation Factors

In general, the risk of suicide goes up in situations that increase the amount of change, stress, and/or emotional pain a person is experiencing, or that reduce his or her ability to cope with stress, or both. These types of situations include the following:

1. Divorce or breakup of a serious relationship: This is the single highest situational risk factor for suicide.
2. Severe financial problems: These can affect every area of a person's life and damage his or her self-esteem and feeling of being a competent adult, parent, spouse, and so on.
3. Loss of a job, serious problems at work, or retirement: In addition to the financial impact of losing a job, our culture teaches us to base our identity and self-esteem on our work. Feeling like a failure at this important part of life can be devastating. Even retirement can lead to a loss of identity and a feeling that one's main worth in the world is gone.
4. Recent death of a loved one (especially if by suicide), or an anniversary of a death: Losing a parent, sibling, partner, child, or close friend often triggers the kind of emotional pain that can lead to suicide. If that person died by suicide, it can strongly influence others in the same direction. Anniversaries of deaths are painful reminders, especially for a person whose grief has not healed.
5. Serious illness or physical injury or disability: Beyond being painful and frightening, and therefore very stressful, medical problems of this kind are devastating to the self-image of many people, when they suddenly see themselves as no longer whole, attractive, or able to do many things they used to do.
6. Recent geographical move: This often includes financial stress, a change of job, and a sudden isolation from supportive relationships.
7. Recent change of jobs (including promotions): Even a long-hoped-for promotion is stressful, and can be either disappointing or tougher to handle than expected.
8. Recent change of supervisor at work: This is often more stressful than we realize. It requires a lot of adjustment and brings much uncertainty in a relationship with a person who has great power in our lives.

Lifestyle Factors

A number of factors in a person's lifestyle make him or her more vulnerable to stress and less capable of coping with difficulties, resulting in higher risk of suicide under any conditions but especially in high-stress situations like those just listed:

1. Use of alcohol and/or other drugs: A large proportion of suicides are under the influence of alcohol or other drugs when they kill themselves, and a large percentage of alcoholics kill themselves or try to do so. Alcohol is a depressant drug; depressants reduce control over impulses and impair judgment.

2. Social isolation: Being a loner means a person has few supportive relationships to lean on when he or she is in emotional pain. This may also be a source of pain in itself, due to loneliness and feelings of failure and inadequacy.

3. Working in a high-stress job: Especially in the case of jobs that have a "macho" image and role expectations, such as law enforcement and the military, the combination of high stress and the belief that one should not ask others for help with personal problems can be deadly.

4. Frequent conflicts with others: This can be a sign of ongoing emotional pain, poor "people skills," an attitude of not caring about the consequences of one's actions, poor impulse control, or all of the above.

5. Owning or having easy access to firearms: Suicide is often an impulsive act, especially in younger people, and having a gun available can make the difference between acting on an impulse or being delayed long enough to have second thoughts.

6. Engaging in high-risk sports or other activities: Recklessness in other areas and thrill-seeking behavior is often found in people who commit or attempt suicide.

Warning Signs

There are a number of common behavior patterns in people who are thinking about killing themselves or who have decided to do so:

1. Talking or hinting about suicide or death: Most suicides repeatedly tell people they are thinking about killing themselves before they actually do so. This may take the form of hints such as talking about wanting to go to sleep and never wake up, to go away and never come back, and similar types of remarks. Always take this seriously and ask the person what he or she meant by the remark—getting the person to talk about it is more likely to keep him or her from acting on the idea than anything else you can do.

2. Frequent anxiety, anger, or depression, followed by sudden improvement of mood when the situation has not improved: This can mean that the person is no longer feeling trapped in the situation because he or she plans to escape by suicide.

3. Frequent preoccupation: If a person who is in a very stressful situation suddenly becomes absentminded and often seems mentally somewhere else, this in combination with other factors listed can mean the person is considering suicide.

4. Making arrangements for loved ones' needs: If a person suddenly starts buying personal insurance policies, making a will, settling debts, and doing similar things, these actions may be preparations for his or her own death.

5. Giving away cherished possessions: This can be a sign that the person knows he or she won't be around much longer.

6. Saying goodbyes: This may not be put into words, but if a person suddenly starts making visits to favorite people and places, it may mean he or she is saying goodbye.

7. A sudden increase in conflicts with authority and others: This can mean a person has stopped caring about consequences because he or she doesn't plan to be around to face them.

8. A sudden increase in drinking and/or drug use: This can mean that a person is becoming overwhelmed; in any case, it lowers the ability to cope with stress and resist impulses.

It is important to remember that all of these situational factors, lifestyle factors, and warning signs are merely indicators, and many of them have other explanations. They become most meaningful when several of them are seen together in a pattern.

CONCLUSION

There is a significant connection between substance abuse and suicide; other groups such as adolescents and elders are also at greater risk than average for suicide. Beyond these factors, this presentation discussed the suicidal state of mind, life situation factors, and lifestyle factors that increase the risk of suicide, and behavior patterns that can be warning signs that a person is considering suicide or has decided to take his or her own life. The next presentation in this program will discuss what clients can do if someone they know appears to be at risk for suicide.

REVIEW OF LEARNING GOALS

Upon completion of this presentation, participants should demonstrate:

1. Understanding of suicide factors and warning signs by listing, without notes or references, at least four factors in a person's life situation that would increase the risk of suicide.

2. Understanding of suicide factors and warning signs by listing, without notes or references, at least four factors in a person's lifestyle that would increase the risk of suicide.

3. Understanding of suicide factors and warning signs by listing, without notes or references, at least four warning signs that might indicate that a person was in increased danger of suicide.

QUESTIONS/DISCUSSION BEFORE POSTTEST

ADMINISTER POSTTEST

QUESTIONS/DISCUSSION AFTER POSTTEST

1. The Suicidal State of Mind: The following four factors are almost always present in suicide:

    a. Intense _____ _____.

    b. A belief that one cannot _____ this emotional pain.

    c. A feeling that there is no way to _____ the _____ except by dying.

    d. A feeling of being _____ , that _____ _____ understands
or cares very much.

    If any of these four factors is reduced or eliminated, the risk of suicide drops dramatically. This can happen in four ways:

    1) The emotional pain is _____.

    2) The person comes to believe that he or she _____ _____ the painful situation.

    3) The person comes to believe there is a way to reduce or end the emotional pain _____
_____ .

    4) The person comes to feel a strong _____ _____ to, and to feel
_____ by, another person or people.

2. Life Situation Factors: In general, the risk of suicide goes up in situations that increase the amount of change, stress, and/or emotional pain a person is experiencing, or that reduce his or her ability to cope with stress, or both. These types of situations include the following:

    a. _____or _____ of a serious _____ : This is the single highest situational risk factor for suicide.

    b. Severe _____ problems

    c. Loss of a _____, serious problems at _____ , or _____

    d. Recent _____ of a _____ _____ (especially if by suicide),
or an _____ of a _____

    e. Serious _____ or _____ _____ or _____

    f. Recent _____ _____

    g. Recent change of _____ (including _____)

    h. Recent change of _____ at work

3. Lifestyle Factors: There are a number of factors in a person's lifestyle that make him or her more vulnerable to stress and less capable of coping with difficulties, resulting in higher risk of suicide under any conditions but especially in high-stress situations like those just listed:

    a. Use of _____ and/or _____ _____

    b. _____ _____

    c. Working in a _____ - _____ job

    d. Frequent _____ with others

e. Owning or having easy access to _____

f. Engaging in _____ - _____ sports or other activities

4. Warning Signs: There are a number of common behavior patterns in people who are thinking about killing themselves, or who have decided to do so:

a. _____ or _____ about suicide or death: Always take this seriously and ask the person what he or she meant by the remark — getting the person to talk about it is more likely to keep him or her from acting on the idea than anything else you can do.

b. Frequent _____ , _____ , or _____ , followed by sudden of mood when the situation has not improved

c. Frequent _____

d. Making arrangements for _____ _____ _____

e. Giving away _____ _____

f. _____

g. A sudden increase in _____ with authority and others

h. A sudden increase in _____ and/or _____ _____

It is important to remember that all of these situational factors, lifestyle factors, and warning signs are merely indicators, and many of them have other explanations. They become most meaningful when several of them are seen together in a pattern.

In the next presentation in this program, we will discuss what to do if someone appears to be at high risk for suicide based on these factors.

Name: _____   Date: ____/____/____

Pretest/Posttest
Suicide Awareness and Prevention,
Part 1: Factors and Warning Signs

1. List four life situation factors that increase the risk of suicide:

_____

_____

_____

_____

2. List four lifestyle factors that increase the risk of suicide:

_____

_____

_____

_____

3. List four behaviors that may be warning signs that a person is considering or planning suicide:

_____

_____

_____

_____

Name: _____   Date: ____/____/____

Facilitator's Guide
Suicide Awareness and Prevention, Part 2: Prevention and Response

INTRODUCTION

Subject and Why It Is Important

Ask how many group members feel they have the knowledge and skills to effectively handle a potential or actual suicidal crisis in someone close to them. Review the facts mentioned in Part 1 that substance abusers are at higher than average risk for suicide, also that group members may have family members or friends that belong to other high-risk groups such as teenagers and seniors, and recall any relevant personal experiences participants described in Part 1. Note that whereas Part 1 taught participants about contributing factors and warning signs of suicidal risk, this presentation contains information about what participants can do if and when they see the signs they learned about in Part 1.

Group Policy

Explain to participants that they will be evaluated on their accomplishment of these goals.

LEARNING GOALS Upon completion of this presentation, participants should demonstrate understanding of suicide prevention strategies by listing, without notes or references, at least four actions they can take to safeguard a potentially suicidal person (someone who is considering or threatening suicide, makes a suicidal gesture, or attempts suicide) in the short term.

Upon completion of this presentation, participants should demonstrate understanding of suicide prevention strategies by listing, without notes or references, at least four actions they can take to permanently reduce the risk of suicide with a suicidal person after a short-term crisis has passed.

Upon completion of this presentation, participants should demonstrate understanding of suicide response strategies by listing, without notes or references, three actions they can take in response to a suicide attempt, gesture, or completed suicide to effectively help family members, friends, and coworkers of a suicidal person.

QUESTIONS As the presenter, you may ask participants to hold their questions until the end or to ask them at any time during the presentation. If participation is a high priority, we recommend allowing questions at any time; if brevity is more important, it works better to hold questions until the end.

PRETEST Pass out the pretest if you choose to use it, asking participants to fill out and turn in their answer sheets without putting names on them; tell them the posttest will be done at the end of the presentation.

Background and Lead-In

Recall the first question asked in the introduction to this presentation, about who feels they have the knowledge and skills to effectively handle a potential or actual suicidal crisis in someone close to them. Ask participants to recall what Part 1 said was the most common behavior pattern seen as a warning sign that someone was considering suicide: if no one responds with the correct warning sign, supply the answer that the most common warning behavior is talking about suicide either directly or in hints. Ask group members who they imagine the suicidal person would approach to talk about this; after getting feedback, answer that the typical suicidal person talks about it with people he or she trusts and feels close to, usually family members or close friends. Note that this means that the person who realizes the danger and needs to act will probably be someone like them, a family member or friend, rather than someone like the presenter, a trained professional.

Suggested analogy: Compare this with the fact that most of the time when a person is hurt physically, the first people on the scene are not doctors or nurses or paramedics, but family, friends, and neighbors, and that they can save a life by doing first aid that keeps the person intact until the trained professionals arrive. Conclude the lead-in by drawing the parallel that the aim of this presentation is not to make the group members trained psychologists or doctors, but to teach them mental and emotional first aid for suicide so they can keep a person intact until the trained professionals have a chance to do their part. Emphasize that this presentation is not meant to make the participants capable of handling a suicidal crisis on their own, but only to give them the tools to keep someone alive long enough to get them to professionals for more in-depth help.

SUICIDE PREVENTION AND RESPONSE STRATEGIES

Short-Term Strategies When Someone Is Considering or Threatening Suicide, Makes a Suicidal Gesture, or Attempts Suicide

First we will define these terms:

- Considering suicide means just that: it is a serious option a person may decide to act upon.
- A suicide threat is a statement not yet put into action.
- A suicidal gesture is an action that could be harmful, but is taken without the real belief that one will die as a result, such as shallow cuts on a wrist that don't reach any major blood vessels or a small overdose of a nonlethal medicine.
- A suicide attempt is an action taken with the sincere belief that one will die as a result, a genuine try at killing oneself. If the participants come to have a strong feeling that someone may be at risk for suicide, based on the information presented in Part 1, there are several things they should do:

1. Act on your concerns: The first thing you must do is choose to act on that feeling. Ask for reasons why a person might fail to say or do anything; write answers on the board, then discuss the following:
   a. Fear of embarrassment (what if I'm wrong and he or she laughs or gets mad?)
   b. Feeling someone else should do it (especially if you have little in common with the person)
   c. Feeling that people should be able to handle their own situations
   d. Fear of making a mistake and making it worse
   e. Hope it will get better without your needing to act

2. Ask directly and get them talking: A common fear is that talking about suicide may trigger someone to act, but this is not what happens. Actually, the more a person talks about it, the less likely he or she is to follow through with action. This seems to be partly because the fact that someone is listening in an accepting way reduces one of the four key mental states, the feeling of isolation and not being understood or accepted. It also seems to be partly because in talking about the situation, the person may see hope or options overlooked before. Some factors to keep in mind:
   a. Listening is the most important thing you can do, not coming up with answers. The motto here is "Get them talking and keep them talking."
   b. Don't argue, belittle the person's feelings, make comparisons, or try to use logic; none of these work, and any such response is likely to be seen as rejection. Just listen and make occasional comments reflecting what you heard or asking for clarification.

c. In as calm and matter-of-fact a way as possible, ask for details about the person's suicidal thinking. Do they have a specific method planned? Do they have the means? How lethal or dangerous is the method they have thought about? How quickly can they act on it? The more specific, lethal, and available their planned method, the more danger they are in. For example: A person who has thought about "ending it all" but has not come up with a specific plan is in much less danger than the person who replies that he would shoot himself with a pistol and that he has the loaded pistol in the glove compartment in his car.

3. Offer understanding encouragement: Don't tell the person he or she shouldn't feel that way, but do the following:

   a. Encourage the person to remember past hard times and how he or she got through them.

   b. Help the person remember situations where he or she is helpful to others and needed and loved by them.

   c. Let the person know that you're glad he or she told you, and that you believe this was a healthy way of trying to keep himself or herself safe.

4. Make it safe: If possible, persuade the person to turn over any weapons, and remove dangerous items such as broken glass or alcohol or other drugs. Set up safeguards to keep the person away from windows and balconies if on an upper floor.

5. Stay: If the person is actively thinking about suicide, *don't leave him or her alone!* Either call for professional help and wait until it arrives, or go with the person to a hospital or other place where you know he or she will be safe.

6. Make an anti-self-harm contract: Ask the person to agree that before acting on any desire to kill or hurt self, he or she will talk with you and/or a professional or crisis hotline worker. If possible, put this in writing and get the person to sign it.

Long-term Strategies for Reducing the Risk of Suicide

Once an immediate crisis is past, you may feel relief, but unless long-term change occurs, the risk may rise instead of diminishing. The person's problems are probably unchanged, and he or she may even feel embarrassment and a sense of failure at not having committed suicide. You can contribute to the kind of long-lasting change that really will reduce the danger by doing the following:

1. Stay in contact, keep checking back: Following through on your initial interest will go a long way to permanently break down that sense of isolation.

2. Get other friends and family involved: When you have heard about someone close to you having a serious problem, how did you feel? If you are like most of us, you wanted to help in some way. Others feel the same, and the caring they show will also reduce isolation.

3. Keep the person busy: Having something constructive to do keeps the mind busy so there is less time to dwell on problems and reduces the feeling of helplessness and uselessness to others that contributes to the risk of suicide.

4. Help the person stay clean and sober: Reducing or eliminating use of alcohol or other drugs will automatically lower suicide risk by a large margin.

5. Help the person learn needed skills: For example, if you know someone who has financial problems and never learned how to manage money, teaching him or her how to balance a checkbook and how to manage credit cards may do more good than years of counseling. The same can apply with communication skills, parenting skills, job skills, and so on.

6. Encourage basic self-care: Just getting proper rest, food, and exercise makes a big difference in ability to handle stress.

7. Encourage professional help: Counseling or therapy may be a big help in dealing with the underlying problems that trigger a suicidal crisis.

8. Encourage increased social activity: This will help keep the person busy and break down his or her emotional isolation.

Strategies for Effective Response to Help Friends, Family, and Coworkers after a Suicide Threat, Gesture, Attempt, or a Completed Suicide

If any participants have described being strongly affected by another's suicidal speech or actions, recall their experiences: if not, emphasize that suicide has a devastating and lasting impact on those left behind. They commonly experience many disturbing emotions and thoughts, including any of the following:

- Feelings of responsibility and self-blame
- Blaming others in the family/group
- Guilt
- Anger
- Hurt
- Shame
- Embarrassment
- Confusion
- Intensified grief
- Thoughts of suicide of their own

To minimize the negative impact on the other people affected, some simple steps are very helpful:

1. Encourage them to talk about their thoughts and feelings: This is especially important with children, who are even more likely than adults to blame themselves for what happens around them.
2. Encourage them to seek professional help if necessary: The people close to a suicide may need counseling of their own to overcome their emotional pain in the aftermath.
3. Emphasize supportive relationships: This helps others avoid the feelings of isolation that contribute to suicidal thinking and behavior.

CONCLUSION

In Part 2, we have covered effective actions to take as preventive measures and in response to a suicidal threat, gesture, attempt, or completed suicide, both for surviving suicidal individuals and for their friends, families, and coworkers.

REVIEW OF LEARNING GOALS

Upon completion of this presentation, participants should demonstrate:

1. Understanding of suicide prevention strategies by listing, without notes or references, at least four actions they can take to safeguard a potentially suicidal person (someone who is considering or threatening suicide, makes a suicidal gesture, or attempts suicide) in the short term.
2. Understanding of suicide prevention strategies by listing, without notes or references, at least four actions they can take to permanently reduce the risk of suicide with a suicidal person after a short-term crisis has passed.
3. Understanding of suicide response strategies by listing, without notes or references, three actions they can take in response to a suicide threat, gesture, attempt, or completed suicide to effectively help family members, friends, and coworkers of the suicidal person.

QUESTIONS/DISCUSSION BEFORE POSTTEST

ADMINISTER POSTTEST

QUESTIONS/DISCUSSION AFTER POSTTEST

Participant Handout
Suicide Awareness and Prevention, Part 2: Prevention and Response

1. Suicide Prevention and Response Strategies

    a. Short-term strategies when someone is considering or threatening suicide, makes a suicidal gesture, or attempts suicide:

    Definitions of these terms:

    _____ _____ means just that: treating it as a serious option a person may decide to act upon.

    A _____ _____ is a statement not yet put into action.

    A _____ _____ is an action that could be harmful, but is taken without the real belief that one will die as a result, such as shallow cuts on a wrist that don't reach any major blood vessels or a small overdose of a nonlethal medicine.

    A _____ _____ is an action taken with the sincere belief that one will die as a result, a genuine try at killing oneself. If the participants come to have a strong feeling that someone may be at risk for suicide, based on the information presented in Part 1, there are several things they should do:

    1) _____ on their concerns

    2) Ask _____ and get them _____ : A common fear is that talking about suicide may trigger someone to act, but actually, the more a person talks about it, the less likely he or she is to follow through with action.

    (a) _____ is the most important thing you can do, not coming up with answers. "Get them talking and keep them talking."

    (b) Don't _____, belittle the person's feelings, make comparisons, or try to _____ _____ .

    (c) In as calm and matter-of-fact a way as possible, ask for _____.

    3) Offer understanding encouragement:

    (a) Encourage the person to remember _____ _____ _____ and how he or she _____ _____ _____ .

    (b) Help the person remember situations where he or she is _____ to others and _____ and _____ by them.

    (c) Let the person know that you're glad he or she told you, and that you believe this was a healthy way of trying to keep himself or herself safe.

    4) _____ _____ _____ : If possible, persuade the person to turn over any weapons, and remove dangerous items such as broken glass or alcohol or other drugs. Set up safeguards to keep the person away from windows and balconies if on an upper floor.

    5) _____ _____ _____ : If the person is actively thinking about suicide, don't leave him or her alone! Either call for professional help and wait until it arrives, or take the person to a hospital or other safe place.

    6) Make an anti-self-harm _____ : Ask him or her to agree that before acting on any desire to kill or hurt self, he or she will talk with you and/or a professional or crisis hotline worker. If possible, put this in writing and get the person to sign it.

b. Long-term strategies for reducing the risk of suicide: Once an immediate crisis is past, you may feel relief, but unless long-term change occurs, the risk may rise instead of diminishing. The person's problems are probably unchanged, and he or she may even feel embarrassment and a sense of failure at not having committed suicide. You can contribute to the kind of long-lasting change that really will reduce the danger by doing the following:

1. _____ _____ _____ , keep checking back.

2. Get other _____ and _____ involved.

3. Get them _____ and keep them _____ .

4. Help them stay _____ and _____ .

5. Help them _____ _____ they need.

6. Encourage _____ _____ - _____ .

7. Encourage seeking _____ _____ .

8. Encourage increased _____ _____ .

2. Strategies for Effective Response to Help Friends, Family, and Coworkers After a Suicide Threat, Gesture, Attempt, or Completed Suicide: Suicide has a devastating and lasting impact on those left behind. They commonly experience many disturbing emotions and thoughts, including any of the following:

Feelings of _____ and _____ - _____

_____ others in the family/group

Guilt

_____

Hurt

_____

Embarrassment

Confusion

Intensified grief

Thoughts of _____ of their own

To minimize negative impacts on others affected, some simple steps are very helpful:

a. Encourage them to _____ _____ _____ _____

and _____ : This is especially important with children.

b. Encourage them to seek professional help if necessary.

c. Emphasize _____ relationships.

Name: _____ Date: ____/____/____

Pretest/Posttest
Suicide Awareness and Prevention,
Part 2: Prevention and Response

1. List four effective short-term actions you could take to safeguard someone at risk of suicide and who has made a suicide threat, gesture, or attempt:

_____

_____

_____

_____

_____

_____

_____

_____

_____

2. List four effective longer-term actions you could take to permanently reduce the risk of suicide for someone who has made a suicide threat, gesture, or attempt:

_____

_____

_____

_____

_____

_____

_____

_____

_____

3. List three effective actions you could take to help friends, family members, and coworkers of a person who threatened suicide, made a suicidal gesture or attempt, or committed suicide:

_____

_____

_____

_____

_____

_____

Name: _____   Date: ____/____/____

INTRODUCTION

Subject and Why It Is Important

Start with a practical example: Pass out blank pieces of paper to participants. On another piece of paper, write "make a paper airplane" and hold it up toward the participants too quickly for them to read it. Whisper the same words too quietly to be heard clearly while facing away from the class. Turn around, wait about 30 seconds, then ask the group, "What's the matter, don't any of you like airplanes?" Wait another 30 seconds and say "Why aren't you doing what you're supposed to do?" After a few more seconds, announce "Everybody failed," and walk out of the room.

Return to the room and ask the participants what they are thinking and feeling about what has just happened; write their answers on a board, flip chart, or transparency sheet. Then tell the group that they were supposed to make paper airplanes out of the sheets of paper they received. Ask how many participants are capable of making a paper airplane, are willing to make a paper airplane, and want to succeed in this program. Then ask why they failed to do so. They, of course, will point out that the presenter didn't tell them what to do. Reply that the presenter did indeed give them written and verbal instructions. They will reply along the lines that they weren't given enough time to read the instructions and that the verbal instructions were not audible.

Acknowledge that the task was indeed impossible short of psychic powers as it was presented. Point out that the presenter knew exactly what the participants were supposed to do and was thinking about it; note that the problem was not inability or unwillingness or that the presenter didn't express the information, but that the information was not given in a clear and understandable form. Then ask how many times the participants have seen anger and frustration result when someone failed to communicate clearly what he or she wanted others to do. Ask how many participants think this could lead to stress and relationship problems. Ask how many think stress and relationship problems could affect recovery from alcoholism and addiction.

Group Policy

Explain to participants that they will be evaluated on their accomplishment of these goals.

LEARNING GOALS Upon completion of this presentation, participants should demonstrate understanding of communication skills by listing, without notes or references, the four necessary basic elements of the communication process.

Upon completion of this presentation, participants should demonstrate understanding of communication skills by listing, without notes or references, four skills related to effective communication.

Upon completion of this presentation, participants should demonstrate understanding of communication skills by demonstrating use of a specific active listening and feedback process.

QUESTIONS As the presenter, you may ask participants to hold their questions until the end or to ask them at any time during the presentation. If participation is a high priority, we recommend allowing questions at any time; if brevity is more important, it works better to hold questions until the end.

PRETEST Pass out the pretest if you choose to use it, asking participants to fill out and turn in their answer sheets without putting names on them; tell them the posttest will be done at the end of the presentation.

Background and Lead-In

Refer to the introductory exercise and restate that this was an example of poor communication. Ask the following discussion questions, write participants' answers on a board, flip chart, or transparency sheet, and facilitate brief discussion: "What are some forms of communication?" (Possibilities include verbal, through choice of words and manner of speaking; written; nonverbal, including facial expressions, gestures, posture, and other actions; and omission, or what is not said, written, or done.) "What are some causes of poor communication?" (Possibilities include language differences, failure to listen, poor expression of ideas, expectations of mind reading, fear of speaking directly, lack of desire to communicate, and deliberate dishonesty.)

COMMUNICATION SKILLS

Basic Elements of the Communication Process

Present items 1–4 below, then ask participants for examples of how these might be lacking; discuss.

1. Sender: The sender must have a message and the desire and ability to send it. Lack of a sender with all of those factors makes communication impossible.
2. Receiver: The receiver must have the willingness and ability to receive the message. Lack of a receiver with these traits also makes communication impossible.
3. Message: The message must contain information in a form having a meaning known to both sender and receiver. If the message lacks information, is in a form that is not understandable to both parties, or has different meanings to the two parties, accurate communication will not take place.
4. Medium: The medium must be accessible to both sender and receiver; if it is not, the message cannot be carried from one to the other.

Guidelines for Effective Communication

1. Stay as positive as practical:
   a. Avoid name-calling.
   b. Avoid sarcasm.
   c. Avoid yelling, threatening, and intimidation.
   d. Separate criticism of actions from attacks on people.
   e. When possible, offer solutions.
   f. Use the "sandwich method" for criticism or correction—say something positive, then offer the criticism or other information likely to be perceived as negative, then finish with another positive statement. Example: A shop teacher says to a student: "I like the energy and enthusiasm you bring to this class. I would like you to be more careful, because this morning when you were so eager to get to work on your project, you didn't put on your safety goggles before you started using the drill press. However, I know you try really hard to do things the right way and you're a fast learner, so I have a lot of confidence that you'll remember and not make that mistake again."
2. Be clear and specific:
   a. Make your point clearly—ask for what you want, tell how you feel.
   b. Avoid saying people "always" or "never" do things.
   c. If you quote someone's words, be accurate.
   d. If you talk about other's actions, give times, dates, and places.
   e. Avoid exaggeration.

    f. Stick to what's relevant.

    g. Ask for feedback—"Please tell me what you understood me to say."

    h. Rephrase/restate your message if necessary until the other understands.

3. Talk from your own point of view:

    a. No mind-reading or attribution of motives or feelings to others—"Just the facts ma'am"; avoid saying things like "you just think that . . ." or "you just wanted to . . ."

    b. Own your own feelings—no "you made me mad/sad/etc."

    c. Use "I" statements.

    d. Avoid statements like "I know how you feel," "You know . . ."

4. Keep conversation a two-way process:

    a. Don't monopolize.

    b. Stop often enough to let others respond while they can remember what's on their minds.

    c. Make one point at a time.

5. Stay on the subject:

    a. Organize your thoughts in a clear order before starting.

    b. Discuss one topic at a time.

    c. Don't bring up already settled incidents and issues.

    d. Avoid "kitchen-sinking" (bringing up every problem and issue you have with the other person all in the same conversation).

6. Be a good listener:

    a. Listen with full attention, rather than rehearsing your next words.

    b. Actively listen—attend to posture, tone, expression, as well as words.

    c. Don't interrupt.

    d. Ask questions when you aren't sure you understand something.

    e. Give feedback—paraphrase message back to sender, and ask if you understood the meaning correctly; if not, ask for a restatement.

A Structured Communication Process: Active Listening and Feedback

Explain that this process is used to discuss subjects that are likely to cause strong emotions. When it was taught to couples in a premarital communication skills course, it resulted in graduating couples having a divorce rate over 10 years that is 50% lower than average.

1. Preparation:

    a. Agree to discuss an issue at a time when both are prepared to do so.

    b. Decide who will be the sender (speaker) first and who will be the receiver (listener).

2. Procedure:

    a. The speaker speaks: He or she makes a brief (one- or two-sentence) statement, on one topic, being specific and using the A-B-C format (event, result, emotions: "When you did A, B happened, and I felt C.").

    b. The receiver listens closely without interrupting while the sender speaks, then gives feedback, that is, responds by rephrasing the sender's message in the receiver's own words and asking whether it is accurate—this doesn't mean the receiver is agreeing, just that he or she understands! During this stage, the receiver doesn't respond, explain, or argue. His or her turn is coming to present the other side.

    c. The sender responds to the receiver's feedback: If it is accurate, the sender says so. If it is inaccurate or incomplete, the sender restates any part that wasn't understood, and the receiver responds again.

    d. Switch places once the receiver gives accurate feedback to the sender, and repeat the process.

3. Things to avoid in this process:

    a. "You" statements—"you always," "you never," "you made me . . ."

    b. Attacks—yelling, name-calling.

    c. Stating thoughts as feelings—"I feel that . . ." is not a feeling! Feelings are emotions, not views or opinions.

4. Results: People report the following experiences with this method:

    a. Less frustration—both people feel they have been heard

    b. Getting communication out of argument ruts

    c. Clearing up or avoiding misunderstandings

    d. Avoiding angry blowups

    e. Greater empathy both ways

CONCLUSION

This presentation has provided information on communication skills to help participants avoid stress and relationship problems that would lower their quality of life and make it harder to stay clean and sober. We have covered the elements of the communication process, effective communication skills, and a structured communication method using active listening and feedback to discuss emotional subjects without getting into fights.

REVIEW OF LEARNING GOALS

Upon completion of this presentation, participants should demonstrate:

1. Understanding of communication skills by listing, without notes or references, the four necessary basic elements of the communication process.
2. Understanding of communication skills by listing, without notes or references, four skills related to effective communication.
3. Understanding of communication skills by demonstrating use of a specific active listening and feedback process.

QUESTIONS/DISCUSSION BEFORE POSTTEST

ADMINISTER POSTTEST

QUESTIONS/DISCUSSION AFTER POSTTEST

1. Basic Elements of the Communication Process:

    a. _____ : The sender must have a message and the desire and _____ to send it. Lack of a sender with all of those factors makes communication impossible.

    b. _____ : The receiver must have the _____ and ability to receive the message. Lack of a receiver with these traits also makes communication impossible.

    c. _____ : The message must contain _____ in a form having a meaning known to both sender and receiver. If the message lacks information, is in a form that is not understandable to both parties, or has different meanings to the two parties, accurate communication will not take place.

    d. _____ : The medium must be accessible to both _____ and _____ ; if it is not, the message cannot be carried from one to the other.

2. Guidelines for Effective Communication:

    a. Stay as _____ as practical:

        1) Avoid _____ - _____ .

        2) Avoid _____ .

        3) Avoid _____ , _____ , and intimidation.

        4) Separate criticism of _____ from attacks on _____ .

        5) When possible, offer _____ .

        6) Use the " _____ method" for criticism or correction—say something positive, then offer the criticism or other information likely to be perceived as negative, then finish with another positive statement.

    b. Be _____ and specific:

        1) Make your point _____ —ask for what you want, tell how you feel.

        2) Avoid saying people " _____ " or " _____ " do things.

        3) If you quote someone's words, be _____ .

        4) If you talk about other's actions, give _____ , _____ , and _____ .

        5) Avoid _____ .

        6) Stick to what's _____ .

        7) Ask for _____ —"Please tell me what you understood me to say."

        8) Rephrase/restate your message if necessary until _____ _____ _____ .

    c. Talk from your own _____ _____ _____ :

        1) No _____ - _____ or attribution of motives or feelings to others—"just the facts, ma'am"; avoid saying things like "you just think that . . ." or "you just wanted to . . ."

        2) _____ your own _____ —no "you made me mad/sad/etc."

        3) Use " _____ " statements.

        4) Avoid statements like "I know _____ _____ _____ ," "you know . . ."

    d. Keep conversation a _____ - _____ process:

        1) Don't _____ .

        2) Stop often enough to let others _____ while they can remember what's on their minds.

        3) Make _____ _____ at a time.

e. Stay on the _____ :

    1) _____ your thoughts in a clear order before starting.

    2) Discuss _____ at a time.

    3) Don't bring up _____ - _____ incidents and issues.

    4) Avoid " _____ - _____ " (bringing up every problem and issue you have with the other person all in the same conversation).

f. Be a _____ :

    1) Listen with _____ _____ , rather than rehearsing your next words.

    2) _____ —attend to posture, tone, expression, as well as words.

    3) Don't _____ .

    4) _____ when you aren't sure you understand something.

    5) Give _____ —paraphrase message back to sender, and ask if you understood the meaning correctly; if not, ask them to restate.

3. A Structured Communication Process: Active Listening and Feedback

a. _____ :

    1) Agree to discuss an issue at a time when both are prepared to do so.

    2) Decide who will be the sender (speaker) first and who will be the receiver (listener).

b. _____ :

    1) The sender speaks: He/she makes a brief (one- or two-sentence) statement, on one topic, being specific and using the A-B-C format (event, result, emotions: "When you did A, B happened, and I felt C.").

    2) The receiver listens closely without interrupting while the sender speaks, then gives feedback, that is, responds by rephrasing the sender's message in the receiver's own words and asking whether it is accurate—*this doesn't mean the receiver is agreeing, just that he or she understands!* During this stage, the receiver doesn't respond, explain, or argue. His or her turn is coming to present the other side.

    3) The sender responds to the receiver's feedback: If it is accurate, the sender says so. If it is inaccurate or incomplete, the sender restates any part that wasn't understood, and the receiver responds again.

    4) Switch places once the receiver gives accurate feedback to the sender, and repeat the process.

c. Things to _____ in this process:

    1) "You" statements—"you always", "you never," "you made me . . ."

    2) Attacks—yelling, name-calling.

    3) Stating thoughts as feelings—"I feel that . . ." is not a feeling! Feelings are emotions, not views or opinions.

d. Results: People report the following experiences with this method:

    1) Less frustration—both people feel they have been heard.

    2) Getting communication out of argument ruts.

    3) Clearing up or avoiding misunderstandings.

    4) Avoiding angry blow-ups.

    5) Greater empathy both ways.

Pretest/Posttest
Communication Skills

1. List the four elements of the communication process that must be present for any communication to exist: _____ , _____ , _____ , and _____ .

2. List four techniques of effective communication: _____

_____

_____

_____

_____

_____

_____

_____

_____

3. Describe active listening and feedback as you understand them: _____

_____

_____

_____

_____

_____

_____

_____

_____

_____

_____

_____

_____

_____

_____

_____

_____

_____

Name: _____ Date: ____/____/____

Facilitator's Guide
Dual Diagnosis

INTRODUCTION

Subject and Why It Is Important

Ask participants to think of the challenges and difficulties they are coming to see connected with overcoming substance abuse problems, then ask them to think instead about the problems facing people who are mentally ill. Then ask them to consider what life is like for people who face both problems together. State that this is commonly called dual diagnosis, and that many people are dually diagnosed.

If there are any group participants who have dual diagnoses, their experiences may be helpful if they are willing to share them and if, in their therapists' judgment, this would not be detrimental for those clients. These questions should be investigated ahead of time, so that if you want to ask these clients to talk about their experiences with dual diagnoses, you have cleared it with their therapists and talked with the clients about it in advance. If you have dual diagnosis clients in this group and you ask them to share their experiences, allow them each a few minutes to talk and answer questions. It has been our experience that this can be a strongly therapeutic experience for these clients because of the impact of the interest, support, and acceptance of their fellow group members; but, again, this should be considered with caution.

Tell the group that this presentation will contain information about how substance abuse problems interact with some common mental disorders. Tell them that the purpose of this information is to enable them to cope more effectively with dual diagnosis situations if they face them themselves or if someone they know is in this situation.

Group Policy

Explain to participants that they will be evaluated on their accomplishment of these goals.

LEARNING GOALS Upon completion of this presentation, participants should demonstrate basic awareness of common mental disorders by listing, without notes or references, at least four common mental disorders that frequently coexist with substance abuse problems.

Upon completion of this presentation, participants should demonstrate basic knowledge of ways substance abuse and mental illness can be connected by listing, without notes or references, at least four ways one of these problems can cause or intensify the other.

Upon completion of this presentation, participants should demonstrate basic knowledge of specific patterns of dual diagnosis by matching, without notes or references, at least four common mental disorders with the types of psychoactive drugs most commonly abused by people suffering from those mental disorders.

QUESTIONS As the presenter, you may ask participants to hold their questions until the end or to ask them at any time during the presentation. If participation is a high priority, we recommend allowing questions at any time; if brevity is more important, it works better to hold questions until the end.

PRETEST Pass out the pretest if you choose to use it, asking participants to fill out and turn in their answer sheets without putting names on them; tell them the posttest will be done at the end of the presentation.

Background and Lead-In

Ask clients for their estimates as to what percentage of the population suffers significant effects of mental disorders sometime during their lives, then the same question about substance abuse disorders. Tell them that according to a national survey in 1990, both categories were at approximately 20% of the population.

Next, give them the following statistics: According to the same study, among those diagnosed with serious mental illnesses, 29% also had drug or alcohol problems, and of those who had substance abuse disorders, 53% also suffered from psychiatric disorders; other studies reported even higher percentages for people with both types of problems. Finally, note that among people in prisons, mental hospitals (both over 80%, meaning that of people having either mental illnesses or substance abuse problems, over 80% also had the other type of problem), and nursing homes (over 60%), the percentage of dual diagnosis patients is higher yet. In summary, this is a widespread problem that causes even greater devastation to its victims' lives than either mental illness alone or substance abuse alone.

DUAL DIAGNOSIS

Common Mental Disorders That Often Coexist with Substance Abuse and Dependence

1. Mood disorders: These are mental disorders in which a person's moods are disturbed to a degree that interferes with his or her life. The disturbance is in the form of general moods that are either too "high" or too "low." The most common examples are what was formerly called manic depression, now called bipolar disorders, and depression.

2. Anxiety disorders: These are similar to mood disorders, except that instead of the person's mood being generally too far up or down, the person's life is disrupted by feelings that are specifically anxious or fearful. Common examples include panic attacks, obsessive-compulsive disorder, and posttraumatic stress disorder (PTSD).

3. Thought disorders: In a thought disorder, either the person's beliefs and thinking processes are impaired, which is called being delusional, or his or her sensory experiences are distorted (hallucinations), such as hearing imaginary voices or seeing things that aren't there. The most common form of thought disorder is schizophrenia.

4. Personality disorders: A personality disorder is a distorted and dysfunctional style of relating to others, the self, and the world. The example most commonly found coexisting with abuse of alcohol and other drugs is antisocial personality disorder, which, as its name indicates, is demonstrated by actions that consistently show disregard for law, consequences, and the rights and feelings of other people.

How Substance Abuse and Mental Illness Affect Each Other

1. Substance abuse can induce mental illness: Sometimes the use of alcohol and other drugs contributes to mental illness. This can happen in more than one way:

   a. Increased vulnerability: People under the influence of alcohol and other drugs are much more likely than sober people to get into dangerous situations, and less capable of coping with those situations when they happen. This can lead to traumatic experiences that contribute to mental illness.

   b. Direct causation: Drugs can also directly create forms of mental illness, such as psychosis induced by various drugs, especially hallucinogens and stimulants. When you consider that the definition of psychosis describes it as distortion in thinking, sensory perception, or both, and consider that drugs often cause exactly those effects, you can say that drugs cause temporary psychosis, which under some conditions can become permanent.

2. Mental illness can induce substance abuse: Different forms of mental illness often lead to substance abuse either because the person is self-medicating, seeking relief of symptoms of mental illness, or because the mental illness leads the person to pleasure-seeking or thrill-seeking behavior without regard for consequences; this behavior often includes drinking and other forms of drug use.

3. Other factors can induce both substance abuse and mental illness:

   a. Heredity: Research shows strong indications of hereditary factors in both substance abuse and mental illness. Some people may be more likely to have both problems because they are "programmed" that way by genetics, by their childhood family environments, or by a combination of both.

   b. Other causes: Traumatic experiences can sometimes create conditions that incline people toward both substance abuse and mental illness. For example, a person who was severely injured in a traffic accident could, as a result, experience both PTSD due to the emotional impact of the experience, and chronic severe physical pain from injuries, which could lead to substance abuse as a form of self-medication for pain.

4. Dual diagnosis makes treating both problems more difficult:

   a. Combination of symptoms: Because the symptoms of both problems can combine to create more problems and make them worse than would be the case with either substance abuse or mental illness alone, the combination is harder to treat, and relapse into both types of problems is a greater problem. Each problem can also conceal and distort symptoms of the other and make accurate diagnosis and treatment more confusing.

   b. Training of therapists: Many treatment professionals are trained to provide either substance abuse therapy or mental health therapy, but not both, so the person may have to be treated by more than one professional.

   c. Program policies: Reflecting the same split in thinking as the training of therapists just mentioned, many treatment programs address one problem or the other, but not both, again leading to the client's having to seek treatment from more than one source.

Patterns of Dual Diagnosis

Certain types of mental illness are most often found together with the abuse of certain types of drugs; also, some types of mental illness are more likely to coexist with substance abuse than others.

1. Mood disorders: People suffering from depression and bipolar disorders most often abuse stimulants as a form of self-medication. Of all the people surveyed who were diagnosed with any mood disorder, 32% also had diagnoses of chemical dependence or abuse; for bipolar disorder sufferers in particular, this figure was over 60%.

2. Thought disorders: People suffering from schizophrenia and related disorders most often abuse illegal drugs of various kinds; the fact that the drugs are illicit seems to be the common factor. Forty-seven percent of schizophrenics are also diagnosable with substance abuse disorders.

3. Anxiety disorders: PTSD sufferers and others with anxiety disorders abuse alcohol and other depressant drugs more often than other types of drugs, like those with mood disorders as a way of self-medicating their distressing symptoms. For all anxiety disorder sufferers surveyed, the rate of dual diagnosis was around 24%.

4. Antisocial personality disorders: People with this disorder tend to be thrill-seekers who abuse opiates such as heroin and stimulants like methamphetamine, amphetamines, and cocaine, and over 83% have dual diagnoses.

What We Can Do about Dual Diagnosis

The most effective approach seems to be to integrate treatment for both problems at once, and to integrate treatment with other activities such as participation in Alcoholics Anonymous or other community support groups. If you suffer from a dual diagnosis, you can get better treatment by doing the following:

1. Keep treatment professionals informed: Make sure that when you deal with a doctor, therapist, or other professional, you tell him or her about both your mental illness diagnosis and your substance abuse disorder.
2. Get integrated treatment: If possible, seek treatment programs and professionals that work with both issues in an integrated way.

CONCLUSION

Dual diagnosis, or the experience by one person of both a serious mental illness and a substance abuse problem, affects a substantial portion of the population and can intensify the problems and suffering of those who experience this as well as others affected by those people. Dual diagnosis can also make therapy more difficult for both problems. This presentation has briefly discussed some common mental disorders that often coexist with substance abuse problems, some ways substance abuse and mental illness can be connected, patterns in dual diagnosis, and information about what treatment approaches seem most effective.

REVIEW OF LEARNING GOALS

Upon completion of this presentation, participants should demonstrate:

1. Basic awareness of common mental disorders by listing, without notes or references, at least four common mental disorders that frequently coexist with substance abuse problems.
2. Basic knowledge of ways substance abuse and mental illness can be connected by listing, without notes or references, at least four ways one of these problems can cause or intensify the other.
3. Basic knowledge of specific patterns of dual diagnosis by matching, without notes or references, at least four common mental disorders with the types of psychoactive drugs most commonly abused by people suffering from those mental disorders.

QUESTIONS/DISCUSSION BEFORE POSTTEST

ADMINISTER POSTTEST

QUESTIONS/DISCUSSION AFTER POSTTEST

1. Common Mental Disorders That Often Coexist with Substance Abuse and Dependence:
    a. _____ disorders: These are mental disorders in which a person's moods are disturbed to a degree that interferes with his or her life. The disturbance is in the form of general moods that are either too "high" or too "low." The most common examples are what were formerly called manic depression, now called disorders _____ , and _____ .

    b. _____ disorders: These are similar to mood disorders, except that instead of the person's mood being generally too far up or down, the person's life is disrupted by feelings that are specifically _____ or _____ . Common examples include _____ attacks, obsessive-compulsive disorder, and posttraumatic stress disorder (PTSD).

    c. _____ disorders: In a thought disorder, either the person's beliefs and thinking processes are _____ , which is called being delusional, or his or her _____ experiences are distorted, with these distortions being what we call _____ , such as hearing imaginary voices or seeing things that aren't really there. The most common form of thought disorder is _____ .

    d. Personality disorders: A personality disorder is a distorted and dysfunctional style of _____ to _____ , the _____ , and the world. The example most commonly found coexisting with abuse of alcohol and other drugs is _____ personality disorder, which, as its name indicates, is demonstrated by actions that consistently show disregard for law, consequences, and the rights and feelings of other people.

2. How Substance Abuse and Mental Illness Affect Each Other:
    a. Substance abuse can _____ mental illness: Sometimes the use of alcohol and other drugs contributes to mental illness. This can happen in more than one way:

    1) Increased _____ : People under the influence of alcohol and other drugs are much more likely than sober people to get into _____ situations, and less capable of coping with those situations when they happen. This can lead to traumatic experiences which contribute to mental illness.

    2) _____ causation: Drugs can also directly create forms of mental illness, such as _____ induced by various drugs, especially hallucinogens and stimulants. When you consider that the definition of psychosis describes it as distortion in thinking, sensory perception, or both, and consider that drugs often cause exactly those effects, you can say that drugs cause temporary psychosis, which under some conditions can become permanent.

    b. Mental illness can induce substance abuse: Different forms of mental illness often lead to substance abuse either because the person is _____ , seeking _____ of symptoms of mental illness, or because the mental illness leads the person to pleasure-seeking or thrill-seeking behavior without regard for _____ ; this behavior often includes drinking and other forms of drug use.

    c. Other factors can induce both substance abuse and mental illness:

    1) _____ : Research shows strong indications of hereditary factors in both substance abuse and mental illness. Some people may be more likely to have both problems because they are "programmed" that way by genetics, by their childhood family environments, or by a combination of both.

2) Other causes: _____ _____ can sometimes create conditions that incline people toward both substance abuse and mental illness. For example, a person who was severely injured in a traffic accident could, as a result, experience both PTSD due to the emotional impact of the experience and chronic severe physical pain from injuries, which could lead to substance abuse as a form of self-medication for pain.

     d. Dual diagnosis makes treating both problems _____ _____:

       1) Combination of symptoms: Because the symptoms of both problems can combine to create more problems and make them worse than would be the case with either substance abuse or mental illness alone, the combination is harder to treat, and _____ into both types of problems is a greater problem. Each problem can also _____ and _____ symptoms of the other and make accurate diagnosis and treatment more confusing.

       2) _____ of therapists: Many treatment professionals are trained to provide either substance abuse therapy or mental health therapy, but not both, so the person may have to be treated by more than one professional.

       3) Program policies: Reflecting the same split in thinking as the training of therapists just mentioned, many treatment programs address one problem or the other, but not both, again leading to the client having to seek treatment from more than one source.

3. Patterns of Dual Diagnosis: Certain types of mental illness are most often found together with the abuse of certain types of drugs; also, some types of mental illness are more likely to coexist with substance abuse than others.

     a. Mood disorders: People suffering from depression and bipolar disorders most often abuse _____ as a form of self-medication. Of all the people surveyed who were diagnosed with any mood disorder, 32% also had diagnoses of chemical dependence or abuse; for bipolar disorder sufferers in particular, this figure was over 60%.

     b. Thought disorders: People suffering from schizophrenia and related disorders most often abuse _____ drugs of various kinds; the fact that the drugs are illicit seems to be the common factor. Forty-seven percent of schizophrenics are also diagnosable with substance abuse disorders.

     c. Anxiety disorders: PTSD sufferers and others with anxiety disorders abuse alcohol and other _____ drugs more often than other types of drugs, like those with mood disorders as a way of self-medicating their distressing symptoms. For all anxiety disorder sufferers surveyed, the rate of dual diagnosis was around 24%.

     d. Antisocial personality disorders: People with this disorder tend to be thrill-seekers who abuse _____ such as heroin and _____ like methamphetamine, amphetamines, and cocaine, and over 83% have dual diagnoses.

4. What We Can Do About Dual Diagnosis: The most effective approach seems to be to integrate treatment for both problems at once, and to integrate treatment with other activities such as participation in _____ _____ or other _____ _____ _____ .
If you suffer from a dual diagnosis, you can get better treatment by doing the following:

     a. Keep treatment professionals _____: Make sure that when you deal with a doctor, therapist, or other professional, you tell him or her about both your mental illness diagnosis and your substance abuse disorder.

     b. Get _____ treatment: If possible, seek treatment programs and professionals that work with both issues in an integrated way.

Name: _____   Date: ____/____/____

Pretest/Posttest
Dual Diagnosis

1. List four common mental disorders that frequently coexist with substance abuse problems:

_____

_____

_____

_____

_____

_____

_____

_____

2. List four ways one of these problems (substance abuse/dependence and mental illness) can cause or intensify the other:

_____

_____

_____

_____

_____

_____

_____

_____

3. Match the following common mental disorders with the types of psychoactive drugs most commonly abused by people suffering from those mental disorders:

Mood disorders (depression, bipolar disorder)	Alcohol and other depressants
Thought disorders (schizophrenia)	Stimulants
Anxiety disorders (panic attacks, PTSD)	Illicit drugs of any kind
Antisocial personality disorder	Opiates

Name: _____   Date: ____/____/____

Facilitator's Guide
Codependency and Addictive Relationships

INTRODUCTION

Subject and Why It Is Important

Ask participants for their definition of the term "codependency." Write answers on a board, flip chart, or transparency sheet. Then offer this definition: *Codependency is a pattern of trying to control others for their own good, which ends up being bad for oneself and the relationship.* Compare with answers on board, looking for common points. Ask group members what kinds of actions would be examples of codependent behaviors; briefly discuss answers. Finally, ask group members how this might affect their ability to remain clean and sober; briefly discuss answers.

Group Policy

Explain to participants that they will be evaluated on their accomplishment of these goals.

LEARNING GOALS Upon completion of this presentation, participants should demonstrate understanding of codependency by listing, without notes or references, at least four typical codependent behavior patterns and at least four healthy relationship behaviors as counterparts to those codependent behavior patterns.

   Upon completion of this presentation, participants should demonstrate understanding of codependency and addictive relationships by listing, without notes or references, at least three sources of information and help for people seeking to change codependent behavior patterns into healthy patterns.

QUESTIONS As the presenter, you may ask participants to hold their questions until the end or to ask them at any time during the presentation. If participation is a high priority, we recommend allowing questions at any time; if brevity is more important, it works better to hold questions until the end.

PRETEST Pass out the pretest if you choose to use it, asking participants to fill out and turn in their answer sheets without putting names on them; tell them the posttest will be done at the end of the presentation.

Background and Lead-In

Refer to the impact of codependency on recovery, as briefly discussed in the introduction. State that codependent behavior by family and friends, though well-intentioned, can contribute to continued drinking/drug use and to relapse once a person does give up alcohol and other drugs. State that this presentation's aim is to provide information so that group members and their families and friends can avoid this trap in present and future relationships.

CODEPENDENCY

What Causes Codependency?

In the definition above, we said that *Codependency is a pattern of trying to control others for their own good, which ends up being bad for oneself and the relationship.* The key phrase regarding cause is "for their own good." When codependents engage in the behaviors we will discuss in a moment, they are trying to help the alcoholics, addicts, or other compulsive people with whom they are in relationships. The roots of codependency are often in the following feelings and beliefs:

1. The desire to help
2. A sense of responsibility, usually caused by feeling that something needs to be done and no one else is doing it
3. A belief that the alcoholic or addict is not capable of getting along without the codependent
4. A belief that it is important to protect the image of the family, the couple, and/or the other person by hiding problems
5. A belief that the codependent can change another person and a sense of having both the right and the duty to do so
6. A feeling that the codependent has no right to say no or to withhold help
7. Self-esteem based on doing things for others
8. A feeling of superiority and strength when the codependent rescues others or cleans up after them

Typical Codependent Behavior Patterns and Healthy Counterparts

1. Enabling/rescuing—protecting the addiction: The codependent often goes to great lengths to clean up after the alcoholic or addict and rescue him or her from the consequences of addictive behavior. The effect is to make it easy and convenient to keep on behaving the same way, which means this actually delays the sick person's getting uncomfortable enough to change. *The healthy counterpart* to this is to let others deal with their own problems as much as possible.
2. Overresponsibility and martyrdom: The codependent often takes on responsibility for the actions, feelings, and thoughts of others, then feels as if he or she is being victimized by the problems those others create. *The healthy counterpart* to this is to take responsibility for oneself and expect other adults, and children as far as is reasonable to do the same.
3. Manipulation and control: A natural result of feeling responsible for others is a tendency to try to control their behavior, either without letting them know (manipulation) or by direct command (control). *The healthy counterpart* to this is mutual respect and self-determination, with partners openly asking for what they want and accepting the other's decision rather than trying to trick or bully the partner into acting as they wish.
4. Parentification of children: Children in these families tend to grow up early, especially older children, and end up taking care of adults much of the time. *The healthy counterpart* to this is for adults to handle their responsibilities and let children be children without dealing with adult concerns.
5. Isolation and family secrets: The belief that the family's image must be protected leads to restricting contacts with "outsiders" and teaching children to "keep things in the family" even when they are obviously problems with which the family needs help. *The healthy counterpart* to this is a balance between privacy and openness, with the freedom to go outside the family for help if necessary and healthy friendships outside the family.
6. Denial and "no-talk" rules: Even within the family, many subjects are off-limits, and often the codependent will not acknowledge even obvious problems, leading to the "elephant in the living room" syndrome (a huge problem no one talks about because no one wants to bring it up, but everyone sees it and has to keep walking around it). *The healthy counterpart* to this is for all family members to feel free to bring up problems and concerns and talk about them.
7. Resentment and self-pity: Because the codependent is doing so much for others (whether they want it or not) and feels unappreciated, he or she often comes to feel burned out, resentful, and self-pitying. *The healthy counterpart* to this is a refusal to take on others' responsibilities, thus avoiding these reactions.
8. Undermining of recovery: Although the codependent may say, and believe, that he or she wants the recovery of the alcoholic or addicted partner very much, when this starts to happen the codependent may (without realizing it) act in ways that undermine the recovery and push the other back toward addictive behaviors. *The healthy counterpart* to this is to treat recovery as a team effort and work on one's own issues while being supportive of positive changes in others.

Sources of Information, Help, and Support for Healthy Change

1. Therapy: Either group, couple, or individual therapy or counseling may be a big help in identifying codependent patterns in one's life and learning healthy behaviors to change those patterns.

2. 12-Step groups: Just as Alcoholics Anonymous, Narcotics Anonymous, Cocaine Anonymous, and other 12-Step groups exist to help alcoholics and addicts, there are 12-Step groups to help their family and friends with issues of codependency. These include Al-Anon, Nar-Anon, Love and Sex Addicts Anonymous, CoDependents Anonymous, and Adult Children of Alcoholics.

3. Other support groups: Many communities have other support groups for help with relationship issues, usually listed in newspapers. They will have names such as Women Who Love Too Much and Addictive Relationships.

4. Healthy examples among family and friends: If you know people who have relationships that match the characteristics listed above as healthy counterparts to codependency, seeking their advice or just spending time with them and learning from their examples may be useful.

5. Self-improvement literature: A wide array of information on this subject is available in popular books and workbooks, videotapes, audiotapes, and on the Internet.

CONCLUSION

Because alcoholism and addiction run in families and people raised in addictive environments often tend to become codependent, and because being in a relationship with a nonrecovering codependent can undermine a newly clean and sober person's abstinence, this presentation's goal is to help group members avoid problems caused by codependency in their relationships. We have covered the following areas: causes of codependency; typical codependent behaviors and their healthy counterparts; and sources of information, help, and support for healthy change for anyone who wants to improve their relationship skills.

REVIEW OF LEARNING GOALS

Upon completion of this presentation, participants should demonstrate:

1. Understanding of codependency by listing, without notes or references, at least four typical codependent behavior patterns and at least four healthy relationship behaviors as counterparts to those codependent behavior patterns.

2. Understanding of codependency by listing, without notes or references, at least three sources of information and help for people seeking to change codependent behavior patterns into healthy patterns.

QUESTIONS/DISCUSSION BEFORE POSTTEST

ADMINISTER POSTTEST

QUESTIONS/DISCUSSION AFTER POSTTEST

1. Definition: Codependency is a pattern of trying to _____ others for _____ _____ _____ , which ends up being bad for oneself and the relationship.

2. What Causes Codependency? The roots of codependency are often in the following feelings and beliefs:

    a. The desire to _____

    b. A sense of _____ , usually caused by feeling that something needs to be done and no one else is doing it

    c. A belief that the alcoholic or addict is not capable of getting along _____ _____ _____

    d. A belief that it is important to protect the _____ of the family, the couple, and/or the other person by _____ problems

    e. A belief that the codependent can _____ another person and a sense of having both the _____ and the _____ to do so

    f. A feeling that the codependent has no right to _____ _____ or to _____ _____

    g. Self-esteem based on _____ _____ _____ _____

    h. A feeling of _____ and _____ when the codependent rescues others or cleans up after them

3. Typical Codependent Behavior Patterns and Healthy Counterparts:

    a. _____ / _____ — protecting the addiction: The codependent often goes to great lengths to clean up after the alcoholic or addict and rescue him or her from the consequences of addictive behavior. The effect is to make it easy and convenient to keep on behaving the same way, which means this actually delays the sick person's getting uncomfortable enough to change.
    The healthy counterpart to this is to let others _____ _____ _____ _____ _____ as much as possible.

    b. _____ and _____ : The codependent often takes on responsibility for the actions, feelings, and thoughts of others, then feels as if he or she is being victimized by the problems those others create.
    The healthy counterpart to this is to take responsibility for _____ and expect other adults and children as far as is reasonable, to do the same.

    c. _____ and _____ : A natural result of feeling responsible for others is a tendency to try to control their behavior, either without letting them know (manipulation) or by direct command (control).
    The healthy counterpart to this is _____ _____ and _____ _____ , with partners openly asking for what they want and accepting the other's decision rather than trying to trick or bully the partner into acting as they wish.

d. Parentification of _____ : Children in these families tend to grow up early, especially older children, and end up taking care of adults much of the time.

The healthy counterpart to this is for adults to handle their responsibilities and let children _____ _____ without dealing with adult concerns.

e. _____ and family _____ : The belief that the family's image must be protected leads to restricting contacts with "outsiders" and teaching children to "keep things in the family" even when they are obviously problems with which the family needs help.

The healthy counterpart to this is a balance between _____ and _____ , with the freedom to go outside the family for help if necessary and healthy friendships outside the family.

f. _____ and " _____ - _____ " rules: Even within the family, many subjects are off-limits, and often the codependent will not acknowledge even obvious problems, leading to the "elephant in the living room" syndrome (a huge problem no one talks about because no one wants to bring it up, but everyone sees it and has to keep walking around it).

The healthy counterpart to this is for all family members to _____ _____ to bring up problems and concerns and talk about them.

g. _____ and _____ - _____ : Because the codependent is doing so much for others (whether they want it or not) and feels unappreciated, he or she often comes to feel burned out, resentful, and self-pitying.

The healthy counterpart to this is a refusal to take on others' _____ , thus avoiding these reactions.

h. _____ of recovery: Although the codependent may say, and believe, that he or she wants the recovery of the alcoholic or addicted partner very much, when this starts to happen the codependent may (without realizing it) act in ways that undermine the recovery and push the other back toward addictive behaviors.

The healthy counterpart to this is to treat recovery as a _____ _____ and work on one's own issues while being supportive of positive changes in others.

4. Sources of Information, Help, and Support for Healthy Change:

a. _____ : Either group, couple, or individual therapy or counseling may be a big help in identifying codependent patterns in one's life and learning healthy behaviors to change those patterns.

b. _____ - _____ groups: Just as Alcoholics Anonymous , Narcotics Anonymous, Cocaine Anonymous, and other 12-Step groups exist to help alcoholics and addicts, there are 12-Step groups to help their family and friends with issues of codependency. These include Al-Anon, Nar-Anon, Love and Sex Addicts Anonymous, CoDependents Anonymous, and Adult Children of Alcoholics.

c. Other _____ groups: Many communities have other support groups for help with relationship issues, usually listed in newspapers. They will have names such as Women Who Love Too Much and Addictive Relationships.

d. _____ _____ among family and friends: If you know people who have relationships that match the characteristics listed above as healthy counterparts to codependency, seeking their advice or just spending time with them and learning from their examples may be useful.

e. Self-improvement _____ : A wide array of information on this subject is available in popular books and workbooks, videotapes, audiotapes, and on the _____ .

Name: _____   Date: ____/____/____

Pretest/Posttest
Codependency

1. List four behaviors that are examples of codependency in a marriage or family relationship:

_____

_____

_____

_____

_____

_____

_____

_____

2. List four healthy relationship behaviors that would be the counterparts to the codependent behavior patterns you listed for question 1:

_____

_____

_____

_____

_____

_____

_____

_____

3. List three sources of information and help for people seeking to change codependent behavior patterns into healthy patterns:

_____

_____

_____

_____

_____

_____

_____

Name: _____   Date: ____/____/____

INTRODUCTION

Subject and Why It Is Important

Ask each participant to briefly state the three most important changes he or she hopes to see in his or her life as a result of becoming clean and sober. List answers on a board, flip chart, or transparency sheet, indicating duplications by putting check marks next to answers given by more than one person.

Discuss how many of the desired changes listed have to do with relationships (romantic, family, friendship, or work). Ask participants how many of the desired changes are likely to occur if they stop using alcohol or other drugs but make no other major changes in their lifestyles, then briefly discuss the idea that recovery involves many changes above and beyond abstinence from psychoactive substance use.

Group Policy

Explain to participants that they will be evaluated on their accomplishment of these goals.

LEARNING GOALS Upon completion of this presentation, participants should demonstrate understanding of healthy relationship skills by listing, without notes or references, at least four skills for finding and developing healthy relationships.

Upon completion of this presentation, participants should demonstrate understanding of healthy relationship skills by listing, without notes or references, at least four skills for maintaining healthy relationships.

Upon completion of this presentation, participants should demonstrate understanding of healthy relationship skills by listing, without notes or references, at least four specific problem areas to watch for in relationships.

QUESTIONS As the presenter, you may ask participants to hold their questions until the end or to ask them at any time during the presentation. If participation is a high priority, we recommend allowing questions at any time; if brevity is more important, it works better to hold questions until the end.

PRETEST Pass out the pretest if you choose to use it, asking participants to fill out and turn in their answer sheets without putting names on them; tell them the posttest will be done at the end of the presentation.

Background and Lead-In

Ask participants what effect their success or failure in their relationships might have on their success in recovery, and on their quality of life and happiness. Ask how many feel they have all the knowledge and skills they need in this area. Reiterate that the approach of this presentation is to assume they have the motivation needed and that any problems in their past or present are mostly due to their not knowing how to achieve what they hope to accomplish in relationships. This presentation aims to increase their chances of success by giving them more tools, based on the experiences of many others before them.

HEALTHY RELATIONSHIP SKILLS

Finding and Developing Healthy Relationships

Participants' relationship goals may be directed toward either current relationships or future ones they hope to develop. This first section will address skills that are useful in starting relationships. In general, these will apply not only to romantic relationships but also to other friendships and work relationships.

1. Becoming capable of healthy relationships: It is a cliché but very true that the relationships we form can't be any healthier emotionally than the people in those relationships, namely, ourselves and our relationship partners. It is also true that we tend to attract, and be attracted to, others who are at about our own levels of emotional health. Therefore, before we become capable of participation in a good relationship, we must be functioning in a healthy way as individuals on our own. This means using the tools presented throughout treatment and in support groups and allowing time to work on and change our addictive and unhealthy lifestyle patterns. This is why newly recovering people often receive the advice that they should avoid making major relationship decisions or commitments for at least their first year of recovery; it takes most people that long to become stable enough to make healthy choices.

2. Selecting and screening partners and friends: There is nothing wrong with being cautious and picky or with screening people out when we feel they aren't right for us. Many people who become alcoholics or addicts were themselves raised in dysfunctional environments in which they may not have learned that they have the right to say no: It is important to remember that *no one is obligated to go out with anyone else, or become romantically or sexually involved, or even to become friends, just because the other person wants this or is in need.* While actively abusing chemicals and during recovery, we are likely to meet many people who are truly needy but who are not able to be in healthy relationships. It is important to be able to choose not to get into relationships when we feel it is unhealthy, unsafe, or inappropriate. Also, sometimes a relationship may seem to start out well, then later we may have experiences with others that change our feelings about being in relationships with them. Again, we have the right at that time to screen people out, to decide to end those relationships, or to reduce our level of involvement in them.

3. Controlling pace and stages in relationship development: Rome wasn't built in a day, and neither was any healthy relationship. A common pattern in unhealthy relationships is a rapid progression to high levels of emotional and/or sexual intimacy. This is not safe, because it takes time to get to know another person well enough to tell how stable and dependable he or she is (see "Risk management" below). By contrast, a healthy relationship develops at a slow enough pace that both partners are able to get to know one another at deeper and deeper levels of intimacy and trust as the levels of openness and vulnerability in the relationship increase.

4. Risk management: This is the art of being neither too reckless nor too cautious as a relationship develops, so that we don't get hurt too badly too often, but we don't deny ourselves the chance to experience good relationships. There are two key principles here:

   a. Don't risk more than you're willing to lose—Don't take a chance by making yourself physically or emotionally vulnerable unless you can accept the odds that the other person will let you down and the consequences if he or she does so.

   b. Don't risk much more than the other person is risking—If you are making yourself very open emotionally, sharing your feelings, dreams, and fears, and the other person is withholding this type of disclosure, something is out of balance. An imbalance of vulnerability creates an unhealthy imbalance of power in a relationship.

5. Watching for repetition of unhealthy patterns: Many of us find, reviewing our life histories, that we have certain patterns of behavior that have caused us problems over and over. In relationships, these can be patterns such as being drawn to certain types of people who hurt us or engaging in certain types of relationship-destroying behavior of our own. It is wise to first review our own pasts to identify such patterns, then to watch for their coming up again and to get the feedback of others we trust to help us do this watching. If we see the old patterns being replayed, we have two choices: We can either do something different (cut the relationship short or keep it at a different level from past patterns, or choose to change our own behaviors as the relationship develops) or we can do the same thing again *and probably get the same results we have gotten in the past.*

6. Warning signs—knowing when to back away: These are some near universal signs that a developing relationship is unhealthy or becoming that way. One of the skills in finding and developing healthy relationships is identifying these signs and distancing oneself or getting completely out of the relationship, whichever is most appropriate:

   a. You and the other person want significantly different types of relationship (e.g., you want a nonromantic friendship and he or she wants to become lovers), and neither of you is willing to change your goals for the relationship.

   b. The other person becomes abusive, intrusive, manipulative, demanding, or controlling. This includes physical and sexual coercion, pressure, or violence; open or implied threats; guilt-inducing statements such as anything starting with "If you care about me . . ." or similar words; demands or pressure to account for time or activities; demands or pressure to cut back or give up other family or friendship relationships or other activities.

   c. The other person becomes consistently needy and you find yourself frequently rescuing him or her, solving his or her problems, or otherwise "fixing" the person.

   d. You become aware that the other person is being dishonest, secretive, or unethical (by your standards) and is unwilling to discuss this and/or change these behaviors.

   e. You consistently notice that friends or family whom you consider to be healthy and to have good judgment perceive the other person as unhealthy or unsafe.

   f. You find yourself feeling pressured or unsafe, or find yourself doing things you don't really want to do in the relationship out of a feeling of obligation or pity. This includes situations in which you feel pressure to violate your values or standards for fear of losing the relationship. It is best to let it go and wait for someone with whom you can be yourself and still be in a relationship.

Maintaining Healthy Relationships

For group members who are in relationships they wish to make or keep healthy, or for use in future relationships, these skills are important after relationships are formed.

1. Communication skills: This is the most important area in most relationships. We learn to talk more or less automatically as children, but we don't learn good communication skills automatically unless our parents or caregivers role-model them for us. These are covered in detail in separate presentations. Good communication skills include:

   a. Active listening and feedback skills

   b. Staying positive

   c. Being clear and specific

   d. Staying on the subject

   e. Avoiding "you" statements, mind-reading, and attacks

2. Acceptance and being supportive: We often find that when a partner or friend tells us about a problem, we feel obligated to solve it. This can lead to the following problems:

   a. The listener being uncomfortable and changing the subject

   b. Cutting off the person speaking and giving advice

   c. Minimizing, comparing, or belittling the problem

   What people usually want from their friends or partners is not a solution, but support. In a healthy relationship, partners practice listening, offering understanding and support, and letting the other person find his or her own solution. This is also much easier than trying to solve another person's problems for him or her.

3. Balancing togetherness and individuation: In a healthy relationship, there are three categories of time and activities: yours, mine, and ours. Partners in friendship or love do some things together and others on their own; they have some mutual friends and some friends they don't share.

4. Being interdependent: We all want to feel needed, but none of us has the strength or resources to adequately manage more than one life at a time. In a healthy relationship, partners need one another but can function alone, and there is a balance of needs. In other words, I need my partner in this way, and he or she needs me in that way.

5. Balancing work and play: In a healthy relationship, work and play are both important, and partners share some of both. Work is necessary for both partners to contribute to the relationship (work can be anything from a paid job to maintaining a household), and shared play is necessary to keep love and enjoyment of one another active.

6. Handling conflicts: Every relationship includes conflict. Having conflict does not mean a relationship is unhealthy. In healthy relationships, people accept that conflict is natural and find ways to resolve it so that both partners are satisfied with the results over time, and they remember that although they are in conflict they care about each other more than they care about the conflict. This means that in a healthy relationship, partners can disagree, argue, and work out conflicts in a loving and respectful way. This is also addressed in detail in separate presentations. Some specific conflict resolution skills are:

   a. Checking for miscommunication and clarifying when it is found

   b. Working to see the other's point of view

   c. Seeking compromises acceptable to both partners

   d. Practicing putting the relationship ahead of winning the conflict

   e. Using time-outs to allow tempers to cool when necessary

   f. Making appointments to discuss touchy topics at times when both partners are prepared to do so

   g. Working on one area of conflict at a time

Dealing with Specific Problems

Some particular types of problems occur in many relationships. Here are some of these specific problems:

1. Misunderstandings and disappointments: If you have chosen a partner who is dependable and honest, problems of this type will probably result from poor communication and wishful thinking. The primary solutions in a healthy relationship are to practice good communication skills and to examine our own thinking about our partners to make sure our expectations are reasonable and based on real experience with those partners rather than on our untested ideas or impressions about them, especially when a relationship is new and we don't know each other very well yet.

2. Violations of rights or boundaries: Again, if you have chosen a healthy partner, these will usually result from poor communication and differing expectations. Two partners may have grown up with different beliefs about rights, roles, and boundaries between partners. And again, the healthy relationship solutions are good communication and frequent self-examination of motives, expectations, and beliefs.

3. Jealousy and possessiveness: This is an unhealthy pattern, but is present to some degree in nearly every relationship, even comparatively healthy ones. It is typically based on insecurity and fear of abandonment. The healthy solution is for partners in a relationship to address these underlying concerns, as well as the jealous and possessive behavior, and resolve both in a way both are satisfied with.

4. Children: We and our partners will always have different experiences, beliefs, and expectations about proper child rearing because of having grown up in different families. In a healthy relationship, these differences are openly addressed, preferably before having children, and resolved by finding compromises acceptable to both partners.

5. Money: Again, we and our partners are likely to have learned different habits and views about managing money, and in a healthy relationship will discuss this openly and reach a compromise acceptable to both partners. If either or both partners lack skills or experience in managing money, information and training are available from community agencies.

6. Change in general: Changes are always stressful, and because we and our partners are different people, we see and experience these changes differently. This sometimes leads to honest differences of opinion about how to handle them. Because people are less patient and tolerant when under more stress, and because change is stressful, this can trigger emotional conflicts. In a healthy relationship, partners work at their conflict resolution skills, use them to manage conflict resulting from change, and anticipate problems when they know major changes are coming in their situation.

CONCLUSION

Many of the goals people have for their recoveries are connected to relationships, but it takes more than abstinence from substances to create healthy connections with others. This presentation has introduced skills for finding and developing healthy relationships, for maintaining them, and for coping with specific types of problems that arise in many relationships.

REVIEW OF LEARNING GOALS

Upon completion of this presentation, participants should demonstrate:

1. Understanding of healthy relationship skills by listing, without notes or references, at least four skills for finding and developing healthy relationships.

2. Understanding of healthy relationship skills by listing, without notes or references, at least four skills for maintaining healthy relationships.

3. Understanding of healthy relationship skills by listing, without notes or references, at least four specific problem areas to watch for in relationships.

QUESTIONS/DISCUSSION BEFORE POSTTEST

ADMINISTER POSTTEST

QUESTIONS/DISCUSSION AFTER POSTTEST

1. Skills that are useful in finding and starting relationships (not only romantic relationships but also other friendships and _____ relationships):

    a. Becoming _____ of healthy relationships: It is a cliché but very true that the relationships we form can't be any healthier emotionally than the people in those relationships, namely, ourselves and our relationship partners. It is also true that we tend to attract, and be attracted to, others who are at about our own levels of emotional health.

    b. _____ and _____ partners and friends: There is nothing wrong with being cautious and picky, or with screening people out when we feel they aren't right for us. Many people who become alcoholics or addicts were themselves raised in dysfunctional environments in which they may not have learned that they have the right to say no: it is important to remember that *no one is obligated to go out with anyone else, or become romantically or sexually involved, or even to become friends, just because the other person wants this or is in need.*

    c. Controlling _____ and _____ in relationship development: A common pattern in unhealthy relationships is a rapid progression to high levels of emotional and/or sexual intimacy. This is not safe, because it takes time to get to know another person well enough to tell how stable and dependable he or she is. By contrast, a healthy relationship develops at a slow enough pace that both partners are able to get to know one another at deeper and deeper levels of intimacy and trust as the levels of openness and vulnerability in the relationship increase.

    d. Risk _____: This is the art of being neither too reckless nor too cautious as a relationship develops, so that we don't get hurt too badly too often, but we don't deny ourselves the chance to experience good relationships. There are two key principles here:

        1) Don't risk more than you're _____ _____ _____ .

        2) Don't risk _____ _____ than the other person is risking.

    e. Watching for _____ of _____ _____: Many of us find, reviewing our life histories, that we have certain patterns of behavior that have caused us problems over and over. In relationships, these can be patterns such as being drawn to certain types of people who hurt us or engaging in certain types of relationship-destroying behavior of our own. It is wise to first review our own pasts to identify such patterns, then to watch for their coming up again, and to get the feedback of others we trust to help us do this watching. If we see the old patterns being replayed, we have two choices: We can either do something different (cut the relationship short or keep it at a different level from past patterns, or choose to change our own behaviors as the relationship develops) or we can do the same thing again *and probably get the same results we have gotten in the past.*

    f. Warning signs — knowing when to _____ _____: These are some near universal signs that a developing relationship is unhealthy or becoming that way. One of the skills in finding and developing healthy relationships is identifying these signs and distancing oneself or getting completely out of the relationship, whichever is most appropriate:

        1) You and the other person want significantly _____ types of relationship.

        2) The other person becomes _____ , _____ , _____ , demanding, or _____ . This includes physical and sexual coercion, pressure, or violence; open or implied threats; guilt-inducing statements such as anything starting with "If you care about me . . ." or similar words; demands or pressure to account for time or activities; demands or pressure to cut back or give up other family or friendship relationships or other activities.

3) The other person becomes consistently _____ and you find yourself frequently _____ him or her, solving his or her problems, or otherwise "fixing" the person.

4) You become aware that the other person is being _____ , secretive, or unethical (by your standards) and is unwilling to discuss this and/or change these behaviors.

5) You consistently notice that friends or family whom you consider to be healthy and to have good judgment perceive the other person as _____ or _____ .

6) You find yourself feeling _____ or _____ , or find yourself doing things you don't really want to do in the relationship out of a feeling of _____ or _____ . This includes situations in which you feel pressure to violate your values or standards for fear of losing the relationship. It is best to let it go and wait for someone with whom you can be yourself and still be in a relationship.

2. Maintaining Healthy Relationships: These skills are important after relationships are formed.

a. _____ skills: This is the most important area in most relationships. Good communication skills include:

1) Active _____ and feedback skills

2) Staying _____

3) Being _____ and specific

4) Staying _____ _____ _____

5) Avoiding " _____ " statements, mind-reading, and _____

b. _____ and being supportive: We often find that when a partner or friend tells us about a problem, we feel obligated to solve it. This can lead to the following problems:

1) The listener being uncomfortable and changing the subject

2) Cutting off the person speaking and _____ _____

3) Minimizing, comparing, or belittling the problem

What people usually want from their friends or partners is not a solution, but _____ . In a healthy relationship, partners practice listening, offering understanding and support, and letting the other person find his or her own solution. This is also much easier than trying to solve another person's problems for him or her.

c. Balancing _____ and individuation: In a healthy relationship, there are three categories of time, activities, and outside friendships: _____ , _____ , and _____ .

d. Being _____ : We all want to feel needed, but none of us has the strength or resources to adequately manage more than one life at a time. In a healthy relationship, partners need one another but can function alone, and there is a balance of needs. In other words, I need my partner in this way, and he or she needs me in that way.

e. Balancing _____ and _____ : In a healthy relationship, work and play are both important, and partners share some of both.

f. _____ conflicts: Every relationship includes conflict. Having conflict does not mean a relationship is unhealthy. In healthy relationships, people accept that conflict is natural and find ways to resolve it so that both partners are satisfied with the results over time, and they remember that although they are in conflict they care about each other more than they care about the conflict. This means that in a healthy relationship, partners can disagree, argue, and work out conflicts in a loving and respectful way. Some specific conflict resolution skills are:

1) Checking for _____ and clarifying when it is found

2) Working to see the other's _____ _____ _____

3) Seeking _____ acceptable to both partners

4) Practicing putting the relationship ahead of _____ the conflict

5) Using _____ - _____ to allow tempers to cool when necessary

6) Making _____ to discuss touchy topics at times when both partners are prepared to do so

7) Working on _____ area of conflict at a time

3. Dealing With Specific Problems: Some particular types of problems occur in many relationships. Here are some of these specific problems:

a. Misunderstandings and disappointments: The primary solutions in a healthy relationship are to practice good _____ skills and to examine our own thinking about our partners to make sure our expectations are reasonable and based on real experience with those partners.

b. Violations of _____ or boundaries: Again, if you have chosen a healthy partner, these will usually result from poor communication and differing expectations. Two partners may have _____ _____ with different beliefs about rights, roles, and boundaries between partners. And again, the healthy relationship solutions are good communication and frequent self-examination of motives, expectations, and beliefs.

c. _____ and _____ : This is an unhealthy pattern, but is present to some degree in nearly every relationship, even comparatively healthy ones. It is typically based on insecurity and fear of abandonment. The healthy solution is for partners in a relationship to address these underlying concerns, as well as the jealous and possessive behavior, and resolve both in a way that satisfies both partners.

d. _____: We and our partners will always have different experiences, beliefs, and expectations about proper child rearing because of having grown up in different families. In a healthy relationship, these differences are openly addressed, preferably before having children, and resolved by finding compromises acceptable to both partners.

e. _____: Again, we and our partners are likely to have learned different habits and views about managing money, and in a healthy relationship will discuss this openly and reach a compromise acceptable to both partners. If either or both partners lack skills or experience in managing money, information and training are available from community agencies.

f. _____ in general: Changes are always stressful, and because we and our partners are different people, we see and experience these changes differently. This sometimes leads to honest differences of opinion about how to handle them. Because people are less patient and tolerant when under more stress, and because change is stressful, this can trigger emotional conflicts. In a healthy relationship, partners work at their conflict resolution skills, use them to manage conflict resulting from change, and anticipate problems when they know major changes are coming in their situation.

Name: _____   Date: ____/____/____

Pretest/Posttest
Healthy Relationship Skills

1. List four skills for finding and developing healthy relationships:

_____

_____

_____

_____

_____

_____

_____

_____

2. List four skills for maintaining healthy relationships:

_____

_____

_____

_____

_____

_____

_____

_____

3. List four common problem areas to watch for in relationships:

_____

_____

_____

_____

_____

_____

_____

_____

Name: _____ Date: ____/____/____

Facilitator's Guide
Grief and Loss

INTRODUCTION

Subject and Why It Is Important

Ask participants what connections they think may exist among grief, loss, and substance abuse; write answers on board, flip chart, or transparency sheet. If it is not given as an answer, ask how many participants drank or used to cope with unhappy feelings, and ask how many feel that there is some event that would be so upsetting that they would feel they had to drink or use to handle it; if anyone says there is, ask what that event would be. Tell the group that the purpose of this presentation is to explain the process of grief experienced by most people after significant losses so that when (not if) they find themselves grieving, they can better understand what they are going through and how to cope with it in non-self-destructive ways.

Group Policy

Explain to participants that they will be evaluated on their accomplishment of these goals.

LEARNING GOALS Upon completion of this presentation, participants should demonstrate understanding of grief and loss by listing, without notes or references, at least four types of losses that often cause intensive grief.

Upon completion of this presentation, participants should demonstrate understanding of grief and loss by listing, without notes or references, the five typical stages of grieving over loss described by Elisabeth Kubler-Ross.

Upon completion of this presentation, participants should demonstrate understanding of grief and loss by listing, without notes or references, at least four healthy coping skills for dealing with grief and loss.

QUESTIONS As the presenter, you may ask participants to hold their questions until the end or to ask them at any time during the presentation. If participation is a high priority, we recommend allowing questions at any time; if brevity is more important, it works better to hold questions until the end.

PRETEST Pass out the pretest if you choose to use it, asking participants to fill out and turn in their answer sheets without putting names on them; tell them the posttest will be done at the end of the presentation.

Background and Lead-In

As mentioned earlier, many newly recovering people feel that they would be unable to remain clean and sober if some particular event happened to them. Most often, this event is a loss of some kind, such as a death of someone they love or the loss of a relationship. In many cases, this is a loss that is guaranteed to happen eventually, such as the death of a parent. Point out that this means that these people have already made a plan to relapse—the only thing they don't know is when. In other cases, the losses feared aren't inevitable, but it is beyond the recovering person's control to prevent them. Even here, they are placing their life or death under the control of people or situations outside themselves. The goal of this presentation is to enable participants to cope with losses while maintaining their sobriety and abstinence, not only from substance abuse but from other self-destructive behavior.

GRIEF AND LOSS

Types of Losses

Ask participants to name types of events they would consider significant losses, ones that would cause feelings of grief. Write their answers after other class feedback written down earlier, then discuss connections. To the list of losses given by group members, add any of the following that are missed:

1. Death of a family member, friend, or other significant person: This is the most obvious answer and will probably have been the first response. Discuss the idea that the pain and loss felt are less for the dead person, who is not suffering, than for oneself and the loss of having that person in one's life.

2. Miscarriages and abortions: These are often ignored or minimized as losses, but are often felt as deeply as the loss of a child carried to term—even in the case of voluntary abortions. Acknowledging the loss and experiencing the grief seem necessary here as much as in other deaths.

3. Divorces and other relationship endings: Again, this will probably have been given as a response by participants. Note that, after death of a spouse, divorce is often considered the second most stressful life event people experience, and one whose effects may last for years.

4. Loss of a job: This is also a highly stressful event that affects self-esteem deeply as well as forcing changes and secondary losses in other areas such as security, work friendships, and plans and goals.

5. Death of a pet: People become strongly attached to animals, and their deaths often result in grief as intense as that resulting from human deaths, but society is less likely to recognize and respect this kind of grief.

6. Major illness or injury to oneself or a loved one: Even when no one has died, the loss of physical strength and health, sometimes the permanent loss of abilities, has a deep impact on the person suffering the loss and others close to him or her.

7. Geographical moves: Loss of familiar places and routines, even when replaced by new ones just as satisfactory, is a major life change and often triggers significant grief. This can be confusing because we may not be able to understand where the feeling of loss comes from.

8. Retirement: This is a major loss of identity, often a loss of self-esteem, sometimes a serious loss of financial and material security. The period shortly before and after retirement is a time of increased risk of suicide, especially in cultures like ours that place great emphasis on our work as the most important thing about us.

9. Other major life transitions: Changing from one stage of life or situation to another is always a loss, even when the change is one we want and have worked to bring about. This applies to graduation, marriage, the birth of a child, job promotion, and other similar events. Even when we have also gained, we have lost whatever is left behind, and we seem to need to go through a grieving process even in these cases.

10. Getting clean and sober: Yes, this is a loss! An addiction is a major part of a person's life. It may have provided a big part of one's identity and is almost always the primary coping tool for dealing with many situations. Even when we recognize that the use of alcohol or other drugs (or a compulsive behavior such as gambling) has stopped being a source of pleasure and has become painful and destructive, we often feel a terrible sense of loss at giving it up. This is normal. It does not mean we are "doing recovery wrong" or that we are going to relapse.

Stages of Grief

Elisabeth Kubler-Ross studied people who were dying of fatal illnesses to find out how they adapted to their own impending deaths. She found that the people she talked with usually experienced five stages of grieving, and that these apply in other situations of loss as well. People may not experience these stages in exact sequence, and they may move forward and backward in the process, slipping back into an earlier stage at times. Some people, because of insufficient time or because they resist the process, are unable to complete the stages of grieving and remain stuck somewhere in the midst of the process, sometimes until they die. The five stages are:

1. Denial: A common first reaction to loss, either one that has happened or one that is coming, is to refuse to believe it. This may be hard to understand for others watching this reaction. This is a first way to control one's experience and avoid suffering the loss, but it doesn't usually last long because the denial is difficult to maintain in the face of facts, unless one is or becomes delusional and therefore seriously mentally ill.

2. Anger: The most common second stage, once denial starts to wear off, is anger. This anger may be felt toward anyone or anything. People often feel angry at doctors and other medical professionals working with a dying or dead person; at other people, often family members or friends; at themselves; and often at the person or thing that is being lost. Often, this anger is intense despite one's having the logical knowledge that it doesn't make sense. This is a second way to keep the pain away, which can last longer than the denial but usually breaks down in turn.

3. Bargaining: In this common stage, people may try to "make a deal" with God, fate, or some person they feel has the power to keep the loss from happening: "God, if you let my wife live, I'll do anything." This is still another attempt to control the situation and avoid the loss. This stage also tends to end when people see that this tactic is not preventing the loss.

4. Depression: This is the stage reached when all efforts to avoid experiencing the loss fail and we realize that we can't escape this painful experience. Depression may be experienced not only as a "down" mood, but as apathy, withdrawal, loss of interest in many parts of life, loss of energy, loss of appetite or increase in eating, changes in sleep patterns, difficulty thinking or concentrating, self-hatred, and/or thoughts of death or suicide. People in this stage often become worried that they are falling apart or "going crazy," that their feelings will never return to normal, and that they are not reacting normally, but this is a common experience. After a time, as we adjust to the loss we are experiencing and it starts to become a normal part of our world, we can move on to the final stage (though, as mentioned, in many cases, people fail to reach the last stage for various reasons).

5. Acceptance: This is the last stage, in which we begin returning to normal. The loss we have experienced becomes part of the past and the changes in our world and life become what we think of as normal. Thinking of the loss becomes less painful, though it will probably still cause sad feelings for a long time, possibly for the rest of our life.

Connections among Grief, Loss, and Substance Abuse

1. Recovery as a loss to be grieved: As mentioned above, the very act of giving up the use of alcohol and/or other drugs is one of the losses alcoholics and addicts must experience as part of early recovery.

2. Past patterns of using substances to cope with emotional pain: Accepting pain, anger, and depression and dealing with them drug-free may be very difficult, if only because it's a new task and the newly recovering person may never have done it before.

3. Cultural connections: In many cultures, and many subcultures including families, there may be traditions of drinking or other drug use at times of loss. Beyond this, our culture generally encourages looking for quick fixes and escaping pain and discomfort in any way we can rather than accepting them as normal parts of life.

4. Lack of a support system: Maintaining abstinence can be difficult without the support of others, especially early in recovery. Because our culture is uncomfortable with loss, even others who would be supportive in some situations may avoid a person who is grieving a loss, and people may minimize the loss, tell the grieving person he or she needs to "put it behind you and get over it," refuse to discuss the loss, or avoid contact with the grieving person. This can undermine an important resource for staying clean and sober just at a time when stresses that can influence a recovering person toward relapse are heightened.

Healthy Coping Skills for Grief and Loss

Having healthy alternatives is one of the most effective factors in maintaining abstinence from addiction and other compulsive behaviors, and that is true in this area as in others. Some healthy coping skills for grief and loss, which can reduce the risk of relapse, include the following:

1. Maintain and rely on a support system: Both within a recovery program such as Alcoholics Anonymous and in other situations, it is vital to find people who are supportive—who will listen to and spend time with someone who is suffering—and to turn to them when one has the kind of painful feelings that led to drinking, drugs, or other excesses. For some of us, our habit has been to isolate ourselves, and it may take deliberate and uncomfortable effort to go to others. It is especially helpful to join with others feeling the same loss for mutual support.

2. Understand and accept the grieving process: Learn about the information in this presentation, and see that feeling you are falling apart or going crazy is normal and not a sign that you aren't handling the situation adequately.

3. Remind yourself that the pain is temporary: As people often say, "This, too, shall pass." It may not lessen the hurt in the present to remember this; however, one aspect of depression and grief is the feeling that life will always be sad and painful, and this can lead to despair. Remembering how past pain eventually healed can be a source of hope and strength.

4. Slow down: When we are grieving, we don't function as well in any area of life. We are less effective at work, more prone to problems in relationships, more likely to get physically sick, more accident-prone. It is important not to expect as much of ourselves as we normally would.

5. Concentrate on basics: We may tend to neglect self-care in times of grief. It is important at these times to make sure we eat properly, get enough rest, and get regular exercise of some kind. Failure to do these things makes us vulnerable to stress and depression even under normal conditions, and in a time of loss can set us up for relapse.

6. Turn to spiritual sources of support: Whether through participation in an organized religion or a private relationship with a personal higher power, faith and reliance on something larger than oneself for support can be a literal lifesaver. In circumstances of loss, the application of some of the tools and principles of 12-Step recovery programs can be as useful to cope with grief as to avoid relapse.

CONCLUSION

Grief and loss can have a major impact on recovery from addiction and other compulsive behaviors. In this presentation we have covered types of experiences that can trigger feelings of grief and loss; the typical stages of grief; connections among grief, loss, and substance abuse; and healthy coping skills for dealing with grief and loss. Our goal in presenting this information has been to increase group members' ability to cope with grief and loss while maintaining abstinence and recovery.

REVIEW OF LEARNING GOALS

Upon completion of this presentation, participants should demonstrate:

1. Understanding of grief and loss by listing, without notes or references, at least four types of losses that often cause intensive grief.
2. Understanding of grief and loss by listing, without notes or references, the five typical stages of grieving over loss described by Elisabeth Kubler-Ross.
3. Understanding of grief and loss by listing, without notes or references, at least four healthy coping skills for dealing with grief and loss.

QUESTIONS/DISCUSSION BEFORE POSTTEST

ADMINISTER POSTTEST

QUESTIONS/DISCUSSION AFTER POSTTEST

1. Types of Losses That Can Cause Intense Grief:

a. _____ of a _____ _____ , _____ , or other significant person: Much of the pain and loss we feel may be less for the person who has died, who is not suffering, than for ourselves and the loss of having that person in our lives.

b. _____ and _____ : These are often ignored or minimized as losses, but are often felt as deeply as the loss of a child carried to term — even in the case of voluntary abortions. Acknowledging the loss and experiencing the grief seem necessary here as much as in other deaths.

c. _____ and other _____ endings: After death of a spouse, divorce is often considered the second most stressful life event people experience, and one whose effects may last for years.

d. Loss of a _____: This is also a highly stressful event affecting self-esteem deeply as well as forcing changes and losses in other areas such as security, work friendships, and plans and goals.

e. Death of a _____ : People become strongly attached to animals, and their deaths often result in grief as intense as that resulting from human deaths, but society is less likely to recognize and respect this kind of grief.

f. Major _____ or _____ to oneself or a loved one: Even when no one has died, the loss of physical strength and health, sometimes the permanent loss of abilities, has a deep impact on the person suffering the loss and others close to him or her.

g. _____ _____ : Loss of familiar places and routines, even when replaced by new ones just as satisfactory, is a major life change and often triggers significant grief. This can be confusing because we may not be able to understand where the feeling of loss comes from.

h. _____: This is a major loss of identity, often a loss of self-esteem, sometimes a serious loss of financial and material security. The period shortly before and after retirement is a time of increased risk of suicide, especially in cultures like ours that place great emphasis on our work as the most important thing about us.

i. _____ _____ : Changing from one stage of life or situation to another is always a loss, even when the change is one we want and have worked to bring about. This applies to graduation, marriage, the birth of a child, job promotion, and other similar events.

j. Getting _____ and _____ : Yes, this is a loss! An addiction is a major part of a person's life. It may have provided a big part of one's sense of identity and is almost always the person's primary coping tool for dealing with many situations. Even when we recognize that the use of alcohol or other drugs (or a compulsive behavior such as gambling) has stopped being a source of pleasure and has become painful and destructive, we often feel a terrible sense of loss at giving it up. This is normal. It does not mean we are "doing recovery wrong" or that we are going to relapse.

2. Stages of Grief: Elisabeth Kubler-Ross studied people who were dying of fatal illnesses to find out how they adapted to their own impending deaths. She found that the people she talked with usually experienced five stages of grieving, and that these apply in other situations of loss as well. People may not experience these stages in exact sequence, and they may move forward and backward in the process, slipping back into an earlier stage at times. Some people, because of insufficient time or because they resist the process, are unable to complete the stages of grieving and remain stuck somewhere in the midst of the process, sometimes until they die. The five stages are:

a. _____ : A common first reaction to loss, either one that has happened or one that is coming, is to refuse to believe it. This is a first way to control one's experience and avoid suffering the loss, but denial is difficult to maintain in the face of facts.

b. _____ : The most common second stage, once denial starts to wear off, is anger. People often feel angry at doctors and other medical professionals working with a dying or dead person; at other people, often family members or friends; at themselves; and often at the person or thing that is being lost. This is a second way to keep the pain away, which can last longer than the denial but usually breaks down in turn.

c. _____ : In this common stage, people may try to "make a deal" with God, fate, or some person they feel has the power to keep the loss from happening. This is still another attempt to control the situation and avoid the loss. This stage also tends to end when people see that this tactic is not preventing the loss.

d. _____ : This is the stage reached when all efforts to avoid experiencing the loss fail and we realize that we can't escape this painful experience. Depression may be experienced not only as a "down" mood, but as apathy, withdrawal, loss of interest in many parts of life, loss of energy, loss of appetite or increase in eating, changes in sleep patterns, difficulty thinking or concentrating, self-hatred, and/or thoughts of death or suicide. People in this stage often become worried that they are falling apart or "going crazy," that their feelings will never return to normal, and that they are not reacting normally, but this is a common experience.

e. _____ : This is the last stage, in which we begin returning to normal.

3. Connections among Grief, Loss, and Substance Abuse:
   a. Recovery as a _____ to be _____ .
   b. _____ _____ of using substances to cope with _____ _____ :
   c. _____ connections: In many cultures, and many subcultures including families, there may be traditions of drinking or other drug use at times of loss. Beyond this, our culture generally encourages looking for quick fixes and escaping pain and discomfort in any way we can rather than accepting them as normal parts of life.
   d. Lack of a _____ _____ : Maintaining abstinence can be difficult without the support of others, especially early in recovery.

4. Healthy Coping Skills for Grief and Loss: Having healthy alternatives is one of the most effective factors in maintaining abstinence from addiction and other compulsive behaviors, and that is true in this area as in others. Some healthy coping skills for grief and loss, which can reduce the risk of relapse, include the following:
   a. Maintain and rely on a _____ _____ : It is especially helpful to join with others feeling the same loss for mutual support.
   b. Understand and accept the _____ process.
   c. Remind yourself that the pain is _____ . Remembering how past pain eventually healed can be a source of hope and strength.
   d. _____ _____ : When we are is grieving, we don't function as well in any area of life. We are less effective at work, more prone to problems in relationships, more likely to get physically sick, more accident-prone.
   e. Concentrate on _____ : It is important at these times to make sure we eat properly, get enough rest, and get regular exercise of some kind.
   f. Turn to _____ sources of support.

Name: _____   Date: ____/____/____

Pretest/Posttest
Grief and Loss

1. List four types of losses that often cause intensive grief:

_____

_____

_____

_____

_____

_____

_____

2. List the five typical stages of grieving over loss described by Elisabeth Kubler-Ross:

_____

_____

_____

_____

_____

_____

_____

_____

_____

_____

_____

3. List four healthy coping skills for dealing with grief and loss:

_____

_____

_____

_____

_____

_____

_____

_____

Name: _____   Date: ____/____/____

Bibliography and Suggested Reading

Aiken, L. R. (1997). *Questionnaires & inventories: Surveying opinions and assessing personality.* New York: Wiley.

Alcoholics Anonymous World Services, Inc. (1976). *Alcoholics Anonymous: The story of how many thousands of men and women have recovered from alcoholism* (3rd ed.). New York: Alcoholics Anonymous World Services.

Beck, A. T., Emery, G., Rush, A. J., & Shaw, B. F. (1979). *Cognitive therapy of depression.* New York: Guilford Press.

Bedell, J. R., & Lennox, S. S. (1997). *Handbook for communication and problem-solving skill training.* New York: Wiley.

Berg, I. K., & Miller, S. D. (1992). *Working with the problem drinker: A solution-focused approach.* New York: Norton.

Carlton, P. L. (1983). *A primer of behavioral pharmacology.* New York: Freeman.

Center for Substance Abuse Prevention. (1993). *Measurements in prevention: A manual on selecting and using instruments to evaluate prevention programs.* Rockville, MD: U.S. Department of Health and Human Services.

Center for Substance Abuse Treatment. (1994a). *Treatment Improvement Protocol (TIP) Series 8: Intensive outpatient treatment for alcohol and other drug abuse.* Rockville, MD: U.S. Department of Health and Human Services.

Center for Substance Abuse Treatment. (1994b). *Treatment Improvement Protocol (TIP) Series 9: Assessment and treatment of patients with coexisting mental illness and alcohol and other drug abuse.* Rockville, MD: U.S. Department of Health and Human Services.

Center for Substance Abuse Treatment. (1995). *Treatment Improvement Protocol (TIP) Series 14: Developing state outcomes monitoring systems for alcohol and other drug abuse treatment.* Rockville, MD: U.S. Department of Health and Human Services.

Center for Substance Abuse Treatment. (1997). *Treatment Improvement Protocol (TIP) Series 25: Substance abuse treatment and domestic violence.* Rockville, MD: U.S. Department of Health and Human Services.

Clancy, J. (1996). *Anger and addiction: Breaking the relapse cycle—a teaching guide for professionals.* Madison, CT: Psychosocial Press.

Corcoran, K., & Fischer, J. (1994). *Measures for clinical practice: A sourcebook* (Vols. 1 & 2). New York: Free Press.

Cruse, J., Mende, C., Radcliffe, A., Rush, P., & Scott, C. F. (1993). *The pharmer's almanac: II. An updated training manual on the pharmacology of psychoactive drugs.* Denver, CO: Mac.

Eisenberg, A., Eisenberg, H., & Mooney, A. J. (1992). *The recovery book.* New York: Workman.

Evans, K., & Sullivan, J. M. (1995). *Treating addicted survivors of trauma.* New York: Guilford Press.

Farberow, N. L., Litman, R., & Shneidman, E. (1994). *The psychology of suicide: A clinician's guide to evaluation and treatment.* Northvale, NJ: Aronson.

Foy, D. W. (Ed.). (1992). *Treating PTSD: Cognitive-behavioral strategies.* New York: Guilford Press.

Gause, D. C., & Weinberg, G. M. (1989). *Exploring requirements: Quality before design.* New York: Dorset House.

Heggenhougen, H. K. (1997). *Reaching new highs: Alternative therapies for drug addicts.* Northvale, NJ: Aronson.

Howard, K. I., Lish, J. D., Lyons, J. S., & O'Mahoney, M. T. (1997). *The measurement & management of clinical outcomes in mental health.* New York: Wiley

Bibliography and Suggested Reading

Kübler-Ross, E. (1969). *On death and dying: What the dying have to teach doctors, nurses, clergy, and their own families.* New York: Macmillan.

Matsakis, A. (1994). *Post-traumatic stress disorder: A complete treatment guide.* Oakland, CA: New Harbinger.

Matsakis, A. (1996). *I can't get over it: A handbook for trauma survivors* (2nd ed.). Oakland, CA: New Harbinger.

McFarlane, A. C., van der Kolk, B. A., & Weisaeth, L. (Eds.). (1996). *Traumatic stress: The effects of overwhelming experience on mind, body, and society.* New York: Guilford Press.

McMillin, C. S., & Rogers, R. L. (1989). *The healing bond: Treating addictions in groups.* New York: Norton.

Miller, W. R., & Rollnick, S. (1991). *Motivational interviewing: Preparing people to change addictive behavior.* New York: Guilford Press.

National Institute on Drug Abuse. (1993). *Diagnostic source book on drug abuse research and treatment.* Rockville, MD: U.S. Department of Health and Human Services.

National Institute on Drug Abuse. (1994a). *Clinical report series: Assessing drug abuse among adolescents and adults: Standardized instruments.* Rockville, MD: U.S. Department of Health and Human Services.

National Institute on Drug Abuse. (1994b). *Clinical report series: Mental health assessment and diagnosis of substance abusers.* Rockville, MD: U.S. Department of Health and Human Services.

Ortman, D. (1997). *The dually diagnosed: A therapist's guide to helping the substance abusing, psychologically disturbed patient.* Northvale, NJ: Aronson.

Paymar, M., & Pence, E. (1993). *Education groups for men who batter: The Duluth model.* New York: Springer.

Schaeffer, B. (1987). *Is it love or is it addiction?* Center City, MN: Hazelden.

Shapiro, F. (1995). *Eye movement desensitization and reprocessing: Basic principles, protocols, and procedures.* New York: Guilford Press.

Trimpey, J. (1996). *Rational recovery: The new cure for substance addiction.* New York: Pocket Books.

Wiger, D. E. (1997). *The clinical documentation sourcebook.* New York: Wiley.

Woititz, J. G. (1983). *Adult children of alcoholics.* Pompano Beach, FL: Health Communications.

About the Authors

The authors, James R. Finley, M.A., and Brenda S. Lenz, M.S., are experienced addiction therapists, educators, and program managers whose years building and running successful treatment programs and working with addicts and alcoholics in a variety of settings has taught them that a well-structured and effectively run treatment program can produce dramatic recoveries even in clients who have tried and failed time and again to overcome their addictions.

Practice Planners™ offer mental health professionals a full array of practice management tools. These easy-to-use resources include *Treatment Planners*, which cover all the necessary elements for developing formal treatment plans, including detailed problem definitions, long-term goals, short-term objectives, therapeutic interventions, and DSM-IV diagnoses; *Homework Planners* featuring behaviorally-based, ready-to-use assignments which are designed for use between sessions; and *Documentation Sourcebooks* that provide all the forms and records that therapists need to run their practice.

Practice *Planners*™

For more information on the titles listed below, fill out and return this form to: John Wiley & Sons, Attn: M.Fellin, 605 Third Avenue, New York, NY 10158.

Name _____

Address _____

Address _____

City/State/Zip _____

Telephone _____ Email _____

Please send me more information on:

- ❑ The Complete Psychotherapy Treatment Planner / 176pp / 0-471-11738-2 / $39.95
- ❑ The Child and Adolescent Psychotherapy Treatment Planner / 240pp / 0-471-15647-7 / $39.95
- ❑ The Chemical Dependence Treatment Planner / 208pp / 0-471-23795-7 / $39.95
- ❑ The Continuum of Care Treatment Planner / 208pp / 0-471-19568-5 / $39.95
- ❑ The Couples Therapy Treatment Planner / 208pp / 0-471-24711-1 / $39.95
- ❑ The Employee Assistance (EAP) Treatment Planner / 176pp / 0-471-24709-X / $39.95
- ❑ The Pastoral Counseling Treatment Planner / 208pp / 0-471-25416-9 / $39.95
- ❑ The Older Adult Psychotherapy Treatment Planner / 176pp / 0-471-29574-4 / $39.95
- ❑ The Behavioral Medicine Treatment Planner / 176pp / 0-471-31923-6 / $39.95
- ❑ The Complete Adult Psychotherapy Treatment Planner, Second Edition / 224pp / 0-471-31922-4 / $39.95
- ❑ TheraScribe® 3.0 for Windows®: The Computerized Assistant to Psychotherapy Treatment Planning Software / 0-471-18415-2 / $450.00 (For network pricing, call 1-800-0655x4708)
- ❑ TheraBiller™ w/TheraScheduler: The Computerized Mental Health Office Manager Software / 0-471-17102-2 / $599.00 (For network pricing, call 1-800-0655x4708)
- ❑ Brief Therapy Homework Planner / 256pp / 0-471-24611-5 / $49.95
- ❑ Brief Couples Therapy Homework Planner / 256pp / 0-471-29511-6 / $49.95
- ❑ The Child & Adolescent Homework Planner / 256pp / 0-471-32366-7 / $49.95
- ❑ The Psychotherapy Documentation Primer / 224pp / 0-471-28990-6 / $39.95
- ❑ The Clinical Documentation Sourcebook / 256pp / 0-471-17934-5 / $49.95
- ❑ The The Forensic Documentation Sourcebook / 0-471-25459-2 / 224pp / $75.00
- ❑ The Couples & Family Clinical Documentation Sourcebook / 240pp / 0-471-25234-4 / $49.95
- ❑ The Child Clinical Documentation Sourcebook / 256pp / 0-471-29111-0 / $49.95

Order the above products through your local bookseller, or by calling 1-800-225-5945, from 8:30 a.m. to 5:30 p.m., est. You can also order via our web site: www.wiley.com/practiceplanners

WILEY Publishers Since 1807

About the Disk

DISK TABLE OF CONTENTS

About the Disk

About the Disk

Page	File Name	Title
11.59	CH1124	Healthy Relationship Skills, Pretest/Posttest
11.60	CH1125	Grief and Loss, Facilitator's Guide
11.65	CH1126	Grief and Loss, Participant Handout
11.67	CH1127	Grief and Loss, Pretest/Posttest

INTRODUCTION

The forms on the enclosed disk are saved in Microsoft Word for Windows version 7.0. In order to use the forms, you will need to have word processing software capable of reading Microsoft Word for Windows version 7.0 files.

SYSTEM REQUIREMENTS

- IBM PC or compatible computer

- 3.5″ floppy disk drive

- Windows 95 or later

- Microsoft Word for Windows version 7.0 or later or other word processing software capable of reading Microsoft Word for Windows 7.0 files.

    NOTE: Many popular word processing programs are capable of reading Microsoft Word for Windows 7.0 files. However, users should be aware that a slight amount of formatting might be lost when using a program other than Microsoft Word. If your word processor cannot read Microsoft Word 7.0 files, unformatted text files have been provided in the TXT directory on the floppy disk.

HOW TO INSTALL THE FILES ONTO YOUR COMPUTER

To install the files, follow the instructions below.

1. Insert the enclosed disk into the floppy disk drive of your computer.

2. From the Start Menu, choose **Run.**

3. Type **A:\SETUP** and press **OK.**

4. The opening screen of the installation program will appear. Press **OK** to continue.

5. The default destination directory is C:\FINLEY. If you wish to change the default destination, you may do so now.

6. Press **OK** to continue. The installation program will copy all files to your hard drive in the C:\FINLEY or user-designated directory.

USING THE FILES

Loading Files

To use the word processing files, launch your word processing program. Select **File, Open** from the pull-down menu. Select the appropriate drive and directory. If you installed the files to the default directory, the files will be located in the C:\FINLEY directory. A list of files should appear. If you do not see a list of files in the directory, you need to select **WORD DOCUMENT (*.DOC)** under **Files of Type.** Double click on the file you want to open. Edit the file according to your needs.

Printing Files

If you want to print the files, select **File, Print** from the pull-down menu.

Saving Files

When you have finished editing a file, you should save it under a new file name by selecting **File, Save As** from the pull-down menu.

USER ASSISTANCE

If you need assistance with installation or if you have a damaged disk, please contact Wiley Technical Support at:

Phone: (212) 850-6753

Fax:　(212) 850-6800 (Attention: Wiley Technical Support)

Email: techhelp@wiley.com

To place additional orders or to request information about other Wiley products, please call (800) 225–5945.